AF538817

# BIODIVERSITY AND ECOLOGY

INTERNATIONAL ENVIRONMENTAL ECONOMICS

# BIODIVERSITY AND ECOLOGY


*Edited by*

**Dr. Ram Krishna Mandal**

*Associate Professor of Economics*

*Dera Natung Govt. College*

*Itanagar – 791 113*

*Arunachal Pradesh*

*(India)*

*e-mail: rkm_1966@yahoo.co.in*

**DISCOVERY PUBLISHING HOUSE PVT. LTD.**

**NEW DELHI-110 002**

*Published by:*
**Tilak Wasan**

**DISCOVERY PUBLISHING HOUSE PVT. LTD.**
4383/4B, Ansari Road, Darya Ganj
New Delhi-110 002 (India)
*Phone* : +91-11-23279245, 43596064-65
*Fax* : +91-11-23253475
*E-mail* : parul.wasan@gmail.com
discoverypublishinghouse@gmail.com
*web* : www.discoverypublishinggroup.com

***First Edition:* 2012**
**ISBN: 978-93-5056-152-2**

**Biodiversity and Ecology**



***Printed at:***
***Shree Balaji Art Press***
***Delhi***

*to*

*Mrs. Archana Mandal (Wife)*
*Miss Anusree Krishna Mandal (Daughter)*
*Master Avinandan Krishna Mandal (Son)*

# PREFACE

The present study is an attempt at a comprehensive and critical analysis for the role of *Biodiversity and Ecology* for the protection of natural resources in the world. The unlimited greed of man is threatening the healthy and diverse biological order that needs immediate correction. Man is exploiting both biological and other precious natural resource beyond the replacement levels, besides polluting them badly thereby posing greater danger to the future generation's smooth survival. In an effort to save erosion of natural resources, several threatened regions are declared as biodiversity hotspots, which includes the Western Ghats and the Eastern Himalayan that are treasure houses for several flora and fauna. It is time to make man realise the negative impact of nature on 'biodiversity' and make him act as a 'trustee' or 'conservator' of nature in true sense. Otherwise, a day may not be far off when our future generation would be compelled to face several risks including shortage of food and other requirements. The time is most appropriate to realise the importance of biodiversity conservation for the good of all species. It also calls for a well planned strategy to adequately compensate people involved in biodiversity conservation by foregoing benefits of opportunity costs accruing from commercial crops or exploitation of natural resources.

Forest is the most important resource in the world. This can also be called 'primary source' in the words of Norman Myers, the famous ecologist. This resource is the mother of unique culture and traditions of local tribes and is also at the root of abundance of water, biodiversity and soil formation. Forestry is a multi-faceted business and the Department of Environment and Forest is committed to manage forestry resources in a balanced way so that a full range of benefits (economic, social and environmental) are delivered not only today but for generations to come.

Trees in a variety of ethno-forestry and agro-forestry systems contribute to food security, rural income generation through diversity of products and services, and can enhance nutrient cycling, improve soil productivity, soil conservation and soil faunal activities. Nonetheless, trees in agro-forestry systems can also cause competition with the associated food crops. The contribution of agro-forestry systems in India are in the areas of (*i*) biodiversity conservation; (*ii*) yield of goods and services to society; (*iii*) augmentation of the carbon storage in agro-ecosystems; (*iv*) enhancing the fertility of the soils, and (*v*) providing social and economic well-being to people.

The present volume is a collection of papers contributed by eminent scholars, academicians, policy-makers, bureaucrats and thinkers from different parts of the world. The publication of this book would not have been possible without their contributions. Their work is based on diverse source materials which consist of official reports, published journals, books and findings of field work. Most of their writings are based either on the social structural aspects or on the social dynamism and rapid regional socio-economic transformation. I have felt the need to put some of their writings together so as to enable the readers to get an overall idea about the aspect. Some of their writings have been updated, revised and edited for the purpose. I hope that the readers will find it relevant for understanding the present problem raised by globalization. I hope, this book will benefit immensely the students, researchers, teachers, young scholars, planners and administrators in the area of sustainable rural development and common property resources. I am conscious of the bulk of the work which becomes largely inevitable on account of the intrinsic sweep of the subject. I acknowledge my gratitude to all contributors, whose works are consulted in the preparation of this volume.

I would be failing in my duty if I do not extend my gratitude to my Principal, Shri Tomar Ete, Dera Natung Govt. College, Itanagar, Arunachal Pradesh, India for generating in me an interest to edit this book.

I also acknowledge my beloved teacher and guide, Prof. Chandan Kumar Mukhopadyaya, Department of Economics, University of North Bengal, West Bengal for the inspiration I received from him. I extend my gratitude to him.

I have received support and cooperation from my colleagues Dr. A.I. Singh and Mrs. Madhuparna Bhattacharjee, I acknowledge a deep sense of gratitude to them.

I am also taking the opportunity to thank profusely to Mr. Tilak Wasan, Managing Director, Discovery Publishing House Pvt. Ltd., New Delhi for publication this book.

Lastly, I am grateful to the members of my family: Mrs. Archana Mandal (wife), Miss Anusree Krishna Mandal (Daughter) and Master Avinandan Krishna Mandal (son) for their untiring support and patience during the work of this volume.

**Dr. Ram Krishna Mandal**

# CONTENTS

*Preface*

*List of Contributors*

1. Biodiversity, Benefit Sharing: Towards a Better Reality ............. 1

    — *Prof. G. Rajasekar*

2. Thinking Outside the Box?: A Paradigmatic Shift in the Study of Environmental Scarcity, Conflict and Ecological Security in Malaysia ............. 11

    — *Dr. Sharifah Munirah Alatas*

3. Ethics of Biodiversity Conservation in Landscape Planning: A Case for Integrated Habitat in Non-Protected Areas ............. 27

    — *Dr. Faiza Abbasi*

4. Biological Diversity, Environmental Ethics and Traditional Ecological Knowledge: Concerns in Northeast India ............. 39

    — *Mr. Bal Krishan Choudhary*

5. Floristic Diversity of Northeast India and its Conservation ......... 61

    — *Mr. Krishna Upadhaya, Mr. Hiranjit Choudhury and Mr. Nripemo Odyuo*

6. Mount Saramati: Ideal Site for Biodiversity Conservation and Ecotourism in Nagaland, Northeast India ............. 72

    — *Mr. Nripemo Odyuo, Mr. Krishna Upadhaya and Mr. S.A. Jamir*

7. Tribal Relation with Nature: A Case of the Lepchas of West Bengal ............. 82

    — *Dr. Dulal Chandra Roy*

8. Indigenous People, Traditional Knowledge in Respect of Ownership Issues in Biodiversity ............. 102

    — *Dr. Bindu Vijay, Mr. Vivek Dubey and Mr. Amartya Saha*

9. Aquatic Organisms as Bio-indicators ............. 123

    — *Mr. Vinod Kumar Verma and Ms. Amita Saxena*

10. E-Waste—A Major Threat to Environment .................................. 129

*— Ms. Kamlesh Agrawal, Ms. Sai Prasanna and Ms. J. Saujanya*

11. An Introduction to Ecotaxation and Environmental Levy ............ 139

*— Dr. Md. Samsur Jaman*

12. Biodiversity: A Threat Perception to Sustainable Development in Arunachal Pradesh of India .................................................. 148

*— Dr. Ram Krishna Mandal*

*Index* .................................................................................. 193

# LIST OF CONTRIBUTORS

**Prof. G. Rajasekar,** Department of Legal Studies, University of Madras, Chennai, Tamil Nadu, India

**Dr. Sharifah Munirah Alatas,** Strategic Studies and International Relations Programme, Faculty of Social Sciences and Humanities, National University of Malaysia, UKM Bangi, Bangi, Selangor, Malaysia

**Mr. Bal Krishan Choudhary,** Assistant Professor, Department of Environmental Science, Ambedkar College, Fatikroy, Tripura, India

**Mr. Krishna Upadhaya,** Division of Environmental Science, Department of Basic Sciences and Social Sciences, School of Technology, North-Eastern Hill University, Shillong, Meghalaya, India

**Mr. Hiranjit Choudhury,** Botanical Survey of India, Eastern Circle, Shillong, Meghalaya, India

**Mr. Nripemo Odyuo,** Botanical Survey of India, Eastern Circle, Shillong, Meghalaya, India

**Dr. Faiza Abbasi,** Member, IUCN-CEC, Guest Faculty, Department of Wildlife Sciences, Aligarh Muslim University, Aligarh, U.P., India

**Mr. S.A. Jamir,** Department of Botany, Fazl Ali College, Mokukchung, Meghalaya, India

**Dr. Dulal Chandra Roy,** Associate Professor, Department of Economics, Kalimpong College, Post Kalimpong, District Darjeeling, West Bengal, India

**Dr. Bindu Vijay**, Asst. Prof of Science, Gujarat National Law University, Gujarat, India

**Mr. Vivek Dubey**, Asst. Prof. of Law, Gujarat National Law University, Gujarat, India

**Mr. Amartya Saha**, Gujarat National Law University, Gujarat, India

**Mr. Vinod Kumar Verma**

**Ms. Amita Saxena**

**Ms. Kamlesh Agrawal,** Assistant Professor, Department of Commerce, St. Ann's Degree College for Women, Santosh Nagar Colony, Mehdipatnam, Hyderabad, India

**Ms. Sai Prasanna,** Assistant Professor, Department of Commerce, St. Ann's Degree College for Women, Santosh Nagar Colony, Mehdipatnam, Hyderabad, India

**Ms. J. Saujanya**, Assistant Professor, Department of Commerce, St. Ann's Degree College for Women, Santosh Nagar Colony, Mehdipatnam, Hyderabad, India

**Dr. Md. Samsur Jaman**, Assistant Professor, Department of Economics, Jiri College, Jiribam, Manipur, India

**Dr. Ram Krishna Mandal,** Associate Professor of Economics, Dera Natung Government College, Itanagar-791 113, Arunachal Pradesh, India

# Biodiversity, Benefit Sharing

## *Towards a Better Reality*

— Prof. G. Rajasekar

### Introduction

The link between people and nature are as old as themselves. Long before the growth of modern global society, communities across the globe used the natural resources for their development. Experience shows that continuous utilization of natural resources inevitably brought out rapid changes in the environment. These attitudinal changes of human being led to the rapid environmental degradation on one hand and extinction of species on the other side.

Loss of biodiversity is a threat to civilization resulting incalculable loss. The environmental issues like pollution, global warming and depletion of ozone layer can be overcome but eroded species cannot be brought back. Therefore, once lost species from the earth is lost forever. In order to tackle this issue the international community for the first time came with an instrument known as the Convention on Biological Diversity—1992. The significance of this convention is principle of ethics and equity in both accessing the wealth and sharing the benefits are enshrined. The convention called the signatories to respect, preserve and maintain knowledge, innovations and indigenous communities so as to encourage the equitable sharing of benefits arising from the utilization of such knowledge of innovations and practices. Therefore, it becomes need of the hour to have equilibrium between ecological and social process for coping with issues such as climatic change, biological invasion, biodiversity depletion, land degradation and desertification.

Responding to the call, made by the international community India has enacted certain legislation with an object to check the rapid deterioration of the ecology due to human interference. Thus it goes without saying that a law relating to biological diversity becomes an inevitable one though the regulations and rules of environmental protection are said to be a well developed area of law in India.

The Biological Diversity Act, 2002 is enacted as a comprehensive legislation with an aim and objective of sustainable use of natural resources and sharing of benefits out of it.[1]

## Meaning of Biodiversity

Generally speaking, the term biodiversity is a complex term and it is very difficult to define. But the definition holds that biodiversity is a measure of the relative diversity among organism present in different ecosystem. However this definition is not an exhaustive definition but an illustrative definition. The plain reading of this definition gives an understanding that it includes diversity within the species and among species and comparative diversity and ecosystem[2].

The Biological Diversity Act defines '*biodiversity*' means the variability among living organisms from all sources and includes diversity within species or between species and eco-system.[3] The notion of biodiversity refers to the variety of genetically distinct populations and species of plants, animals and micro-organism and the variety of ecosystems of which they are functioning parts.[4] The Biological Diversity Convention defines biological diversity includes diversity within the species and ecosystems and implies that the regulation of biodiversity seeks to encompass all living beings and their interactions and the ecosystems within which they live.[5] Going by the words of the above definitions one can easily say that it is nothing but a variation of life at all levels of biological organisms.

## Biodiversity and the International Regime

International Community felt that an effective regulatory regime for controlling the access of natural resources in the national and local community is necessitated. Like any other economic activity, it is realized that the genetic resources also have tremendous economic potential over the developmental process.[6] The commercialization of these resources in the name of economic development posed serious challenges in sustenance of these genetic resources. The biodiversity of developing countries is not only about the variability of living organism but also the life and livelihoods of human beings.

The United Nations Convention on Environment and Development (UNCED), 1992 outlines the plan and actions to have a healthy, productive life in accord with nature.[7] Therefore the UNCED explains the effects of environmental degradation on the developmental process. This observation is much reflected in the Preamble of the Convention of Biological Diversity (here in after referred as CBD).[8] It is pertinent to note that the UN General Assembly has also adopted a resolution with reference to the CBD. The resolution runs as follows:

> There remains an urgent need for the conservation and sustainable use of biological diversity and the fair and equitable sharing of benefits arising from the utilization of components of genetic resources. The threat to Biodiversity stems mainly from habitat destruction, over harvesting, pollution and the inappropriate introduction of foreign plants and animals.[9]

The fundamental objectives of the CBD are biodiversity conservations, sustainable use of biological resources and equitable sharing from such use.[10] However strong provisions relating to basic issues such as ownership, access, right to knowledge and resources, sustainability, informed consent and benefits are found missing.[11] The provisions ensuring genetic resources and knowledge associated with the same is no longer can be treated as a free good is found missing. As such there would be an implication for over-use of resources, knowledge, right to property etc. Ultimately there is every chance of clashes between cultures, systems of medicines and agricultural practices.

## Sustainable Use

The concept of sustainable use of biological resources had its lineage from World Conservation Strategy (WCS) 1980. In WCS the concept has been described as analogous to specially the interest whilst keeping capital. However Sustainable use means the use of components of biological diversity in a way and at a rate that does not lead to the long-term decline of biological diversity, thereby maintaining its potential to meet the needs and aspirations of present and future generation.[12]

From the above definition one can easily say that the components of biological diversity can be divided in to ecosystem, species and genetic materials. As such, sustainable use involves the use of each of these components.

Over the years the direct dependence over these resources has considerably reduced since several communities and families changed their occupation or even due to migration. Yet there are numerous communities in all parts of the country are directly and largely depend for their sustenance and survival on these resources. Such peoples and communities have a stake in conserving and using the resources in a sustainable manner.[13] These communities depend on their immediate natural environment for their survival for long and consequently developed a stake in conserving the local resources base.

The existence of customary practices governing the use of biological and natural resources may be observed in the context of forest use practices, traditional water uses and management, landholding patterns, agricultural practices, fisheries.[14] Sustainable use of bio-resources is reflected in the customs of the local and indigenous communities. Knowledge of the community elders regarding the status of resource is translated into a practice which incorporates sustainable harvest or wise use of the resources. This practice over a period of time became the custom transferred from one generation to another for a long time. Customary law and principles followed by traditional knowledge-holders fulfill individual, family and communal needs.[15]

The UN Convention on Biological Diversity requires member countries to share benefits equitably from the use of genetic resources and related knowledge and also to protect and encourage customary use of biological resources in accordance with traditional cultural practice.[16] The practice of treating man as a strand in the web of life was naturally conducive for conservation of nature. This is called as indigenous wisdom.

In State of Bihar *vs.* Subodh Gopal[17] the Supreme Court held that a customary right in the exercise of excavate stones for the purpose of trade (not for domestic or agricultural purpose) by the residents of the locality would *ex facie* be unreasonable, because the exercise of such right ordinarily tends to the complete destruction of the subject matter of the right. The custom was therefore unreasonable. Going by the words of the judiciary it can be easily construed that customary rights can be used only for conservation and not for excavation.

The Supreme Court in M.C. Mehta vs. Kamalnath and others[18] had ruled that the doctrine of Public Trust applies to natural ecosystem and the government as a public trustee should protect the same for the benefit of the society as large and the private commercial and industrial establishment should not be allowed to misappropriate them. The judgment of the court once again people are right to their common.

In the light of the inter-generational rights theory each generation has a right to receive the planet and its cultural and natural resources in an enjoyable condition. Therefore, it is a positive duty of the present generation to preserve and conserve the earth's natural resources for the better utilization of the future generation.

## Permanent Sovereignty over the Natural Resources

One of the Sovereign Right recognized by the International Law principle is sovereign rights over the natural resources.[19] The principle of permanent sovereignty over natural resources dictates that the sovereign state is empowered to exploit the natural resources within its boundary. This can be realized from the following words of the UN General Assembly:

> Every State has the sovereign and inalienable right to choose its economic system, as well as its political, social and cultural systems in accordance with the will of its people, without interference, coercion or threat in any form whatsoever.[20]

It is pertinent to note that earlier there were efforts to declare genetic resources as common heritage of mankind. However, CBD reaffirmed that states have their own biological resources. The sovereign rights over natural resources and the state's right to determine the access to the genetic resources located within the jurisdiction of the state is recognized by Art. 15.1 of CBD.

The law relating to biodiversity works on CBD's premise that the state has the sovereign right over its genetic resources. The authorities under the law at national, state and local levels have to deal with the issues of access to genetic resources.[21]

## Benefit Sharing

One of the goals of CBD is equitable sharing of benefits derived from the use of genetic resources. Benefit sharing is a relatively new notion that has been developed as a consequence of the rapidly changing scenario concerning claims over biological and genetic resources, traditional knowledge and the strengthening of intellectual property to accommodate life patents.[22] In other words, benefit sharing evolved as an indirect recognition that traditional knowledge-holders cannot directly from the strengthening of the intellectual property rights system even where their knowledge constitutes the basis for a product or process which can be protected under existing intellectual property rights.

India is a party to CBD. Recognizing the sovereign rights to use their own biological resources, the convention expects the parties to facilitate access to genetic resources by other parties subject to municipal legislation.

The salient features of Biological Diversity Act, 2002 is (i) to regulate access to biological resources of the country with the purpose of securing equitable share in benefits arising out of the use of biological resources;

(*ii*) to conserve and sustainably use biological diversity; (*iii*) to respect and protect knowledge of local communities related to biodiversity; (*iv*) to secure sharing of benefits with local communities as conservers of biological resources and holders of knowledge and information relating to the use of biological resources; (*v*) conservations and development of areas of importance from the standpoint of biological diversity by declaring them as biological heritage sites; (*vi*) protection and rehabilitation of threatened species; and (*vii*) involvement of institutions of state government.

## Traditional Knowledge

Traditional knowledge refers to the knowledge, innovations and practices of indigenous or local communities or individual embodying traditional life-styles. It represents part of the unregistered and often unappreciated intellectual property of such communities or individual and includes agriculture biodiversity, sustainable land use and natural resource management. This knowledge has been transferred from one generation to other from time immemorial.

The values and benefit of knowledge and traditional practices with regard to the protection and conservation of the natural resources therefore got recognition openly. Traditional knowledge of the indigenous people for conserving biological resources is authorized by the provisions mentioned in Chapter V of the Conservation of Biological Diversity Act and Art. 8 (j)[23] of CBD.

The use of biological resources has gradually led to the development of body of knowledge. Traditional knowledge plays an important role in identifying genetic materials with beneficial characteristics that can be isolated and separated from the original organisms and used in the development of novel products. The CBD provides vital opportunities for countries to introduce new measures to recognize and protect indigenous knowledge and innovations. Further the Draft Declaration on Rights of Indigenous People specifically provides that indigenous people are entitled to the recognition of the full ownership, the control and protection of their cultural and intellectual property.[24]

## Indian Constitution and Equitable Benefit Sharing

The Constitution of India provides that it shall be the duty of the state to apply the Directive Principles in the making of laws. These principles are:

- The State shall strive to promote the welfare of the people by securing and protecting as effectively as it may a social order, in which justice, social, economic and political shall inform all the institutions of the national life.[25]

- The State shall, in particular, direct its policy towards securing-that the ownership and control of the material resources of the community are so distributed as best to subserve the common good.[26]
- The State shall promote with special care the educational and economic interest of the weaker sections of the people and in particular of the Schedule Castes and Schedule Tribes and shall protect them from social justice and all forms of exploitation.[27]
- Urban forestry, protection of the environment and promotion of ecological aspects and Twelfth Schedule.[28]

The combined reading of the above provisions of the Constitution one may easily inferred that it is the duty of the State to secure to its citizen to ascertain their rights of accessing and conserving the natural resources available. The Preamble to the Constitution read with Directive Principles enjoins the state to take up these responsibilities.[29]

The Constitution of India imposes duty not only on the state but also the citizens have to protect and improve the natural environment including forests, lakes, rivers and wildlife, and to have compassion for living creatures.[30]

Economic empowerment is a basic human right. This fundamental right becomes the part of right to live, equality and of status and dignity to the poor, weaker sections, dalits and tribes. Justice is an attribute of human conduct and rule of law is an indispensible foundation to establish socio-economic justice[31].

Duty to act fairly is a part of fair procedure encapsulated under Arts 14 and 21. Every activity of a public authority or those under public duty or obligation must be informed by reason and guided by the public interest.[32]

Further the Constitutional 73rd and 74th Amendments are the step in aid to community conservation based on customary law. These amendments paved the way for self-rule of the local governments. Under Art. 243G, state governments are required to devolve their power and authority to local governments and enable them to function as a self government relating to the matters found in the Eleventh Schedule of the Constitution which includes social and farm forestry, soil and water conservation.[33]

Another interesting aspect is the willingness of the judiciary to impose strictures on a private entity if the activity of such entity infringes the fundamental rights of the people.[34] Here there is a possible argument that the activity of a person seeking access to genetic resources, by its very nature has implications for the rights of the people. This is an enforceable right not only because of contractual or a statutory obligation but of a public duty. Therefore, a *writ of mandamus* can be issued to enforce this right. The question arise here is whether a *Writ of Mandamus* lie against a private entity? While answering for this question the Supreme Court made it clear that a *writ of mandamus* may lie against a private entity depending on the nature of the duty imposed on it. That duty must be judged in the light of the positive obligation owed by the person or authority to the affected party, no matter by what means the duty is imposed.[35] Another crucial position is the lacking of proper legislation. To absolve this critical situation the judiciary came with an answer that international conventions and norms can be relied to the extent of inconsistency with constitutional principles.[36]

## Conclusion

Experience of a decade suggests that economic development positively increased the utilization of biological resources to its maximum. This led to the reduction in its supply and expanded the degradation of environment. Hence, it is needless to say that any discussion relating to economic or political without keeping the issues involving protection of environment or natural resources in mind is senseless. In other words unlike yester years the development is viewed as a wholesome development instead of economic development. Here the sustenance of natural resources required to create an effective framework that cares supplies of resources and controls the demand, so that demand can continue to be shared in future.[37]

The need to sustain one's lifestyle becomes necessary as some of the essential biological resources are either facing extinction or slowly turning unfit for human use.[38] Thus, certain restrictions in using them become inevitable. In this regard it is to say that some duties have been recognized by the community and others are yet to be recognized. Due to the lack of will on the part of the legislature to implement and the absence of effective institutions to monitor the implementation made the enforcement less effective. Moreover one should not forget to notice shared anxiety of mankind that creates or influence the legislative will to preserve and conserve the biological resources for future generations. The realization of the principle Sustainable Development of Biological Resources causes certain environmental implications in the form of environmental duties. Public opinion and cooperation at all levels should be generated for the effective enforcement of these environmental duties; otherwise killing the goose that lays golden eggs.

## REFERENCES

1. The aim and objectives of the Act is to provide for conservation of biological diversity, sustainable use of its components and equitable sharing of its benefits arising out of the use of biological resources, knowledge and four matters connected therewith or incidental thereto. The Biological Diversity Act, 2002 (Act 18 of 2003).

2. Kevin J. Gaston and John I. Speaker, Biodiversity: An Introduction (Second Edition), Blackwell Publishing, p. 4.
3. Sec. 2 (b) The Biological Diversity Act, 2002 (Act 18 of 2003).
4. United Nations, Glossary of Environment Statistics Un Document ST | ESA | STAT | SER F/67 (1997)
5. Article 2, Convention on Biological Diversity, Rio de Janeiro, 5 June 1992, 31 International Legal Materials (1992), p. 818.
6. The Preamble of the Convention of Biological Diversity, 1992, A/CONF.151/26
7. Principle 1 of Rio Declaration.
8. Supra Note 5.
9. UN General Assembly Resolution A/Res/S-19/2dt. Sept.19, 1997.
10. UNDP, Human Development Report, 1999 (Oxford University Press), p. 70.
11. It has been observed that the attempt to create a global market in property rights imposes one conception of ownership and innovation on culturally diverse reality, benefiting private industrial research but not public institutes or farming communities. *Ibid.*
12. Sec. 2 (o) The Biological Diversity Act, 2002 (Act 18 of 2003).
13. Kothari, A.N. Pathak and F. Vania, Where Communities Care: Community based Wildlife and Ecosystem Management in South Asia, 2000 Evaluating Eden Series No. 3
14. Secs.12 to 16 of the Indian Forest Act, 1927 recognizes right to pasture and forest products at the stage of settling rights before a given area of forest is classified as reserve forest.
15. *Ibid.*
16. Supra Note 6.
17. AIR 1968 SC281.
18. (1997)1SCC 388.
19. General Assembly Resolution 1803 (XVII) of 14th December 1962 on Permanent Sovereignty.
20. Arts.1 and 2 of the Charter of Economic Rights and Duties of States.
21. Chapter IV and V of The Biological Diversity Act, 2002 (Act 18 of 2003).
22. Philippe Cullet, *Intellectual Property Protection and Sustainable Development,* Lexis Nexis Butterworths, New Delhi, 2005), p. 163.
23. Art. 8(j) of CBD runs as subject to its National Legislation, respect, preserve and maintain knowledge, innovations and practices of indigenous and local communities embodying traditional lifestyles relevant for the conservation and sustainable use of biological diversity and promote their wider application with the approval and involvement of the holders of such knowledge, innovations and practices and encourage the equitable sharing of the benefits arising from the utilization of such knowledge innovations and practices.
24. Art. 29 Draft Declaration on the Right of Indigenous people, UN Sub-Commission on Prevention of Discrimination and Protection of Minorities, Forty-Sixth Session, 1994, Un Doc E/CN4/Sub2/1994/2/Add1.

25. Article 38 renumbered as Clause (1) thereof by the Constitution (Forty-Forth Amendment) Act,1978, Sec.9 (w.e.f. 20-6-1979).
26. Art. 39 (b), Constitution of India, 1950.
27. Art. 46, Constitution of India, 1950.
28. Ins. by the Constitution (Seventy-Fourth Amendment) Act, 1992 Sec.4 (w.e.f. 1-6-1993), Art 243W Constitution of India, 1950.
29. *Charan Lal Sahu* vs. *Union of India* (1990) 1 SCC 613
30. Art. 51A (g) Ins. by the Constitution (Forty-Second Amendment) Act, 1976, Sec.11 (w.e.f. 3-1-1977).
31. *Muralidhar Dayandeo Kesekar* vs. *Vishwanath Pandu Barde,* 1995 Supp (2) SCC 549.
32. *LIC of India* vs. *Consumer Education* (1995) 5 SCC 482.
33. Entry 2 of the List is Land improvement, implementation of land reforms, land consolidation and soil conservation. Entry 5—fisheries, Entry 6—social forestry and farm forestry.
34. *Indian Council for Environ—Legal Action* vs. *Union of India* (1981) 1 SCC 471.
35. *Anti Mukta Sadguru Shree Mukthajee Vandas Swami suvarana Jayalni Mahostava Smarak Trust* vs. *R. Rudani,* (1989) 2SCC 691, See also *K. Krisnamacharayalu* vs. *Sri.Venkateshewara Hindu College of Engineering,* (1997) 3 SCC 571
36. *Visakha* vs. *State of Rajasthan,* (1997) 6SCC 241.
37. Dr. A. David Ambrose, "Sustainable Development of Natural Resources and Environmental Implications in International Law", *SBRRM Journal of Law,* Vol. 4, p. 32 (1997).
38. *Ibid.*

# Thinking Outside the Box?

## *A Paradigmatic Shift in the Study of Environmental Scarcity, Conflict and Ecological Security in Malaysia*

— Dr. Sharifah Munirah Alatas


### *ABSTRACT*

*This essay provides a fresh approach towards environmental scarcity, conflict and ecological studies, using examples from Malaysia. The ideological foundation of this attempt as a paradigm shift is the concept of ecological philosophy, or ecosophy which identifies environmental deterioration as involving deeper philosophical root. No longer do we speak only of human destruction of the environment, and the facts to support this; no longer do we speak only of steps humans should take to improve the situation. Ecosophy speaks of self introspection, and its interaction with the environment as a means to solving environmental plunder and destruction. It is suggested that the ecosophical approach should be applied to Malaysian society, in anticipation of potential political and societal crises based on diminishing natural resources. An ecosophical approach to identify and mitigate environmental degradation in Malaysia looks at the fundamental values of why environmental preservation and ecological security should be the goal for our planet as a whole. The approach seeks to go beyond the mindset of security-centered environment security thinking, which is still very much interest-driven. This attempt is not an easy one, as its basis is philosophical and normative, rather than empirical.*

## Introduction

The objective of this paper is to provide a fresh approach to the causal relationship between environmental scarcity, conflict and ecological security, using examples from Malaysia. It proposes to investigate the effect of environmental degradation and scarcities of renewable natural resources has on Malaysian society, and in the process, provides a new paradigm in environmental, conflict and ecological studies. The assumptions made here about human nature and actor behavior is that the discourse involves critical, rational debate about the ends of human life, viewed as goals or states of being, to which, humans (ought to) aspire and about the means to achieving these goals. The potential difficulty of this paradigmatic shift is that human behavior is governed by instinct rather than by politics. Throughout this paper, I draw upon the theoretical framework put forth by Leif Ohlsson in his Introductory Chapter, "Environment, Scarcity, and Conflict—A Debate and Its Origin", to the book *Environment, Scarcity and Conflict—A Study of Malthusian Concerns,* (Ohlsson, 1999), as well as upon the seminal work by Thomas F. Homer-Dixon entitled *Environment, Scarcity, and Violence* (Homer-Dixon, 1999). A third document, an issue paper commissioned by the FAO AGLW, entitled *"Water and Social Resource Scarcity"* (Ohlsson, 1998) provides relevant theoretical material on the adaptive capacity of society towards natural resource depletion. While these three works have helped in the general framework of this essay, I am indebted to the works of Arne Naess, for the ideological foundations of this essay, especially with respect to the arguments pertaining to ecophilosophy and ecosophy (Naess, 1974; 1991). I conclude this discourse by attempting an alternative approach to the study of the environmental scarcity-conflict-ecological security nexus, providing specific developments in Malaysian society to support my analysis.

## Clarification of Terminology

***Environment*:** Environment in this essay is defined as the complex of climatic, biotic, social and edaphic (i.e. plant communities that are distinguished by soil conditions rather than by the climate) actors that acts upon an organism and determines its form and survival. These include climate/weather, light, air, water and soil. The environment is a biological construct in which organisms live among one another, sharing their habitat, i.e. their environmental space.

***Ecology*:** Ecology as it is used here is defined as the distribution and abundance of living organisms and how these properties interact with other organisms and their environment. Ecology is the symbiotic relationship between humanity, the natural surroundings (environment), technology and environmental philosophy (ecosophy). The latter term is especially critical in the definition of ecology in that it involves a deep inquiry into values, the nature of the world (ecology) and the self. Ecology, therefore, is the process of how living things harmonize with each other, with their natural surroundings, with human activity, and how all these are determined by values of preservation. Ecosophy involves environmental ethics beyond science and religion. Human activities as a dependent variable in the preservation or destruction of the ecological system are pivotal in the study of environmental scarcity and ecological security. Ecological security takes on a more kaleidoscopic and holistic view of the issues plaguing us, from internal political corruption, to hegemonic domination in the international political environment; from cultural adaptation to advances in technology, industrialization and urbanization, to environmental degradation and scarcity; from the application of philosophical values of the preservation of the Earth to the realization that the fate of humanity is directly linked to how humans interact with each other and with their natural surroundings (Drengson, 1997). Hence, ecological security is the well-being and flourishing of human and non-human life which have value in themselves. This value is based on a holistic biosphere which consists of the interaction of living and non-living (e.g. rivers, mangrove swamps) ecosystems. It is this concept of interaction that could lead to conflict situations, depending on various factors, environmental degradation and scarcity being two of them.

Ecosophy has evolved from the environmental movement, which began with the Stockholm Convention in 1972, progressing on to the Rio Declaration and Agenda 21 in 1992, to the Kyoto Conference and the Kyoto Protocol on climate change in 1997 (to name a few). A very important landmark development in both environmental and ecological awareness was the Malmö Ministerial Declaration of 2000 which identified widespread global environmental deterioration as involving deeper philosophical roots. This declaration institutionalized a more holistic (ecological) approach to tackling the deterioration of the planet. No longer do we speak of 'regional' or 'international' environmental degradation; we speak now of global and planetary ecological destruction. (United Nations Environment Programme, 1972, 1973, 1975, 1979, 1985, 1987, 1988, 1989, 1992, 1995, 1997, 1998, 2000, 2001, 2002, 2004, 2005). Ecosophy as a concept is attributed to Arne Naess, based on a talk he gave in Bucharest in 1972 at the Third World Research Conference. Naess saw two forms of environmentalism: a shallow ecology movement and a long-range deep ecology movement (Naess, 1953). The shallow ecology movement has as its goal, a marriage of health and affluence. The tenets of the long-range deep ecology movement are normative in nature, meaning they ask deep questions about lifes' purposes around the perception of reality beyond science to an intuitive awareness of the oneness of all life. Deep ecology considers the human spirit which feels connected to the cosmos as a whole. Both these concepts will be used in my concluding analysis.

***Natural resources*:** Natural resources can be defined as any material that exists in nature independently of human industry (a road is NOT a natural resource, although most of the material used to construct it is), and that is utilized in some way by humans. Water, natural gas, petroleum, coal, forests and even humans are examples of natural resources.

A distinction must be made between renewable and non-renewable natural resources,[1] because in actuality it is the renewable natural resources that end up being more scarce than the non-renewable resources.[2] The argument is as follows: when petroleum (a non-renewable natural resource) is extracted at a rate that could deplete it, technological advances made by other substitutes (carbon-fiber instead of steel, plastics instead of metal, and fiber-optics instead of copper wires), managed to overcome the apparent scarcity of petroleum. Hence, industrial economies are still able to function efficiently without non-renewable natural resources, which would therefore render the latter 'less scarce'. In this essay, I provide examples of renewable natural resources to validate my analysis as these are most likely to be scarce and disrupt the socio-economic function of societies.

***Scarcity/Environmental Scarcity*:**[3] Throughout this essay, the terms 'scarcity and 'environmental scarcity' will be used in two ways:

(*i*) *As a relative concept and a social construct:* Defined as a decline in, or the degradation of, the level and quality of natural resources from what society has become accustomed to (Ohlsson, 1999: 4). To illustrate this, the air quality in Malaysia's urban metropolises may remain the same for up to 10 years, the needs and expectations of the population during the same period of time may have changed, resulting in a greater demand for cleaner air. The rise in expectations may be a result of a number of factors, including increased education in benchmarking the quality of one's surroundings or external conditions, a rise in the socio-economic status of Malaysians, population growth, the aging of a population and rural-urban migration.

(*ii*) *In economic terms:* Homer-Dixon has defined environmental scarcity as 'a drop in the supply of a key resource, through an increase in demand and through a change in the relative access of different groups to the resource' (Homer-Dixon, 1999: 48). Also, due to overall population growth, economic necessity and rural-urban migration, there would be a need for more urban freshwater consumption rendering that resource 'scarce' among urbanites, as opposed to rural populations. (There may be other reasons why the rural population might *also* face scarcity, but it is not relevant in supporting the point above).

***Security/Ecological Security:*** The concept of security applied in this essay is wide, as opposed to the traditional definition which subjects it to a more *real-politik* interpretation. Here, the meaning of security takes into consideration "any threat of infringement on the choice of individuals, groups or states" (Ohlsson, 1999: 27). Security is freedom from danger, fear, want and deprivation. The previous, less-inclusive definition confines its meaning to one of state-centricism, comprising only military threats to states. To illustrate the point in support of the wider definition of security, it is essential that we look at both the United Nations Conference on Human Environment [UNCHE] (1972) and the UNDP (1994) Declarations.[4] These two declarations emphasized that there is a vital interrelationship between the preservation of the environment and human well being. The first principle of the UNCHE Declaration states that:

> "man has a fundamental right to freedom, equality and adequate conditions of life, in an environment of quality that permits a life of dignity and well being, and he bears solemn responsibility to protect and improve the environment for present and future generations".

This sentiment was repeated in the 1992 United Nations Conference on Environment and Development (UNCED), with a call for citizens' participation in handling environmental issues. Principle 10 of the UNCED declaration proclaimed that:

> "environmental issues are best handled with the participation of all concerned citizens, at all relevant levels. At the national level, each individual shall have appropriate access to information concerning the environment that is held by public authorities, including information on hazardous materials and activities in their communities, and the opportunity to participate in decision-making processes. The state shall facilitate and encourage public awareness and participation by making information widely available. Effective access to judicial and administrative proceedings, including redress and remedy, shall be provided".

These two declarations, including the ideas of Naess outline the essential characteristics of ecological security which gives priority to the basic human rights of people—to provide them protection from the threats of environmental, social, economic, cultural, and political scarcities. Although this may paint a picture of an idealistic existence, it is nevertheless a necessary goal of ecology which could limit conflict over scarce resources.

***Conflict*:** Conflict can be divided into four categories—interstate, intrastate, non-state and one-sided violence. In this essay we concentrate on intrastate conflict and non-state conflict, as well as focus away from interstate-centric definitions (i.e. military threats to states). Specifically, in the Malaysian context, we allude to non-violent conflict, which includes latent conflict and crises (a crisis is defined as tensions below the threshold of violence). The discussion in this essay suggests 'possibilities' for conflict based on perceptions of risks created by environmental scarcity. This analysis, whether it is perceived or real conflict, refers to the clashing of overlapping interests around values and issues between at least two parties. The clash of interests and values has to be of some duration and some magnitude in order to be classified as a conflict. Here we encounter a tautological conundrum of how to define 'some duration' and 'some magnitude'; relative to what benchmark?

The quantitative measures of the clashing of overlapping interests will determine whether these escalate into conflict. The measures of duration and magnitude are such measures that will decide which set of overlapping interests qualify as conflict. Duration analysis of conflict requires that the start and the end of the conflict can be stated in chronological fashion. Usually, trigger events can be chronologized, setting the beginning of the conflict (e.g. the assassination of Rwanda's president on 6 March 1994 marks the start of the civil war). If a conflict ends with the signing of a treaty or agreement, then that represents the end of the conflict.[5] For the purpose of this essay, though, we use the notion of 'perceptions' of the risk of conflict, given a particular situation of environmental scarcity.

## Considerations in Security Studies: Some Observations of its Evolutionary Process

It is appropriate to take a brief look at the contemporary debate concerning the concept of security. Discourses on the environment and ecological security is relevant in strategic and security studies, irrespective of the current Cold War-post-Cold War, bipolar-unipolar debate. From an ecological perspective, this debate focuses on how to relate the post-Cold War geopolitical scenario environmentally and ecologically, with conflict. Since the break-up of the Soviet Union, the re-unification of Germany, and the expansion of both the European Union (EU) and the North Atlantic Treaty Organization (NATO), the discourse among academics and policy decision-makers has focused on defining a new concept of security (i.e. thinking outside the box). This change in focus was largely due to a shift from a bi-polar world to a world which was thought to be multi-polar, with not one, but many centers of power. For example, the EU and a united Germany were thought of as new centers of political and economic power, relegating military power to a lower rung. Further east, the nuclear arsenal testing by both Pakistan and India was another testament to other centers of power, in these cases, nuclear powers. Japan's and China's remarkable rise to economic supremacy demonstrated their soft-power capabilities, unchallenged by other regions.

With 9/11 however, strategic thinking changed again, in order to explain the 'us versus them' response of the United States, represented by George Bush's pre-emptive strike doctrine with respect to the 'war against terrorism'.

The conceptual approach of this paper posits that while academic studies and discourses that feed policy initiatives are influenced by the geopolitical repositioning of 'power politics' there is no need to redefine the concept of security, to either remain 'inside' or 'outside' the security box. This is especially so when we observe developments in environmental and ecological studies. Conflict and insecurity have always existed, whether in a bipolar, multipolar or unipolar context. Countries have always competed for wealth and security; much of this competition has also centered on the need to secure environmentally-scarce 'goods'. In their pursuit of ideological, political and economic leadership, countries have also had to deal with internal problems, deriving from ethnic and tribal rivalries, economic pressure, resource scarcity, religious sectarianism, the narcotics trade or plain political expediency. Several hotspots of conflict in the early 1990s, had their roots in the Cold War period. Examples of these include nations and groups fighting for self-determination (French-Algerian war, Russia-Chechnya, Israel-Palestine), genocides or civil wars fought between ethnic (Central Asia), racial and tribal (Africa), or religious (Middle-East or South Asia) groups. These hotspots did not suddenly emerge because the Soviet Union disbanded into several independent nations, or because the EU and NATO expanded. It can be argued that a Cold War-post-Cold War periodization was created by interest groups to implement shifts in policy (the reasons for these shifts are beyond the scope of this discussion). Most importantly, issues of strategy and security that have had their roots in a Cold War, bipolar world still have to be dealt with.

Following that, it is safe to say that discussions of natural resource scarcity and security, which is part of the ecological security discourse has been present in academia and the larger society, for a long time. Thomas Malthus, about two hundred years ago, had already discussed this in his essay, *An Essay on the Principle of Population* (Malthus, 1798). Post-Cold War power politics has rendered this to the back-burner due to reasons presented in the previous paragraph. Issues associated with ecological security now fall under the rubric of 'non-traditional' security issues, which, in itself is a misnomer. According to the 'followers', 'non-traditional' security issues include human security (as defined by the United Nations Development Program [UNDP] 1994 Annual Report on Human Development), transnational security and drug-trafficking, and environmental security, to name a few. The question that comes to mind, though, is, what is 'non' traditional about these? The discussion here asserts that certain quarters in government, academia, interested grassroots groups and the private sector, with their own respective agendas, have perpetuated the 'non-traditional' security concept in order to justify 'humanitarian', economic, political and to a lesser extant, military initiatives as a way to perpetuate ideological domination in a post-Cold War realm. While debating that terminology such as 'traditional' and 'non-traditional' should not be applied to security studies, we also suggest a refocusing of attention, away from the tri-partite—bipolar, multipolar, unipolar, discourse, to issues of threat against the planet's ecology. Its relevance lies in the possible repercussions that ecological insecurity could have to national, regional and global stability. It is also vital to emphasize the environmental scarcity-conflict nexus, highlighting the potential it has to disrupt harmony within a state.

## ENVIRONMENTAL SCARCITY AND ECOLOGICAL SECURITY IN MALAYSIA

In Malaysia, a developing nation, environmental scarcity and a lack of ecological security are closely related to industrialization and urbanization. Urbanization is defined as an increase in the proportion of people living in urban areas. Urbanization in Malaysia is the result of consistent migration of rural dwellers to urban centers, in search of steadier jobs, and higher standards of living. The United Nations Economic and Social Commission for Asia and the Pacific (ESCAP) together with funding from the United Nations Population Fund (UNFPA) did a study on the rate of urbanization in Asia and the Pacific, and found that between 1995 and 2030, out of 33 of the world's largest cities, 27 will be in Asia, by 2015. Of these 27, the rate of increase will be highest in Southeast Asia (chart 2.1).

**Chart 2.1 : Rate of urbanization in Asia and the Pacific, 1995-2030**

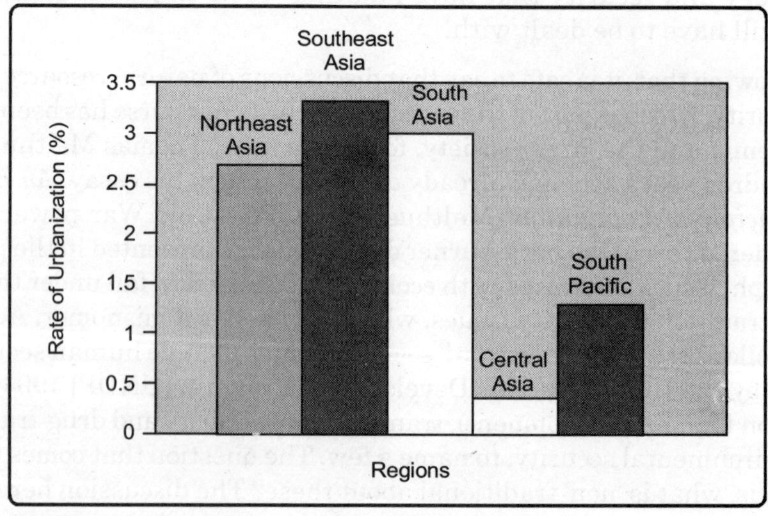


**Source**: United Nations Population Fund 1996 and ESCAP 1999.

The high rate of urbanization in Southeast Asia contributes to environmental degradation and scarcity because the level and quality of natural resources is not enough to meet the needs and expectations of these populations. The term 'expectations' is what explains the social-construct aspect of scarcity, which correctly defines environmental scarcity in Southeast Asia. One of the most destructive activities that has left many Southeast Asian nations in a state of environmental degradation and scarcity is land clearance. This is probably the most irreversible form of 'planet plunder' because it results in severe economic and social hardships. Once the bio-mass is stripped off (in the form of deforestation), species can become extinct, and indigenous groups who depend of forest resources for their culture and livelihood will be displaced. Exposed soils, especially in the tropics, erode rapidly, and, in many cases, are subject to declining fertility and desertification; they also degrade the water quality of downstream communities, often contributing to flooding and silting of rivers and dams. Land clearance often extends to the coastal regions and into the sea itself. This in turn can upset the ocean ecology.

In a recent Malaysian newspaper article entitled "Stop Plundering Mother Nature" (*New Sunday Times*, March 13, 2005), comments by government officials were made about the rapid rate of deforestation that is taking place by Malaysia's urban developers. Several other articles have been published by academics, private citizens and NGOs on the poor state of Malaysia's environment as well as the lack of capacity building programs to overcome environmental degradation. Malaysia's environmental woes can be divided into three main areas: traditional air and water pollution, urban air and water pollution, and solid waste management. Malaysia's traditional pollution of the air and water began about a century ago, when rivers were polluted by tin mine wastewater and sludge. Later, other traditional industries such as rubber and palm oil production further polluted rivers and the surrounding ocean. From the 1960s onwards, Malaysia embarked on a series of industrialization projects which resulted in more industrial waste. Rapid industrialization encouraged rural migration into the urban areas. The expansion of cities led to an increase in the flow of household and human waste into rivers. An increase in fumes generated by vehicles contributed to rising air pollution; this in turn has increased the production of acid rain and greenhouse gases. To date, though, the most serious threat to Malaysia's environment is to freshwater resources. Let us look at Malaysia's largest and most populated urban center, the Klang Valley.

In Malaysia, freshwater to the Klang Valley is supplied by the Klang River, which flows through the heart of Kuala Lumpur city. A river *it is*, but most people would describe it as a 'large monsoon drain'. Again, this is testimony to engineering-driven 'solutions' to riverbank erosion and flooding, and an attempt to manipulate nature, geared towards straightening and widening a river. What is thought to be great engineering feats has turned into expensive 'clean-up' operations for the Malaysian government. On numerous occasions, the Klang 'monsoon-drain' river has overflowed its banks, concrete slabs have cracked, broken and been washed away, and the heart of Kuala Lumpur has been subjected to debilitating floods, human inconvenience and suffering, and traffic congestion (*Star Online*, 2003). Deforestation, dam construction, silt from construction sites, industrial discharges and dumping of solid wastes have undermined the capacity of Malaysian rivers like the Klang River, to carry excessive run-offs to the sea. Having apparently not learnt from mistakes, the Drainage and Irrigation Department (DID) have come up with new proposals to re-meander the river. Although the department claims to be removing the concrete slabs, it remains to be seen how the management of rivers in our urban areas can translate into a more holistic approach to harmonizing nature with urbanization.

Under the Eighth Malaysia Plan, RM1.5 billion has been allocated for flood-relief plans, but the DID is saying this is far from adequate. Be that as it may, will the funding be used appropriately? One positive development is that in 1992, the DID embarked on a clean-up of the Klang River. Subsequently, in 1993, the Malaysian government launched an ongoing 'Love Our Rivers' (*Cintai Sungai Kita*) campaign. After 12 years, it is disheartening to see that Malaysia's urban centers still have clogged-up rivers with animal and domestic waste and industrial effluvia, not to mention the 'monsoon-drain' look! In Malaysia, the freshwater crisis is mounting, and there is more evidence that depletion is taking place at an uncontrollable rate. For example, there are no less than 54 dams in operation in Malaysia. However, the amount of water restored by the dams constitutes only 2 per cent of the total runoff available in a year. Many dams are able to maintain the required water levels throughout the year, only because sufficient surface runoffs are able to reach the impoundment and some sub-surface flows are able to replenish lost water. However, with many more dry spells brought on by changing weather patterns (El Niño weather pattern, for example), many of the dams may not be able to withstand prolonged dry periods. (Dam-construction brings up other debates concerning depletion of forests and natural habitats, which are outside the scope of this paper). Being a tropical and lush country, one would expect Malaysia to have enough water for its needs, on an annual basis. However, this optimism is slowly being compromised by regular shortages, at certain times of the year. The regular flow of water out of domestic taps has diminished and become more precious. This is due to the condition of the sources of the water, i.e. rivers in the highland forests. Rivers in these highlands supply much of the potable water in Malaysia, but the quality, quantity and timing of water is influenced by climate (as we have seen above) and land use. When land use is not properly managed, rivers are subject to pollution, such as eutrophication. Eutrophication of rivers is the result of nitrogen and phosphorus contamination, from fertilizers used in agricultural projects. Similarly, the hazards created by water, such as surface erosion and landslides are influenced by such distribution of contaminants.

The deforestation of tropical forests in East Malaysia has caused landslides and flooding, which in turn has caused homelessness for thousands of inhabitants. For examples, the indigenous peoples (the Penan) in Sarawak have been displaced due to the construction of roads which has cleared forests and destroyed much of their environment, including the pollution of freshwater resources. Although no tension has been reported between logging companies and the Penan, the issue has drawn international attention. What is disheartening is that issues and problems pertaining to the environment are not new in Malaysia. Problems regarding ineffective effluent disposal from mining activities and conflicts of interest between agriculture and wildlife protection were some of the issues that had been drawn out as early as in the 1920s. In those days, interest in environmental quality was confined only to a small number of government officials, academics and special interest groups. At that time, environmental awareness was just emerging, and it was felt that it was the responsibility of the government to bear the brunt of environmental protection. The larger masses were convinced that environmental protection is a luxury and might hinder the development process. Both the government and the people saw problems of the environment through myopic lenses, not realizing that each sector (water, forest, air, etc.) were interconnected, and that one problem fed into another. The picture then was no different with respect to freshwater problems. In 1920, the Waters Enactment was introduced. This was subsequently followed by other legislation, which was largely sectoral and did not focus on a holistic approach to freshwater problems. In 1974, the Environmental Equality Act (EQA) was passed by Parliament, but it did not address freshwater problems as part of the overall deterioration of the environment.

The Malaysian Environmental Quality Report, 2000, the Compendium of Environmental Statistics Malaysia, 2001 and the Eighth Malaysia Plan 2001-2005 put the number of rivers polluted as 45.5 per cent of the total number. This is widely due to population sewage. Statistics from the Asian Development Bank and Water Watch Penang present a similar picture. They claim that, although Malaysia's annual rainfall totals about 2000-5000 mm (one of the highest in the world), the actual amount of water available for use is reduced due to seasonal droughts, deterioration in water quality, wastage and poor management. For instance, on an average, a Malaysian urbanite uses 526 liters per day, and wastes up to 233 liters per day. Wasted water drains back into groundwater deposits which make it costly to tap and reuse. All these statistics are published and available, but what use are they if Malaysian society does not adopt an ecological approach to securing their planet to reduce environmental scarcity?

The case for air pollution in Malaysia is similar. In urban centers, the number of vehicles has increased astronomically. Public transportation systems have lagged behind, leaving city dwellers no choice but to drive their automobiles, not just twice a day (to and from work, or to run daily errands), but sometimes more. Due to affluence, one household may own up to 4 cars, one for each member! Although unleaded gasoline is now the norm in Malaysia, trucks and lorries still use diesel fuel. Public busses are poorly maintained, as are many private vehicles. With regard to the latter, the rate of fatal accidents on Malaysian roads seems to be increasing annually, a sad reminder that there is lax enforcement of laws against poorly-maintained vehicles, and reckless handling of vehicles. The value of recycling non-biodegradable goods was brought up in 2003, when the Prime Minister of Malaysia, Abdullah Badawi declared that all ministries, government departments and agencies, especially those located in the administrative capital, Putrajaya, must place recycling bins in their premises and take steps to cut down on wastage. (*Star Online*, November 10, 2003). At the launching of the National Recycling Day at Dataran Putra, he said,

> "In addition, we can also take steps to cut down on wastage of resources in our offices. As one effort towards a 'paperless government' concept and to save paper, I ask that the Chief Secretary to the Government issues a circular to all ministries and departments to encourage printing on both sides of paper and to ask that staff write or use the blank side of drafts of non-official documents". (*The Star*, 2003)

Three years later, many older and newly-developed neighborhoods in the Klang Valley and other urban centers still lack recycling facilities, and public apathy towards the separation of garbage (plastics, glass and paper) still exists. This is despite the efforts of many NGOs who are actively involved in capacity building activities.[6]

## Ecosophical Approach to A Scarcity-Conflict-Security Nexus in the Malaysian Context

How can we synthesize the information above to conceptualize a scarcity–conflict–security nexus in the Malaysian context? Why is it important to do so? To answer these questions, one must address the fundamental issue of human interaction with its environs. It is this lack of an ecological approach by all layers of society which confronts Malaysia. What Malaysia faces is the anthropogenic impact on the ecosystem. Plainly put, Malaysia's environmental problem is actually an ecological crisis. A number of developments have contributed to this crisis: (*i*) poor governance (in this case, poor implementation of already-tabled laws); (*ii*) lack of political will (related to the former); (*iii*) the pursuit of profits by both local and foreign private enterprises in development projects (which end up plundering natural resources) done in the name of 'globalization', under the pretext of 'modernizing' a society; (*iv*) inadequate capacity building programs; and (*v*) a lack of public awareness (related to the former) of the crisis.

The ecological philosophical (ecosophical) approach, i.e. looking at a crisis from a more holistic, humanistic paradigm, is based on 'harmony' or 'equilibrium'. This humanistic view of environmental change as applied to Malaysia suggests that the only way we can overcome environmental degradation and scarcity within the society is to not only view the 'facts' of pollution, resource depletion, population explosion or poverty, but to focus also on society's 'value priorities'. In Malaysia, as in other Southeast Asian nations, we must cultivate a respect for nature and the 'inherent worth' of other beings. To date, there has been a lot of attention placed on environmentalism, with many heads of states in the region (including Malaysia's) speaking out against natural resource plunder and environmental annihilation, and in the process, accusing multinational corporations of and funders of having a key role. While this may be true, there is a tendency to be one-sided in the analysis. An ecosophical approach would look at the fundamental values of the state, why and how such multinational corporations are allowed, in the first place, to manipulate governments in the developing world for their own profit.

In Malaysia many newspaper articles have carried well-written and soundly thought-out articles on the environment. For instance, an article written in March, 2005, in Malaysia's *Malay Mail* was headlined "River Systems Under Threat". (*The Malay Mail*, March 31, 2005: 4). The article covered the issue of poaching and illegal fishing at the Nenggiri River system (particularly the River Puian), in Kelantan. The poaching method used typically bombing and poisoning, and this in turn has caused fish populations in connecting streams also be affected. Orang Asli (indigenous people of the region) constantly harvest rare fish because it commands a high price in restaurants. In this case, economic necessity is a primary motivator for poaching. The good news is that positive management and re-stocking of the river system has begun to conserve the river and its aquatic life. Logging in the region has been prohibited too, reducing silting. The article ends with a declaration by its chief conservator, who said, "We hope to do the same (i.e. gazette as a heritage area) for the Puian River which is severely depleted of its natural resources".[7] He added further that the Nenggiri River System has a huge potential in terms of eco-tourism, implying that it was critical to conserve the system before Malaysia lags behind in the eco-tourism industry. This is precisely what characterizes 'shallow' ecological values, in Naess' terminology. Malaysia continues to take part in the 'shallow ecology movement', whereby, issues of environmental scarcity and ecological security are viewed in terms of short-term values. A myopic view is obvious when one speaks of 'eco-tourism' in the Nenggiri River system and 'conservation' in re-stocking the Puian River, in the same breath. On the contrary, conservation programs and education must be geared toward constantly asking the right questions of 'why?'—to ultimate values, norms and premises. In fact, this is a concept that could be very applicable to Malaysian society, which is based on religious values, inter-cultural harmony and political stability. Ecological security emphasizes a holistic approach towards avoiding the potential societal conflict that could arise out of environmental scarcity. With a foundation of principles and values such as social justice, peace and non-violence, many societies in the developing world, such as Malaysia would be better equipped to respond to changing environmental situations (i.e. scarcity of natural resources). If a nation has a corrupt political system, which would most likely lead to a whole host of economic and social problems, it would be difficult to realize higher qualities of life as a whole (which is what the environmental movement has been all about).

The nexus between environmental scarcity, conflict and ecological security is based on the social effects that can ensue. In Malaysia, environmental scarcity can produce negative social effects due to the adaptive inability of society. The ecosophical question to ask in this instance is 'why?'. At the risk of being redundant, why should we ask 'why?'? It is necessary in order to be able to find the root causes of such adaptive inability so that we can overcome them. Adaptive inability may be the cause of:

1. lack of understanding of the inherent value of human and non-human life on Earth;
2. inability to understand that the diversity of life itself is a value, and hence to be preserved;
3. lack of understanding that human have no right to reduce the richness and diversity of life on the planet because it is not theirs to plunder.

If different groups in societies such as Malaysia share these common philosophical principles the potential for conflict over diminishing resources may be reduced. Malaysia may not encounter intra- and inter-state conflict.

## REFERENCES

1. Examples of renewable natural resources are freshwater, forests, fisheries, plant and animal species, land/soil and oxygen/clean air. Examples of non-renewable natural resources are petroleum, coal, natural gas.
2. The terms 'renewable' and 'non-renewable' are differentiated by applying the trajectory of time; ultimately all natural resources are renewable, but the non-renewable resources take millennia to replenish themselves, whereas the renewable resources take a much shorter period of time, i.e. within a generation or two. In simple terms, a renewable resource is capable of being replaced by natural, ecological cycles which are more regular than with a non-renewable resource.
3. Environmentalism emerged as a popular grassroots political movement in the 1960s with the publication of Rachel Carson's book *The Silent Spring*. She, and later others were concerned with the detrimental environmental impacts of modern industrial technology.
4. The 1972 United Nations Conference on Human Environment (UNCHE) is one of the most remarkable events in the history of global environmental awareness. It did not, however, provide a deeper focus of the interrelationship between the environment, interaction and humanity (the ecological approach).
5. There are more detailed analyses in the study of conflict. See also Paul Collier and Anke Hoeffler, "Data Issues in the Study of Conflict". Paper prepared for the Conference on "Data Collection on Armed Conflict", Uppsala 8-9 June 2001. First draft: June 6, 2001.t".
6. The National Council of Women's Organizations is one such NGO which is actively involved in recycling projects.
7. Head, Titiwangsa Heritage Sdn Bhd., Mr. Sharifuddin Budin.

## BIBLIOGRAPHY

1. Attan, Ahiruddin, "Stop Plundering Mother Nature". *The New Sunday Times*, March 13, 2005, p. 5.
2. Cheong, Sam., "River Systems Under Threat", *The Malay Mail*, March 31, 2005, p. 4.
3. Drengson, Alan, "Ecophilosophy, Ecosophy and the Deep Ecology Movement: An Overview". *The Trumpeter: Journal of Ecosophy*, Vol. 14, No. 3, Summer 1997.
4. Department of Environment Malaysia. "Environmental Quality Act", 1974.
5. Hildyard, Nicholas, Sarah Sexton and Larry Lohmann, "Carrying Capacity", "Over population" and Environmental Degradation. http:// www.thecornerhouse.org.uk/item.shtml?x=52014
6. Homer-Dixon, Thomas F., *Environment, Scarcity, and Violence*, Princeton University Press, Princeton, New Jersey, 1999.
7. Malthus, Thomas, *An Essay on the Principle of Population*, 1798.

8. Naess, Arne, *Interpretation and Preciseness*, Oslo, Dybwad, 1953.
9. —*Gandhi and Group Conflict*, Oslo, Universitets-Forlaget, 1974.
10. —*Ecology, Community and Lifestyle*, London, Cambridge, 1991.
11. Ohlsson, Leif. *Environment, Scarcity and Conflict—A Study of Malthusian Concerns*, Department of Peace and Development Research, University of Goteborg, 1999.
12. —*Water and Social Resource Scarcity: An Issue,* Paper Commissioned by FAO AGLW. Department of Peace Development Research (Padrigu), University of Goteborg, 1998.
13. United Nations Environment Programme Website.
14. http://www.unep.org/Documents.multilingual/Default.asp? DocumentID=287
15. Sim Leoi Leoi. "Recycle, Abdullah Tells Government Departments". The Star
16. Online, November 1, 2003, http://www.ecologyasia.com/news-archives/2003/nov-03/thestar_20031110_2.htm.

# Ethics of Biodiversity Conservation in Landscape Planning

## *A Case for Integrated Habitat in Non-Protected Areas*

— Dr. Faiza Abbasi

## Introduction: Natural Ecosystems in Distress—A Question of Balance

There are many values attached to biodiversity in terms of ecosystem services, marketable and subsistence survival goods and future insurance, which make natural ecosystems a vital lung for human societies—urban or rural. The status of natural resources in terms of their contribution to social welfare and suggests that even as new elements of biodiversity are discovered, there are genes, species and ecosystems being lost or threatened. The Millennium Ecosystem Assessment, completed in 2005 by more than 1360 scientists working in 95 countries, found that changes in biodiversity due to human activities were occurring more rapidly in the past 50 years than at any time in human history, and that the direct causes of this loss are either remaining steady, showing no evidence of decline over time, or are increasing in intensity. In effect, we are currently responsible for the sixth major extinction event in the history of the Earth, and the greatest since the dinosaurs disappeared, 65 million years ago.

India's forest cover is a mere 19.4 per cent of the total geographical area of the country of which a huge part is under pressure to meet the demand for fuel wood and timber which amounts to many million metric tonnes (Anon, 2000). The ever-increasing human and cattle population further aggravates the situation and brings agricultural land under the purview of agro-forestry to increase biomass production for anthropocentric goals (Kumar *et al.,* 2003). However, the modernization of agriculture has eliminated all other types of biomass besides the rapidly shrinking diversity of chosen crops in the farmland. This trend has reached its zenith with vast grain fields or plantations of mono-crops. This has also fuelled eco-degradation and landscape harmony disruption (Nayar and Jayal, 1991). Added to this is the policy imperative that recognizes and validates local and tribal rights in the protected areas earmarked for endangered wildlife and indigenous biodiversity.

As biodiversity encompasses all organisms, genes and ecosystems in the film of life around earth called biosphere, which is under increasing threat of human development, we should bring the urban landscapes and rural human habitations too under the umbrella of conservation ethics. In this paper, I make a case for those wetlands, which support precious biodiversity in terms of migratory waterfowl and many other aquatic flora and fauna but do not receive any legal protection as a PA. Besides, the importance of the special zones of influence around these area in the rural landscape and the biodiversity facilitated in the urban areas is also stressed upon with world-wide citations. The face of these is rapidly changing for the worse owing to pressures of real estate and agricultural reclamation to meet the growing food and cash demand in the burgeoning economy.

## Development and Biodiversity Conservation

### *Inhospitable Urban, Industrial and agricultural expansions*

The crux of the equation of photosynthesis is simple. Water sunlight, inorganic nutrients and carbon dioxide are all a plant needs to produce food–chlorophyll, are a granted fact for green plants. Planet earth has been sustaining complex life proliferating generation after generation since eons. Yet this cannot be facilitated in multi-storied laboratories so that we have the rest of the earth's landmass for luxurious development—palatial houses, malls, 8 lane carriageways and industries to let GDPs at a soaring high. In the present paradigm of development, it seems that if all the land devoted to traditional agriculture and forests is freed for so-called development projects the problem of homeless, jobless and foodless will be tackled. Yet, it is to be realized that biosphere is not all about food and goods. To be prepared for the unknown hidden in future it is mandatory to preserve the earth's biodiversity. Charles Darwin in his path breaking book *Origin of Species* describes an experiment where he prepares a culture of a bottle of wet mud collected from a water body and counted as many as 314 species of plants and animals. He concludes that wet soil is the most productive medium for the sustenance of the diversity of life forms. Unfortunately, what we see in the plan for a luxurious earth is an exact prohibition of the meeting of water from mud.

Development ironically, is akin to an unruly spread of urban settlements that lures the rural population towards extravagance. Advancement of the building and construction techniques seems hell-bent to change the architecture of the planet from a heaven for life to a dry hot island of concrete and steel apparently for *Homo sapiens* alone. Use of RCC, cement and glazed tiles prohibits the germination of any pioneer living species—in other words converts the piece of land into a smooth desert. Orchestrated political propaganda for unsustainable housing loans, broadening and extension of road networks and progressive measures in markets and industry, simply overlook the fact that human survival is jeopardized in absence of other biodiversity.

Paradoxically after shrugging the atlas with ill-concieved architecture man turns to nature reserves for respite. In villages of Bihar, India the state Government had provided the BPL families with minimal 'decent' shelters in colonies constructed from asbestos roofs and RCC walls. After spending a season in these houses all the occupants moved back to their erstwhile mud and thatch houses leaving the modern accommodations for their cattle. The explanation they gave was that these houses were hot in summer, cold in winters, suffocating in monsoon and away from nature. I add to this that such constructions are also prohibitive for living species of flora and fauna. Cemented earth prohibits absorption of water and ground water recharge. Hence the water crisis of lowering water table in most cities. The after effects are unimaginable for a region like the north Indian Gangetic Plains with highest population density, exponentially growing population, fast eradicating joint and extended families and demand pressures increasing. One may be bound to ask questions like 'will there be room for other life forms?'

## Limitations of the Protected Area Approach

Designating sites for preservation is not the complete answer for a reversal of the ecodegradation that has set in. The protected area approach was viable for the earlier period when man modified cultural landscapes existed as minute islands scattered in the far more extensive natural landscapes. With the situation reversing in these days the small and residual natural communities of flora and fauna cannot exert their modulator or buffering influence on the man altered regions (Nayar and Jalan, 1991). Besides, as biodiversity exists beyond the protected area too, species based conservation against a site based approach has to be included in the holistic picture of biodiversity preservation. For example, out of the 17 pheasant species found in India ten are globally threatened but their conservation strategies can not be site specific since they have diverse habitat requirements for survival and reproduction at various times of the life cycle. Now if this includes a private land the endangered pheasant is bound to local extinction the moment the owner or the government flags of a building and construction related development measure at the site.

The reason behind the rapid population decline of the house sparrow partially lays in the fact that building techniques rely on fast and certain results provided by bulldozers, cranes and cement. It has become increasingly easier to reclaim wilderness and the consequent chrome and glass sky scrappers are an alien substrate to the thatch roof-loving sparrows. Dr. V. S. Vijayan, former Director, Salim Ali Centre for Ornithology and Natural History, Coimbatore asks a more specific question and words a fear too, "Where have all the sparrows gone? It seems as if they have gone the way of the dodo". Sparrow decline is confirmed and amongst the various reasons given by many other bird watchers, Dr. Subramanya from University of Agricultural Sciences, Bangalore attributes the lack of nesting sites in modern concrete buildings disappearing kitchen gardens and the non-availability of a particular larvae (*Helicoverpa armigera*) associated with the field bean. Formerly urban households in India used to buy field beans in pods from the vegetable markets. When the pod was broken larvae came out, to be promptly devoured by sparrows. But now that fresh seeds are available in packets these larvae have disappeared depriving the sparrow of its favorite morsels.

Traditionally, approaches to conservation of biodiversity have focused on designating human-free spaces for wild species, and revolve mostly around large, charismatic mammals. These spaces, however, are inefficient in protecting species, proving too expensive, or impractical, due to high human densities such as in the tropics. Even existing protected areas are under attack thanks to the burgeoning human population, improper planning and execution, and the need for more food production. Li *et al.*, (2006) also suggest that local policy to modify demographic and individual needs can also bring about habitat improvements for the giant panda in the Wolong Nature Reserve in China where the rural households live a lifestyle that degrades the panda habitat.

In India numerous studies have culminated with the outcome that the forest resources have become unsustainable with the use of conventional policy approach and management practices that alienate the local people and cause overall degradation. Khanduri *et al.*, (2002) suggest eco-restoration of degraded forests in the western Himalayan regions of Garhwal and Singh *et al.*, (2002) prefer participatory practices like agro-forestry and eco-development for the upliftment of the Karbi Tribe in Assam who traditionally practice the disastrous *jhum* or shifting cultivation. Biodiversity in India is inextricable from people's lives as the discourse on CBD

(Convention for Biological Diversity) recognizes and puts forth time and again since 1992, (Faizi, 2009). The protection of biodiversity by setting it aside seems to be a concept stuck in a time warp because of evidences out pouring from the scholarly literature. We have 500 species of insects in entomophagy amongst the tribes of the country (Senthilkumar *et al.*, 2008), nationwide community based conservation and bio-prospecting of medicinal plants (Jha, 2003) specially the southern peninsula (Debnath, 2009) and serious management implications arising due to live stock grazing even in biosphere reserves like Khangchendzonga (Singh *et al.*, 2003).

These limitations to protected areas, and the knowledge that a multitude of biodiversity thrive in farmed areas, and other regions in and around the city have led to their exploration for conservation (Brooks *et al.*, 2004). In the following text I review the importance of cohabited landscapes and their planning and management for facilitating wildlife and biodiversity.

## Ethics for Integrated Habitats: A means for Restoring Natural Balance

While, in the real estate boom some see a spiritual sign of the dooms day coming closer, real estate crimes —the most gruesome and grave ones, are on the rise. May be humanity is paying for its injustice to the other co-habitants of the planet. Innovative measures or reverting to old techniques may prevent earth from being a featureless desert. Checks must be deployed before the punishment is peril. Ecology can give us the pertinent factual understanding, but not the moral rules to determine our behavior vis-à-vis nature. These will have to be provided by the society at large taking biological constraints and human needs in to account. These rules are still being developed and there is yet no general consensus as to what they should be. The guiding principle must be the concept of sustainability, which projects that we have an obligation to maintain for the coming generations the productive capacity of the planet including both areas developed for human use as well as the more natural environments.

The need to plan for biodiversity by setting landscape restoration objectives as against or in addition to achieving the conservation requirements of a particular species or site has been recognized in countries like Australia (Crossman *et al.*, 2007) and landscape planning is accommodated in their regional plans. These plans are increasingly more explicit and specific about the goals for vegetation management and conservation. This has been driven not just by landscape ecology principles and theories but also by the nature of top-down funding programs. It is now relatively common for these plans to contain general broad scale targets for protection, restoration and establishment of comprehensive, adequate and representative samples of biodiversity executed by district level integrated natural resource management committees.

### Protecting and Managing Inland Wetlands

Wetlands are important life support systems for the environment as they provide refugia for wetland animals, habitat for migratory species and seed banks for wetland vegetation. They are able to serve as sources for species dispersal and migration to other wetlands within the landscape and hence their relative contributions to habitat support, regional biodiversity and watershed-wide hydrologic functions assume a disproportionate importance. They provide production values and ecosystem services such as consumptive and non-consumptive uses for drinking, irrigation, fishing and eco-tourism for immediate populations and also benefit society located away from it by bearing potential future use and non-use availability of a healthy water resource for generations to come. They moderate hydrological extreme events as when rivers overflow they absorb excess water and when water is scarce, they help maintain the water table. Apart from serving as a harbor to a wide array of wild flora and fauna they also influence the micro-climate. The intergovernmental treaty on wetlands "The Convention on Wetlands of International Importance especially as Waterfowl Habitat", has been in effect since 1971. Better known as the Ramsar Convention (Ramsar Convention Secretariat, 2006) it includes peats, bogs, marshes, lakes and lagoons covering 159 million hectares for the conservation and wise use through local, regional and national actions and international cooperation, as a contribution towards achieving sustainable development throughout the world.

Sadly policy- and decision-makers take development decisions based upon simple monetary cost benefit analysis and the importance of wetlands for the environment and for human societies is under-rated. Stock market values are not assigned to the ecosystem services of wetlands and under the twin pressures of growing population and global climate change they exist as wastelands or fear the fate of reclamation for urbanization and agricultural expansion (MoEF, 2008). Nevertheless, they need constant monitoring and management as they are in a seral stage of ecological succession. To pull back succession and prevent wetlands from reaching the climax of woodlands specific measures are to be taken to mitigate effects of siltation, eutrophication, draining etc. Macro-scale, landscape and system level functions of the wetland are critical for conservation of biodiversity (Gibbs, 1993) yet environment and wildlife protection agencies remain at a loss of good policy, planning and evaluation for decision-making in the absence of biological assessment.

Inland wetlands are the principal source of renewable fresh water for human use, storing water but also purifying it through the removal of excess nutrients and other pollutants. Disruption of wetland purification processes can have devastating impacts at the source and further downstream. The loss of wetlands in the Mississippi watershed of the United States, for example, combined with high nutrient loads from intensive agriculture in the region, has contributed to the creation of a low-oxygen 'dead zone', incapable of supporting animal life, which extends, on average at mid-summer, some 16,000 square kilometres into the Gulf of Mexico. Recent natural disasters underline the reality that by disrupting ecosystem functions, biodiversity loss makes ecosystems more vulnerable to shocks and disturbances, less resilient, and less able to supply humans with needed services. The damage to coastal communities from floods and storms, for example, can increase dramatically following conversion of wetland habitats, as the natural protection offered by these ecosystems against wave action, tidal surge, and water run-off from land is compromised.

One-fourth of the total species of birds found in India depend on wetlands and multiple studies report habitat loss, degradation, pollution and over-exploitation as major threats to wetlands (Raghavaih and Davidar, 2009). The effect is compounded in case of lakes situated in tourist areas specially in mountains where high seasonality of bird activity coincides with that of tourist influx as observed in the Changthang Cold Desert Sanctuary in Ladakh (Hussain and Pandav, 2008). This underscores the importance of small lakes and marshes in the inhabited landscapes that do not receive any legal protection but support valuable aquatic avifauna serving as an indicator of ecosystem health. A handful of amateur bird watchers in and around the National Capital Region of Delhi have brought to the fore several such wetlands in Bhindawas, Dadri, Basai and Mohammadpur. Together with PAs like Okhla Bird Park and Sultanpur Bird Sanctuary some 100 bird watchers identify more than 200 species of birds from these sites on a single bird marathon day (Pers. Obs.). A cause of raised concern is the fact that all of these wetlands are encompassed by urban settlements developing fast. In an Illinois based GIS study Ward *et al.*, (2010) over a quarter of a century none of the wetlands were lost yet avian populations suffered a decline. This was attributed to the increased development within two km of the wetland leading to extreme changes in their structure. Either they tended to lose much of their vegetation and become open ponds, or exist as rank stands of dense vegetation. This turns them into habitats less suitable for waterbirds

## Biodiversity in Urban Green Spaces and the Built Environment

Where large tracts of natural habitat are under distress due to urban and agricultural expansion we have little understanding of the effects of these human activities on the native biodiversity. However, some studies have been conducted to explore the mechanisms that drive species abundance and richness in developing guidelines for urban land management and development policy. In a study conducted along urban gradients in Italy Sorace and Gustin (2010) report that since the habitat of many species is dwindling the urban green spaces may be a refuge for them if conservation efforts in town are made to preserve the presence of mature trees, habitat heterogeneity, availability of insects and suitable nesting sites in the buildings. In an interesting inference drawn from citizen bird monitoring programs Luther *et al.,* (2008) found some species to be associated with urban and vineyard sites—feeding from bird feeders and on berries of ornamental plants in home gardens, only and never visited natural sites. On the other some species were found to be strongly associated with cover and sensitive to edge effect. These are likely to disappear as scrub vegetation gives way to residential and cultivated area and the more ubiquitous generalists would expand leading to an overall decrease in diversity. Based on another study conducted in England Mason (2006) argues that the built environment has potential to hold greater biodiversity than the arable farmland it will replace in the future. However, to achieve this diversity, wildlife conservationists must insist on being involved from the earliest stages of planning so that valuable sites are retained and new ones are created within the housing matrix to the benefit of both wildlife and the future human inhabitations.

At the M S University campus in Baroda, house sparrows have been studied extensively since 1960 using nest boxes. Researchers report that these boxes have been lying vacant since a long time. Despite the gloomy news from all around there are still some rays of solace. Sparrows have been thronging the SACON campus at Anaikatty, Coimbatore. Today there are about 30 of these birds on the campus. This contrary phenomenon may be due to the campus environment friendly buildings designed by renowned architect Lawrie Baker. The ventilators in these buildings offer cozy nesting sites for sparrows. As a result of the extensive building activity over the last 30-40 years, many older towns and city centres have drifted too far away from their former rural surroundings. The decline of sparrows in their traditional breeding sites in the urban areas of larger towns is due to the paucity of appropriate food during the breeding season and suitable nesting venues. It is the same sad story all over the world. Changing lifestyles and architectural evolution have wreaked havoc on the bird habitat and food sources. Modern buildings devoid of leaves and crannies disappearing homes and gardens and crop fields cleaned of insects by pesticides all play a part in denying sparrow nesting sites and food specially for the young.

Urban bird communities are usually characterized by the dominance of a few species of birds, which comprise an important guild in the representation of urban bird communities. Even though population numbers of most species of birds in the built environment are on the decline, a possible goal following the restoration of numbers of dominant species would also be to control the over-abundance and select the rare ones (Fernandez-Juricic and Jokimaki, 2001). Representation of such habitat specialists may be enhanced by increasing food opportunities or interventions of such nest boxes or installing bird baths. Competitions for such artificial habitat improvements should be experimentally assessed pertaining to the target species before setting up any management measure. Theoretical and empirical developments for understanding the functioning of avian species in the built environment open up new perspectives to direct conservation efforts with active public involvement. It is time for action and offering the city people the possibility to learn to live in close proximity to birds.

In view of the rapid extinction of terrestrial species in the tropics Webb and Kabir (2009) equate the importance of home gardens to that of agro-forestry. They call for research that goes beyond the present trend of species compilations into landscape level investigations of ecological processes in determining the viability of home gardens even if it is an option of the last resort in degraded landscapes. Gonzalez-Garcia *et al.*, (2009) also suggest that private urban green spaces called *patios* in Latin America can act as important refuges for wildlife in the scattered growing cities of the tropics.

## *Using Sustainable Agriculture Practices*

While protection and improvement of existing remnant natural landscapes among the agricultural areas remains the most cost-effective management principle for degraded landscapes in extremely fragmented landscapes re-vegetation and sustainable agricultural practices are the only option to achieve high targets of biodiversity rehabilitation (Andren, 1994). Many of India's regions like the densely populated Indo-Gangetic Plains have been subjected to widespread clearing of vegetation and subsequent fragmentation of habitat. Reserve selection in these areas will not be sufficient to conserve biodiversity because remnant habitats are small isolated and subject to disturbance via edge effects. It is in these landscapes that restoration is urgently required to begin the halt of further species decline. However, land in these regions is in high demand from a variety of land uses, particularly in peri-urban regions experiencing rapid population growth and restoration is expensive. Restoration needs to be carefully planned and prioritized to gain maximum ecological benefit while having minimal adverse economic impact. Careful planning is of most necessity in regions where land uses collide.

Spread far and wide all over the variable landscapes are examples of wildlife cohabiting traditional agricultural areas. A very high index of biological diversity has been associated with the rice fields in countries like Spain (Sanchez-Guzman, 2007) and Srilanka (Bambaradeniya *et al.*, 2004).

Studies in Spain even suggest the declaration of rice fields as Special Protection Area for Birds as they mitigate the impact of wetland loss on migratory waterfowl due to their buffering mechanism. In India too the paddy field habitat provides a feeding ground for many waders like egrets, storks and shanks which in turn act as bio-pesticides by feeding upon the insects and rodents which harm the crop. The guano of these birds is also a source of biofertiliser in the rural economy. However, this symbiotic relation between the farmer and the water birds is being disrupted as the traditional agriculture practices are abandoned for the more cash intensive chemical farming. Use of pesticides and fertilizers is polluting the paddy field environment and causing detrimental impact on the birds which utilize the habitat. Egg-shell thinning of many birds has been reported due to pesticides and this reduces their breeding success. On the Indian side of the Sunderban delta in West Bengal the open billed storks inhabit the rice fields for feeding and nest in heronries on the edges of the villages. However, owing to the traditional beliefs of the people in the villages that the storks bring good luck they are welcomed for feeding and breeding despite the deafening noise from the colonial nesting trees. Similarly, the largest population of the endangered Sarus crane *Grus antigone* found in the wetlands of the Etah and Mainpuri districts are considered as harbingers of prosperity (Sundar, 2003). This population survives till date because of the protection from the local people but eliminative agricultural practices aim to drain the land for crop-fields as such marshes are technically considered as wasteland in the revenue books. Such farming is the most dominant land use yet proves to be a threat to biodiversity due to destruction of natural habitats and secondary effects as soil erosion due to pesticides and fertilizers.

## Conclusion

It takes socio-political will to conceptualize a balance between the development and biodiversity conservation, by working out a legal framework of laws and policies as to drawing a line on the sealing of the earth's nasal pores by advanced construction techniques. How much percentage of a construction project should leave the land to respiration, transpiration; and production and sustenance of biodiversity, so that the fertile topsoil is not barred from production. Teasing out which human influences impact species is important for directing land-use planning as well as management and restoration efforts focused on biodiversity conservation. The success of mitigation and restoration efforts requires determining the relative importance of both local habitat and landscape level variables. More research is required to manipulate landscape planning in this regard. Further experimenting on how to implement and achieve the objectives, an ambitious attempt is also to be seen if dismantling the individual ownership of natural resources including land, from the social and economic fabric might have answers to the problem. Space on land may cease to be a coveted commodity and real estate would acquire a new paradigm where biodiversity too has room to thrive and its competition with humans is eased.

## REFERENCES


1. An L., He G., Liang Z., and Liu J., 2006, "Impacts of demographic and socioeconomic factors on spatio-temporal dynamics of panda habitat", *Biodiversity and Conservation,* 15: 2343-2363.
2. Andren, H., 1994, "Effects of habitat fragmentation on birds and mammals in landscapes with different proportions of suitable habitat: A review, *Oikos,* 71: 355-366.
3. Anon, 2000, *State of Forest Report 1999* (summary), Govt. of India, Frest Survey of India, Dehradun.
4. Bambaradeniya, C.N.B., Edirisinghe J.P., De Silva D.N., Gunatilleke C.V.S., Ranawana K.B., and Wijekoon S., 2004, "Biodiversity associated with an irrigated rice ecosystem in Sri Lanka", *Biodiversity and Conservation,* 13: 1715-1753.
5. Brooks, T. M., M. I. Bakarr, M.I., Boucher, T., 2004, "Coverage Provided by the Global Protected Area System: Is it Enough?", *Bioscience,* 54: 1081-1091.
6. Crossman, N. D., Bryan, A. B., Ostendorf B., Collins S., 2007, "Systematic landscape restoration in the rural—urban fringe: Meeting conservation planning and policy goals", *Biodiversity Conservation,* 16: 9180-9188.
7. Debnath, D., 2009, "Stakeholders approach for medicinal plants cultivation: A case from Tamil Nadu", *Indian Forester,* 135(5): 647-653.
8. Faizi, S., 2009, "ABS Negotiations: Sovereignty shall not be compromised", *Square Brackets,* CBD Newsletter for Civil Society, 2 (Nov): 2-3.
9. Fernandez-Juricic E., Jokimaki J., 2001, "A habitat island approach to conserving birds in urban landscapes: Cases studies form southern and northern Europe", *Biodiversity and Conservation,* 10: 2023-2043.
10. Gibbs, J.P. 1993, "Importance of small wetlands for the persistence of local populations of wetland associated animals", *Wetlands,* (13): 25-31.
11. Gonzale-Garcia A., Belliure J., Gomez-Sal A., Davilla P., 2009, "The role of urban greenspaces in fauna conservation: The case of Iguana *Ctenosaura similis* in the patios of Leon city, Nicaragua", *Biodiversity Conservation,* 18: 1909-1920.
12. Jha, M., 2003, "Community based conservation and management of medicinal plants in India, *Indian Forester,* 129(2): 187-197.
13. Khanduri, V.P., Sharma C.M., Ghildiyal S.K., and Puspwan K.S., 2002, "Forest composition in relation to socio-economic status of people at three high altitudinal villages of a part of Garhwal Himalayas", *Indian Forester* 128(12): 1335-1344.

14. Kumar R., Gupta P.K., and Gulati A., 2003, "Agroforestry extension and its impact on scocioeconomic scenario: A casestudy of Yamunanagar District (Haryana)", *Indian Forester,* 129(4): 435-445.

15. Luther D., Hilty J., Weiss J., Cornwall C., Wipf M. and Ballard G., 2008, "Assessing the impact of local habitat variables and landscapes context on riparian birds in agricultura, urbanized and native landscapes, *Biodiversity Conservation,* 17: 1923-1935.

16. Mason, C. F., 2006, "Avian species richness and numbers in the built environment: Can new housing development be good for birds?, *Biodiversity and Cnservation"* 15: 2365-2378.

17. Nair, S.C., and Jayal N.D., 1991, "Biomass Poverty and Land Restoration." The INTACH environmental series, Indian national trust for art and cultural heritage.

18. Raghavaih, P. S., and Davidar, P., 2009, "Status of migratory waterfowl of Pulicat lake, Andhra Pradesh." *Indian Forester,* 133(10): 1312-1317.

19. Senthilkumar, N., Barthakur N.D., and Rao L., 2008, "Bioprospecting with reference to medicinal insects and tribes in India: An overview", *Indian Forester* 134(12):1575-1591

20. Singh, H. B., Sundriyal R.C., Sharma E., 2003, "Livestock Grazing in the Khangchendzonga biosphere reserve of Sikkim Himalaya, India: implications for management, *Indian Forester,* 129(5): 611-623.

21. Singh J., Chandra A., Saikia H.C., and Thakuria G., 2002, "Socio-economic study of Karbi tribe of Silonijan—A case study in Karbi-Anglong District of Assam," *Indian Forester,* 128(4): 403-411.

22. Sprace, A., and Gustin M., 2010, "Bird species of conservation concern along urban gradients in Italy, *Bidiversity Conservation,* 19: 205-221.

23. Sundar, K.S.G., and Choudhury, B.C. 2003, "Conservation of the Sarus Crane *Grus antigone* in Uttar Pradesh, India", *Journal of the Bombay Natural History Society,* 103(2-3): 182-190

24. Sutherland *et. al.,* 2009, One hundred questions of importance to the conservation of global biological diversity, *Conservation Biology,* 23(3): 557-567.

25. Ward M. P., Semel B., Herkert J. R., 2010, "Identifying the ecological causes of longterm declines of wetland-dependent birds in urbanizing landscapes", *Biodiversity Conservation,* 19: 3287-3300.

26. Webb, E. L., and Kabir M. E., 2009, "Home gardening for tropical biodiversity", conservation. *Conservation Biology,* 23(6): 1641-1644.

# Biological Diversity, Environmental Ethics and Traditional Ecological Knowledge

## *Concerns in Northeast India*

— Mr. Bal Krishan Choudhary

## Introduction

The glory of northeast India lies in the variety of the climatic, edaphic and altitudinal variations, that have resulted in a great range of ecological habitats. Situated between 22-30°N latitude and 89-97°E longitude and covering an area of about 2,62,379 km$^2$. Northeast India represents the transition zone between the Indian, Indo-Malayan and Indo-Chinese biogeography regions. The region is the geographical entry to the treasure of India's flora and fauna, and as a consequence, the region is one of the richest in ecological values and biological diversity. The region, being at the confluence of three major bio-geographical realm of the world, is extremely rich in floral and faunal biodiversity with several endemic species. Northeast, with seven states (Arunachal Pradesh, Assam, Manipur, Nagaland, Meghalaya, Mizoram, and Tripura), represents one of the 25 hotspots of biodiversity of the world. All the northeastern states make up for about 8 per cent of the total geographical area of the country, but has about 25 per cent of the country's total forest areas supporting about 30 per cent of the total growing stock of the forest of the country. About 70 per cent of the total geographical area is mountainous and hilly and rest 30 per cent is under Brahmaputra and Barak valley systems. The demographic feature of northeastern states is unique in that there are more than 100 recognized tribes, which inhabit mostly the hill areas and each with distinct culture, ethos, and traditional knowledge systems. The majority of the people survive on subsistence economy based mainly on the agriculture, supplemented with limited horticulture, animal husbandry, crafts/ handloom, etc. Northeast India is blessed with a wide range of physiography and eco-climatic conditions. The forests in the region are extremely diverse in structure and composition and combine tropical and temperate forest types, alpine meadows and cold deserts. There are regions, for example, in the State of Arunachal Pradesh, where the faunal assemblages also change rapidly from tropical to subtropical, temperate, alpine and finally to cold desert forms. After the Andaman and Nicobar Islands and the Western Ghats, Northeast India forms the main region of tropical forests in India, especially the species-rich tropical rain forests. The tropical semi-evergreen and moist deciduous forests in the lowlands of this region extend south and west into the subcontinent, and east into Southern China and Southeast Asia.

## Concept and Value of Biodiversity

The definition of biodiversity is based on conceptual framework, which incorporates three biological levels of organisms—genes, population/ species and communities/ecosystems and three dimensions—completion, structure and function. Genetic diversity is the sum of total genes which expresses into variation of same phenotypes, i.e. gene for gray and black hair. Species diversity is a sum of all the different species of animals, plants, fungi, and microbial organisms living on earth and the variety of habitats in which they live. Ecological diversity is sum to different ecosystem found on earth, i.e. pond, desert forest etc. Scientists estimate that upwards of 10 million and some suggest more than 100 million different species inhabit the Earth. Each species is adapted to its unique niche in the environment, from the peaks of mountains to the depths of deep-sea hydrothermal vents, and from polar ice caps to tropical rain forests. Biodiversity is richest in hot humid tropical environment and further reduces towards temperate climatic conditions and ultimately least distribution is at poles. It is ironical that the regions which are very rich in biodiversity are maximum poverty-struck due to improper acknowledgement. The seemingly unimportant plants of north east India like ferns and mosses are need to be investigated, studied, appreciated and above all, protected, as they serve vital ecological roles as soil protectors; contribute to the recycling of nutrients and water, offer food and shelter to an assemblage of invertebrates and take a part in air purification and carbon sequestration. The value of diversity is widely accepted and well recognized but estimation of the value is influenced by the perception of the experts from different areas. When we go to valuing the biodiversity, perhaps the greatest value of biodiversity is yet to be unknown. Scientists have discovered and named only 1.75 million species, less than 20 per cent of those estimated to exist; and of those identified, only a fraction has been examined for potential medicinal, agricultural, or industrial values. Human population depends upon large number of products and services which are obtained from our environment to survive. Our dependence on these resources is obligate. Resources are the material required to sustain over aesthetic apetite, our health and life. When these resources are biotic in origin we called it biological resources. The scope and definition is dynamic and it changes with time, i.e. paper currency after a period of time; it would not be resource as it would be replaced by plastic currency. Our survival is impossible without supply by the nature and this dependence is forever. Although we are in era of science and technology but it alone can't change our relationship with nature, i.e. our obligate depends upon the product and services provided by nature. We are heavily deviated from our prime objective of what we do to have access of products and services from the nature. The forestry and wildlife resources contribute substantially in meeting even the needs of subsistence economy, which make the dependency of the people on the forestry resources very high. The use of areas rich in forestry and wildlife resources (mainly of practicing shifting cultivation across the region) and extraction of various forest products is in vogue since long past as an accepted practice. 100-150 years ago pressure on biological resources was much less mainly because o controlled population growth. The greed of the *Homo sapiens* is changed greatly but the size of ecosystem, which is determining the biodiversity of the region is becoming restricted.

## Phytodiversity of the Region

The northeastern Seven states together account for about one-fourth of the total forest cover of the country. So far around 47,000 species of plant have been identified and describe but a large number of plants are yet to be explored, identified and describe, With about 1,67,000 km$^2$ area under forest, this region accounts for approximately 7500 species of angiosperms. Out of 315 families of Angiosperms in India, more than 200 are represented in Northeast India and this region accounts for nearly 50 per cent of the total number of plant species in India as a whole. It is of interest to note that about one-third of the flora of Northeast India is endemic to the region. The striking feature of the flora of Northeast India is the presence of many primitive flowering plants, e.g. *Tetracentron sinense, Manglietia sp., Myrica esculenta, Holboellia latifolia, Exbuchlandia populnea, Corylopsis himalayana, Magnolia pealiana* and *M. qustavii*. The *Coriariaceae, Nepenthaceae, Turneraceae, Illiciaceae, Ruppiaceae, Siphonodontaceae* and *Tetracen-traceae* are monogeneric families represented in this region. Furthermore, some of the important gene pools of citrus, banana, mango and rice are reported to have originated from this region. Of these, mango and banana show the maximum diversity in this region. The carnivorous Pitcher Plant (*Nepenthes khasiana*) is endemic to Meghalaya. Siroy Lily (*Lilium mackliniae*), a ground lily that produces beautiful flowers, is a narrow endemic found in the eastern border area of Manipur. The tropical forests found in the Indo-Myanmar border areas have many representative species in the Indian context, such as *Dipterocarpus tuberculatus, D. turbinatus* and *Melanorrhea usitata* to name only a few. Of about 1300 species of orchids, belonging to 158 genera reported from India, northeast India sustains the highest concentration with about 700 species. As many as 34 species of orchids from northeast India are listed among the threatened plants of India. There are 550 species of orchids found in Arunachal Pradesh alone, the highest number in any state. Many species of orchids are of medicinal importance. In the state of Tripura, more than 60 such species are used as vegetables. In Manipur more than 430 species are being used for medicinal purposes. In parts of Assam and Manipur, the tree *Parkia roxburghii* yields good timber and also provides edible flowers and pods that are highly prized. Agarwood (*Aquillaria malaccensis*) that occurs in the tropical forests of the northeastern region is highly priced. Rhododendrons are known for their showy flowers and foliage. Out of 82 species of rhododendrons recorded from Himalaya, 70 species are confined to eastern Himalaya. Out of 136 species of bamboos found in India, 63 species in 22 genera are found in northeast India, spread over an area of 30,500 km$^2$. About 25 species of bamboo are considered rare in northeast India. In northeast India, 28 species of conifers are recorded. *Pinus kesia* is mention worthy as it could be seen growing in pure patches at elevations of 900 to 1800 m. and it is one of the fast growing trees of this region. *Cycas pectinata* is a rare gymnosperm that occurs in Kamrup and *Gnetum gnemon* occurs in Khasi, Jaintia and the Naga hills. *Podocarpus nerifolia*, a broad-leaved gymnosperm is reported from the Khasi hills, but also occurs in the tropical forests of Barak Valley in Manipur state and in Assam. Northeast India is also known for a variety of saprophytic plants like *Monoropa uniflora, Epipogeum roseum, Aeginitia indica* and the giant orchid *Galeola falconeri*. Northeast India also has a high diversity of non-flowering plants. Of about 1000 species of ferns found in India, nearly half are represented in northeastern India. *Platycerium wallichii* (stag horn fern) from Manipur appears to be the first report of its occurrence within India. This epiphytic fern grows in the moist deciduous forests in the Indo-Myanmar border areas in great profusion. Fern-allies such as *Lycopodium* and *Selaginella* are also diverse in this region. The region is exceedingly rich in lichens, mosses and liverworts. In Arunachal Pradesh over 5000 species of flowering plants (both vascular and non-vascular) are found. Out of which 238 are endemic to the state. The state having more than 500 species of orchids, out of 1000 species in India and are known as "Jewels of Arunachal Pradesh". The forest of Arunachal provides some of the rare and endangered plants species like *Hodgsonia macrocarpa, Entada purseatha* etc. Few of the rare species found are *Calamus inermis, Livistona jenkinsiana Calamus inermis, Livistona jenkinsiana Sapria himalayana, Cyathea spp., Angiopteris evecta* etc. There are diversity of oak, bamboos, canes is remarkable *Schizostachyum fuchsianum* is a unique poisonous bamboo found here. *Albizia arunachalensis* is a rare tree found here. It is famous for *Coptis teeta* and *Taxus baccate*. Assam is rich in bamboo diversity, where 10 genera and 42 species can be found. Of the total 50 Red Data Book species belonging to 20 families of northeastern states, the state houses 45 species belonging to 19 families. Report from Botanical Survey of India state that 102 species of flora, belonging to 75 genera, is endemic to the state. Assam is exceptionally rich in citrus and banana germplasm. It is considered by many to be the 'Creator Center' of citrus flora of India. Another unique feature of the state is occurrence of aquatic fruits like *makhana* or gorgon fruit (*Eurale ferox*). Meghalaya is considering being the centre of origin for citrus. More than 35 per cent of Indian mammal species are found in this state. Due to temperature and climatic difference, the state is supposed to be the storehouse of various exotic and endangered species. Plant species like *Nepenthes khasiana* (Pitcher Plant), orchids like, *Vanda sp.*, *Paphiopedilum sp.* and *Cymbydium sp*, trees like *Taxus baccata* etc (Ramakantha *et al.*, 2003).

## Zoodiversity of the Region

There is a paucity of exploration and research concerning the fauna of northeast India. So far 90,000 species of animals have been explored from the region and mammals are often considered the best-known groups, especially the ungulates. However, a new species of barking deer, 'Leaf Deer' (*Muntiacus putaoensis*), which was recently discovered in Myanmar, is reported from the forests of Arunachal Pradesh in the year 2003 as a new record for India. Northeast India sustains 11 species of primates, if we follow the recent revisions in primate taxonomy. It is but unfortunate that except three species, which could be considered common in Assam, they face an uncertain future in this region. The Hoolock (*Bunopithecus hoolock*) is the only ape in India. It occurs in Assam, Arunachal Pradesh, Manipur, Meghalaya, Tripura and Mizoram in northeast India, and its continued existence in the state of Nagaland is uncertain. The Golden Langur (*Trachypithecus geei*) is one of the most localized species, between Manas and Sankosh Rivers in the Himalayan foothills along the Assam–Bhutan border areas. Out of 16 primates in the world, seven are found in Arunachal Pradesh. The Phayeri's Langur (*Trachypithecus phayeri*) assumes high conservation significance, as this species is restricted in distribution to the state with reported existence of a few troops in North Cachar Hills of Assam, adjacent to the northern boundary of Tripura. The Capped Langur (*Trachypithecus pileatus*) is also a rare animal with limited distribution in northeast India. The stump-tailed Macaque (*Macaca arctoides*) and the northern Pigtailed Macaque (*M. leonina*) have sympatric distributions in northeast India and both have become endangered. The Slow Loris (*Nycticebus bengalensis*) is an inhabitant of tropical forests, south of the Brahmaputra river in northeast India. India harbours six largest cats of the world and the state of Arunachal Pradesh prides itself for sustaining four large cats of Asia—the Tiger (*Panthera tigris*), Leopard (*Panthera pardus*), Snow Leopard (*Uncia uncia*) and the Clouded Leopard (*Neofelis nebulosa*). Of these, the Indian population of the Clouded Leopard is restricted to the northeastern region. Tiger has become a very rare animal in the entire region and perhaps Assam provides the safest asylum for this large cat. The Red Panda (*Ailurus fulgens*) is yet another flagship species of this region, restricted to the higher altitudes. All the bear species that occur in India are recorded from the northeastern region. Though, with about 65 species, bats dominate the mammalian fauna of northeast India, reliable information available on them is sparse. Of the 28000 wild elephants in India, about 33 per cent are found in northeast India. In fact, Assam alone accounts for more elephants than Myanmar, Thailand, Indonesia or any other country in Asia. However, elephant population is dwindling sharply in northeast India. There has been a very serious decline in the elephant population in central Assam whereas those in the southern parts have virtually vanished. The population has seriously declined in Tripura and there are only a few elephants left in Manipur and Mizoram and probably none in Nagaland. All India estimation of wild elephant's population is done every five years. Trend shows the decline in the number of elephant every year. Great Indian Rhinoceros (*Rhinoceros unicornis*) is the largest of all the rhinos now inhabiting the world. In northeast India this species is now restricted to Kaziranga, Pabitora and Orang in Assam. Northeast India supports some of the rarest, least known and most sought after birds of the Oriental Region. This region perhaps supports the highest diversity of bird species in the Orient. More than 400 species of birds are recorded from Kaziranga National Park alone in Assam and although not thoroughly explored, the state of Arunachal Pradesh has a record of 665 species of birds. Among the component of reptilian fauna, the Gharial (*Gavialis gangeticus*) found in Brahmaputra river is of great conservation significance. Northeast India has the highest diversity of Turtles. Of the 26 species of non-marine Chelonians reported from India, 19 are found in this region. The Lizard fauna of northeast India is profoundly influenced by the Indo-Chinese connection. Published records indicate 20 Lizard species from the state of Assam, and 18 species from the tiny state of Manipur. Fifty-eight species of snakes have been recorded in Assam and 34 from Manipur. *Python reticulatus*, the largest snake in India, is found in northeast India and *Python Molurus bivittatus* is known from a single specimen from the Arunachal Pradesh, which was a first record for India. Existing records indicate the presence of 64 species of amphibians in the northeast India but this figure again could be a gross under-estimate as they are a poorly studied group in northeast India. Over 24,000 species of fishes are known in the world, and a majority of these are from warm tropical waters. Northeast India is exceptionally rich in freshwater fishes, and it is heartening to note that the region has been extensively surveyed, and accounts for 236 species. From the state of Manipur alone, 167 species of freshwater species belonging to 11 orders, 31 families and 84 genera are recorded. The fish fauna of Loktak Lake in Manipur comprises 64 species. The Biodiversity Strategy and Action Plan for Northeast Ecoregion suggest that 3,624 species of insects and 50 molluscs are recorded from the region. Butterflies and moths are by far the best-studied invertebrate organisms in northeast India, and the region contributes the maximum number of species for the group in the country (Ghosh *et al.*, 1984).

## Ecosystem Diversity

Though northeast India is predominantly mountainous, the region is very rich in aquatic ecosystem diversity. Interspecific interaction is necessary for existence of different species. Intraspecific division is necessary for success of species and its survival in different type of climate and soil. In order to support the survival of different diverse types of ecosystems are necessary. A large number of bheels, ponds and marshlands in the low lying and floodplain areas of Assam, Arunachal Pradesh and Tripura represent the diversity in lentic ecosystems. In Mizoram important lakes are Palak, Tamdil and Rengdil. Dumboor lake in Tripura situated amidst picturesque hill packed with vegetation. Loktak lake is the largest freshwater lake in north-eastern India. It is also called only floating lake in the world due to floating phumdis (heterogeneous mass of vegetation, soil and organic matters at various stage of decomposition) on it. It is also habitat of one of the most endangered deer, the Brown-Antlered Deer (locally known as Sangai), which was once thought to be extinct. Fish yield from the lake is reported to be about 1,500 tones every year. Nearly 116 species of birds and 425 species of animals have been reported from lake including 21 species of migratory waterfowl.

## Biodiversity Loss is Big Concern

About 100 tribes and more than 300 ethnics groups of the northeast India is symbiotically associated with the biodiversity and other natural resources. For the same degree of perturbation they can be affected adversely since their larger dependence on biodiversity. Most biologists agree that life on Earth is now faced with the most severe extinction episode since the event that drove the dinosaurs to extinction 65 million years ago. Species of plants, animals, fungi, and microscopic organisms such as bacteria are being lost at alarming rates, in fact, that biologists estimate that three species go extinct every hour. Scientists around the world are cataloging and studying global biodiversity in hopes that they might better understand it, or at least slow the rate of loss. Conservation means making use of a resource in an intelligent way so that it can sustain over longer period of time. It is a dynamic concept. It aims at constant exploitation so that quality and quantity of resources does not diminish. Preservation is to store something so that it is not reduced. It is a static concept which aims to preserve the resource. The problem of biodiversity degradation is mainly because man himself has created and increased his problem which needs technical aid for solution. In all, at present more than 700 species of plants from the northeast India are facing the threat of survival in the wild. It needs to be emphasized that all these rare animals occupy narrow bands of forests in the hills and valleys of the region, and, living in small populations, they are extremely susceptible to habitat degradation and hunting pressures. Many of the species in lowland forests are already on the brink of extinction as these forests were the first to be occupied, altered and degraded by man. The population at Manas in Assam is believed to have been decimated in recent years. The Water Buffalo (*Bubalus bubalis*) found in northeastern India has a rather alarming genetic problem. A large number of domestic buffalo, most of them genetically a 'cocktail species' bred by man, are grazed in the habitats of the wild buffalo and the interbreeding revitalizes the domestic strain but has the opposite effect on the wild strains. The Banteng (*Bos javanicus*) occurred in the hills of Manipur as late as 1990s, but is now not reported from the state.

## Human and Wildlife Conflict

Conflicts between human beings and wildlife are fast becoming a serious threat to the survival of many endangered species in the world. According to the world conservation union, it occurs when wildlife's requirements overlap with those of human populations, creating cost to residents and wild animals. Direct contact with wildlife occurs in both urban and rural areas, but it is generally more common inside and around the protected areas, where wildlife population density is higher and animals often stray into adjacent cultivated fields or grazing areas. Species most exposed to conflict are also shown to be more prone to extinction because of injury and death caused by humans; these can be either accidental, such as road traffic and railways accidents, retaliatory shooting, poison or capture. Such human induced mortality affects not only the population viability of some of the most endangered species, but also has broader environmental impacts on ecosystem equilibrium and biodiversity preservation. Human can economically affected through destruction and damage to property and infrastructure (e.g., agriculture crops, orchards, grain stores, water installation, fencing pipes), livestock depredation, transmission of domestic animal disease etc. A set of driving force for human wildlife conflict has been recognized viz., human population growth, land use transformation, species habitat loss, degradation and fragmentation, growing interest in ecotourism and increasing access to natural reserve, increasing population of livestock and completion and exclusion of wild herbivores, abundance and distribution of wild pray, increasing wildlife population as a result of conservation programmes, climatic factors etc.

## People-government Conflict

The past decade has witnessed a tremendous increase about the awareness of environment issues. The environmental issues linked with the fear of existence of the communities particularly in slow economy are incidents of intimidation, threats and physical harassment sometimes frighteningly violent is being reported in northeast by environmental activities. The one famous example from the region is members of 'Idu Mishmi' community of Arunachal Pradesh, who were protesting against the non-availability of 'Environment Impact Assessment' report in printed form so that it can be easily accessible to general people. Earlier it was only available on internet in soft form which was inaccessible to the illiterate tribal community. Due to joint effort of the tribes and non-governmental organization, government bound to cancel 3000 Megawatt Hydel Power dam located in Dibag district of Arunachal Pradesh. For more than a year, local tribal community had protested against the authority on the ground that it would devastate the fragile ecology and destroy the culture and livelihood of the Idu Mishmi community numbering only 8000 individuals. The Dibang dam is classical instance of a fight of local community for access to information and participation and a partial victory of the community. Sometimes development projects leads to political dispute, political conflict between Assam and Meghalaya governments over potential uranium discovery in the border area. The Union Minister of State for Rural Development, Agatha Sangma intervened and told as land is precious for indigenous people; the government should not take the hasty decision in starting the project. The students opposing the project fear that uranium mining would affect the natural environment of the area, may have ill effect if not managed properly and it will open the floodgates of infiltration in the state (*Telegraph*, 14th November 2005).

## Factors Responsible for Deterioration of Biodiversity

Biodiversity is important for survival to meet our all economic and aesthetic requirement. It is our ignorance and greed of so-called custodians of nature, which has led to immense loss. Overgrazing, over-exploitation, pollution, habitat destruction indiscriminate killing, hunting/poaching accidental introduction of exotic or invasive species, monoculture, these all have led to reduction in biodiversity. Increasing population and growing consumption of resources have led to a rapid loss of diversity, eroding the capacity of earth's natural systems to provide the essential goods and services necessary for human survival. It is estimated that human activities have raised the rate of extinction to 1,000 times its normal pre-human rates. Already populations of an estimated two of three birds are declining in the worldwide, one of every eight plants species is endangered or threatened, one-quarter of mammals, one-quarter of amphibians and one-fifth of reptiles are endangered or vulnerable.

### *I. Habitat Degradation*

Deforestation and the resultant loss of soil, especially in the hill areas, are leading to increased siltation of rivers and streams in the entire northeast region. The deep pools that favoured habitats of many species are rapidly becoming shallow and choked with silt, leading to a decline in habitat. At the same time, swamps, marshes, and other wetlands are increasingly being reclaimed for urban and agricultural expansion. Bears of the lower elevations are under especially serious threats owing to habitat degradation as well as persecution by man, as the bile of the animal is considered highly medicinal. Heavy loss of prime elephant habitat is an issue of great concern as loss of elephant habitats heralds doom for smaller creatures as well. Historical records suggest that both the one-horned Javan Rhinoceros (*Rhinoceros sondaicus*) and the two-horned Sumatran Rhinoceros (*Didermocerus sumatrensis*) were once found in parts of northeast India. Both the species are now extinct from the region. It is a great tragedy that in many parts of northeast India some people poison the rivers, streams and other water bodies to get good catches of fish. Apart from using plant poisons, lime, DDT, copper sulphate ($CuSO_4$) and, other synthetic chemicals are being used for fishing. Some are even using dynamite and gelatine sticks for the same purpose. This has serious ill-effects on the entire aquatic ecosystems. Fish stocks are being entirely wiped out; several species of amphibians, birds and other fish predators are also being affected in the process; and nothing is known as to what happens to human beings on consuming such poisoned fishes.

## *II. Habitat Loss*

### *(a) Deforestation and lopping*

The deforestation may be due to human activities like development works or naturally. The primary vegetation in extensive areas of the northeast India has been disturbed and modified, and in some places destroyed by seismic activities, frequent landslides and resultant soil erosion. While these natural causes have contributed only marginally to the change in vegetation type, it is the activity of man that has led to the irreversible transformation in the landscapes and has resulted in colossal loss of biodiversity in the entire region. Human influences have pushed many species to the brink of extinction and have caused havoc to natural fragile ecosystems. Such devastations to natural ecosystems are witnessed almost everywhere in the region and is a cause of great concern. Northeast India has 64 per cent of the total geographical area under forest cover and it is often quoted that it continues to be a forest surplus region. However, the forest cover is rapidly disappearing from the entire region. Lopping contributes in habitat loss for birds and animals which are heavily dependent on canopy. With a very long tail for balance and large paws for climbing, the Clouded Leopard is well suited for life in the canopy. Despite the presence of this elusive animal in all the eight states of the region, its habitat is shrinking at an alarming rate. Vast tracts of forests, especially in the state of Arunachal Pradesh, where the animal reigns free, could remain safe for this magnificent animal, provided such forests are kept away from developmental activities, including the construction of roads. This being the case, the statistics of more than 64 % of the total geographic area in this region under forest cover could be misleading. For example, though the forest cover in Manipur extends to 78% of the total geographic area, only 22 per cent of forest area is under dense forest cover and the rest has been converted to open forests. Except in the Brahmaputra and Barak valleys of Assam where substantial areas are under agriculture, little of the land is available for settled cultivation. Hence, shifting agriculture or slash-and-burn agriculture is the major land use in northeast India and extends over 1.73 million ha (FSI, 1999). Different agencies have come up with different figures concerning the total area under shifting cultivation (*jhum*) in the region.

### (b) Fragmentation

Fragmentation restricts the movement and hence approaches to resources of animals. Monogamy, frugivory and adaptation to brachiation make the species highly susceptible to habitat fragmentation and degradation. Most of the tropical forests that harbour this species are subjected to slash and burn or shifting cultivation and therefore, the ape's habitat is highly degraded and fragmented. It is hunted for the pot and the belief that its flesh and blood have medicinal properties has made it a highly prized commodity. It is also highly prized in the pet trade. All these are detrimental to the survival of the species.

### (c) Flood

The forests of Assam once acted as a sponge, absorbing the tremendous impact of the monsoons. The natural drainage of the vast northeastern Himalaya is channelled through Assam and with the loss of thick forest cover, Brahmaputra, one of the largest and fastest flowing rivers of the subcontinent is creating havoc in the state. Floods that have devastating effects are now common to northeast India and protecting the forests is one vital step in containing this terrible problem.

## III. Over-exploitation and Poaching

A vast majority of the indigenous inhabitants of this region are meat-eating in their food habits and almost all communities have expert hunters, trappers and fishermen. One can find bones, skulls and hides of large and small mammals in tribal huts. It should be noted that though the traditional practices of trapping, snaring etc. of animals are carried out in very remote areas, in most parts of northeast India shooting wild animals with guns is

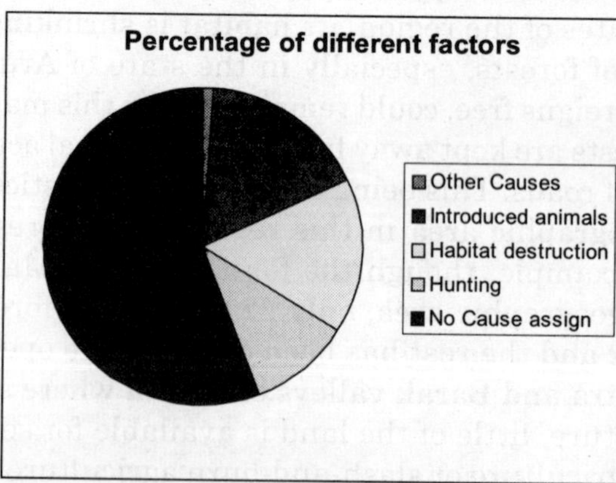


**Fig. 4.1 : Causes of global extinction based on the knowledge of 484 extinct species**

**Source:** World Conservation Monitoring Centre, 1992

prevalent, giving very little chance for the denizens of the forests to recoup from such pressures. Besides, certain meat is valued as medicinal and such animals are persecuted as great efforts are made by a few individuals to seek such animals and bring back home their body parts. In the past, the hunting/trapping was done with considerable prudence with many taboos and restrictions. For example, the Anaal Naga in Manipur did not consume turtle or tortoise meat. The Maram Naga did not eat pork and the Thangkhul Naga did not eat any member of the cat family. Unfortunately, such taboos no more hold any sway among the people now.

## Natural Cause of Extinction Crisis

Species extinction is a natural process but aggravated by anthropogenic activities. Species become extinct when all individuals die without producing offspring. In order to predict what type of human causes are critical in the extinction of wild species, at least seven life history traits have been proposed as factors affecting a species; sensitive to extinction:

*Rarity*: Generally rare species are more prone to extinction than common ones.

*Dispersal ability*: Species that are capable of migrating between fragments of habitat, such as between mainland areas and islands, may be more resistant to extinction.

*Degree of specialization*: It is often thought that organisms that are specialists, for example, those organisms that can only fed on only one type of plant, like pandas, which only fed on a single species of bamboo, are more likely to go extinct.

*Population variability*: Some species with relatively stable populations, that is those that maintain some equilibrium level, may be less prone to extinction than other.

*Trophic status* (animal only): Animals having higher trophic level has lesser population and are more prone to extinction.

*Longevity*: Species with naturally low longevity are more likely to be extinct.

*Intrinsic rate of population increase*: Species that can reproduce and breed quickly may be more likely to recover after severe population decline.

## V. Ecotourism

It is one of the major reasons for biodiversity loss. Pressure of visiting of ecosystem by large populations has a problem of its own because animals have their own privacy. The best attractive wildlife locations are worst affected by tourism. Unrestricted tourism is another major factor which must be restricted..

## Conservation method

### *(i) In- situ Conservation*

In-situ conservation is done in the original habitat of organism. It includes National Parks, Biosphere Reserves and Sanctuaries etc. We mainly focus on the area having very high concentration of organisms. Centre declares National Park/ Sanctuaries by Central/ State Wildlife Act, 1972. Biosphere Reserves need not be showery area but represent all type of ecosystem found in the country together with some specialized area. It is better form of conservation because it is done in natural habitat of the organism. Recovery programme for critically endangered species, e.g. Manipur Brow Antlered Deer (Manipur) is being started. Currently five natural world heritage sites have been identified by UNESCO in India and among them two are from northeastern region viz. Kaziranga National Park and Manas National Park has been recently added to world heritage sites. Assam has three tiger reserves viz. Kaziranga, Manas and Nameri and two in Arunachal Pradesh viz. Namdhapa and Pakke and one in Mizoram viz. Dampa. One elephant reserve, Khasi Elephant Reserve has been accorded by the Ministry of Environment and Forest in Meghalaya. Golden Langur (*Trachypithecus geei*) narrow endemic was discovered in Chakrashilla Hills Reserve in the Dhubri district of Assam, and the area has been turned into a wildlife sanctuary. Within 5.8 per cent of the state's protected area in Tripura, one can count seven species of primates.

**Table 4.1: Elephant Reserves of Northeast India**

| Sl.No. | Elephant Range | Elephant Reserve | States | Total area (sqkm) |
|---|---|---|---|---|
| 1. | North Brahmaputra (Arunachal-Assam) | Kameng | Arunachal | 1892 |
| | | Sonitpur | Assam | 1420 |
| 2. | South Brahmaputra (Arunachal-Assam) | Dihing-Patkai | Assam | 937 |
| | | South Arunachal | Arunachal | 1957.5 |
| 3. | Kaziranga (Assam-Meghalaya) | Karbi Anglong | Assam | 3270 |
| | | Dhansiri-Lungding | Nagaland | 2740 |
| 4. | Eastern Himalaya (Meghalaya) | Garo Hills | Meghalaya | 3500 |
| | | Khasi Hills# | Meghalaya | 1331 |

#Approved by Government of India but not yet notified by the state government.

Areas around National Park/Sanctuaries in Assam are considered for the declaration as eco-sensitive zones and the draft notification in respect of Kaziranga National Park, Bordoibam Beelmukh Bird Sanctuary and Penidehing wildlife sanctuary are in process.

### (ii) Ex-situ Conservation

Ex-situ conservation is done where numbers of plants / animals have diminished and hence to be conserved. Botanical/ Zoological gardens, seed/ pollen/eggs banks etc. are created to fill the purpose. Tissue culture is the best technique helping in it. In Assam state Zoo-cum-Botanical garden is established covering an area of 130 hectares while Botanical garden is spaced out over an area of 82 hectares. It was established in 1982 and has gathered 44 varieties of orchids from northeastern region of the country. The orchids placed in Orchid House of the Botanical garden are rare species that are typical of mountain region. The garden planted palm, conifers, broad leaf plants, variety of herbs and shrubs. The Zoo is supervised by the office of the divisional forest officer. The Zoo has huge collection of reptiles, mammals and aves. The section of reptiles has as many as 358 reptiles of various kinds. The mammal section of the Zoo has a total collection of 37 animals. There are as many as 277 kinds of birds in Zoo.

Here the natural way of growth and process of evolution is restricted because as there is limited number of individuals, hence the chances of inter-breeding are less, so practically no variation over generations. Hence in-situ conservation must be given priorities over ex-situ.

## Moral Ideals behind Conserving Diversity

The world that will exist in 100 and 1000 years will unavoidably be of human design, whether deliberately or haphazard. The principal that should guide this design must be based on science, much of it done only to the date and on ethics. Ethics should not be among other things, apportion cost and benefits between individual and society as a whole and between current and future generations. An alternative apart from ecological evolutionary perspective, known as the resource conservation ethics, was developed by Gifford Pinchot. According to him, the world consists essentially of two components, human being and natural resources, and the latter should be used for the benefit of the former. The proper use of natural resources, according to the resource conservation ethics, is whatever would further "the greatest good of the greatest number (of people) for the longest time". A sustainable world will require on ethics that is ultimately as long lasting as earth will retains its most striking features, its biodiversity only if human have the prescience to do so. This will occur; it seems only if we realize the extent to which we use diversity. Conversationalist emphasizes the need of economic development, it will be virtually impossible, they argue, to stop hunting / exploitation of resources and trade. When no other viable economic alternatives exist for impoverished forest inhabitants. If you are hungry and undernourished, forging a meat meal today for the promise of external aid tomorrow in nothing short of irrational. As rightly told by Leonardo Boff one of the founders of liberation theology, emotions and sensitivity are the essence in the core dimension of human being. It is not reason but feeling that is improve in our first contact with reality and today's great crisis is not economic, political or religions, but a crisis of affect, of the capacity to feel a connection with others. It is indispensable to "take core of all living things", and science shows that co-operation is the "supreme law of the universe". Tribes and people of hill region often lack the physical infrastructure of the institutions, trained personnel and resources to protect their numbers so they are more fragile to environmental alteration. A low income or racial minority community which is surrounded by multiple sources of environmental degradation, waste treatment facilities and landfills face higher average potential environmental risk than residents of clean communities.

## Religious Ethics and Biodiversity Conservation

Indigenous religion traditions in Northeast India seems to have a significant say in ecological ethics, build under the symbiotic association of tribal community and local natural idols in the form of plants, animals and water bodies have considerable effect on popularizing message of conservation. Ecological-Anthropological studies (Gadgil and Guha, 1992) contend that religious mores, folklores and cosmologies of most indigenous societies maintain conservationist ethos in order to sustain their natural resource base. Traditionally in Hindu, Buddhism and other religion the message of natural and climax expression stabilize in forest ecosystem. Traditionally the temples and monasteries were built in the lap of nature to grasp the calm and beauty of nature and they promoted the conservation of natural resources like forest, wildlife and water bodies. Buddhism is very helpful in conserving life of animals including vertebrates and invertebrates (Spansel, 1991).

## Traditional Knowledge and Biodiversity

Berkes (1999) define traditional ecological knowledge (TEK) as a cumulative body of knowledge about the relationships living things (including people) have with each other and with their environment, that is handed down across generations through cultural transmission. TEK includes knowledge, practices and beliefs that are more or less integrated with one another. It is dynamic and evolves as people built on their experiences and observations, experiments learn from others and adapted to changing environmental conditions over time. TEK is placed, based and geographically specific and is most often found among societies that have engaged in natural resources use in a particular place over a long time period, such as indigenous people. The potential for traditional and local ecological knowledge to contribute to biodiversity conservation has been widely recognized. United Nations Convention on Biological Diversity states that the knowledge and practice of indigenous and local communities relevant for conservation and sustainable use of biodiversity should be respected, preserved and applied (Multilateral, 1993). However, new knowledge is created all the time, and indigenous people are not the only ones who have ecological knowledge of value. This more recent local ecological knowledge (LEK) is defined as knowledge practices and beliefs regarding ecological relationships that are gained through extensive personnel observation of and interaction with local ecosystems and shared among local resource users. Local ecological knowledge emerges through process of cultural adaptation to the environment. Learning and identifying it and how TEK and LEK maintain and restore diversity can contribute to biodiversity conservation effort. Integrating TEK and LEK into biodiversity conservation will be difficult if this knowledge does not persist and flourish. The common practice of disregarding the traditional rights and practices of local dwellers in order to establish new conservation area has been termed as "ecocolonialism" because its similarity with the historical abuse of native rights by colonial power of past eras. Cultural diversity is strongly linked with the genetic diversity of crop plants. Mountain dwellers help maintaining the traditional form of agriculture system. In mountain areas, particularly, inaccessible terrain often leads to the development of diverse tribes. The people of these communities develop local plant varieties known as "landraces". These landraces has global significance to conservation and improvement of crop species. There are various biodiversity links TKS for soil fertility management like tribal societies of the region plant nutrient use efficient crops on top of the slopes and less efficient on the bottom to suit soil fertility gradient. In short jhum cycle jhumias are cultivating tuber and vegetable crops rather that cereals in longer cycles. About 20 per cent of weed biomass left in the jhum land to replenish nutrients, traditional eco-technology such as water harvesting system and drip irrigation using bamboos to retain the moisture level of soil (Ramakrishnan, 1992). So there is urgent need to institutionalize the knowledge for economic status of these communities along with conservation of the valuable plant species through public and gender participation mechanism. This effort will serve the multipurpose objective like economic development, conservation of Traditional Knowledge System and medicinal plants. Some of the useful medical formulations derived from the plants are Morgosan-O (*Azadirachta indica*), Reserpine (*Rawalfial sepentina* and *Cammiphora wightii*). So these traditions can be useful in entire conservation process. When we talk about forest conservation, indigenous people use to enhance desirable technique they use to enhance desirable plants species including planting or broadcasting seeds; transporting bulbs and other propagules, shrubs and small trees to make them more abundant and accessible. The problem with tribes is: they don't have the ownership of land if they could; they are in stronger position to save it. Some tribal communities are reluctant to share their knowledge, however because of concerns that other will economically use it, their supremacy may less or other not use it responsibly, the modern form of which is intellectual property rights (IPRs). So these knowledges must be acknowledged and protected for the betterment of the tribal and conservation of biodiversity.

## How to Work

Linking up the cultural diversity with conservation mechanism is the main challenge before policy-makers. I would like to mention an example from Nepal where 14,000 forest groups had been interconnected and result was very assertive in terms of conservation mechanism. Such models can be adopted with some locally suitable modifications. Because the northeast area is large and more diverse, our effort should also be at large scale and decentralized. Initiative should be taken by involving local community and society. One thing we must ensure that community must have role in biodiversity conservation including rule-making, because they understand the local ecology and sub-ecology of particular area. By doing so we also built confidence in local dwellers that we are unifying but giving reason-specific approach. Biggest problem is: areas rich in diversity is also very rich in geogenic resources like coal reserves in Meghalaya and gas reserves in Tripura. In Arunachal Pradesh most of the biologically diversified areas are also suitable for Hydroelectricity generation. These naturally rich lands are inhabited by poor people. We have to scarify because biodiversity matters a lot. We cannot simply destroy it by simply saying that compensatory afforestation will be done, because we know that original status of diversity cannot be maintained by afforestation especially in short time span. So to resolve the issue we have to go for transition and recognition of the local people. We have to look for alternative for our highly ambitious development projects. People must be motivated to conserve the diversity. Efforts should be done to restore biodiversity. It is tough and difficult strategy. It requires specific knowledge about species and surrounding. This strategy includes diagnosis of factors responsible for the decline of species, habitat conservation; captive breeding and restriction of harvesting etc. the strategy include (*i*) reintroduction programmes in the original site of living (*ii*) augmentation programmes to increase the existing population size and genetic diversity of a species, and (*iii*) introduction programmes for new areas. Any biodiversity conservation programme cannot succeed without the awareness and involvement of local people. The theme of the conservation must be in the sentiments of people. It is a crucial thing for success of any conservation programmes. Sustainable development has become key word in every policy of government. But in present population explosion scenario, it is important to provide alternative means to the ever increasing population; otherwise all policies will be eyewash only. The ethnobotanical knowledge among the people of northeast India is praiseworthy. However, colossal deforestation and the loss of species in the region is a matter of serious concern. Some research findings speak contrarily to the widely accepted view that the slash-and-burn type of cultivation is destructive in nature. Whatever are the results of studies on jhum cultivation *per se*, it cannot be ignored that certain ecosystems such as the rain forests are highly susceptible to man-made disturbances and there is a crying need for areas to be free from jhum in order to conserve the region's unique biodiversity. It is recommended that every state shall have at least 5 per cent of the geographical area under National Parks and Wildlife Sanctuaries, which cover natural ecosystems and greater emphasis need be given towards anti-poaching measures in such protected areas. Control on poaching can be done by providing alternate means of living for poachers. The buyers of poached products should be checked, i.e. main source of finance should be controlled. In order to achieve this, there ought to be an increase in forest personnel, who are appropriately trained and equipped, especially in the ranks of Forest Guard, Forester and Range Forest Officer. In areas outside the Protected Area Network, other forms of protection that involves participation of local communities should be followed. The impregnability of certain forests in northeast India is a source of protection, as this factor itself offers some hope for the survival of many species. The remoteness of the region, difficult terrain as well as the severe hunting pressures exerted by the people around their immediate surroundings in many parts of the region make it extremely difficult to document the fauna of the region. Conservation linked developmental initiative should be based upon a value system that indigenous people can realize, appreciate and therefore can participate. Development initiatives that link cultural diversity with biological diversity are seen as the basis for ensuring human security in the socio-ecological fragile system. Development initiatives taken so far and still being pursued are largely centered on textbook knowledge-based approach with experimental models being created in the area of mountain diversity conservation movement or following traditional knowledge system of managing diversity. In such effort community participation and administration of project at village/block level is very important. Over a thousand villages in Nagaland have been organized into Village Development Boards (VDBs), with the specific purpose of the rural development. Using this institution, the highly distorted shifting agricultural system, this indeed is basically as agro-forestry system, but presently operating at subsistence or below subsistence level, is now being redeveloped by strengthening the tree component that has been weakened due to extreme deforestation in the region. The Nepalese alder-based agro-forestry system, with planting of tree done both in space and time, during the cropping and fallow phases of shifting agriculture and maintained for hundreds of years, by some of the local tribes the "Angamis" (Ramakrishnan, 2007). All biological components in nature come under renewable biological resources, which can be replenish with proper initiative. To conserve our resources a detailed research focused on cataloging the biodiversity, their nature and property, factors affecting their distribution etc. at local scale should be done. It should also not be forgotten that the biological diversity is associated with economy and ethnicity of the local dwellers. To manage and conserve our Phytodiversity in particular and Zoodiversity in general we have different classifications. Reserve forests are the areas notified under Indian Forest Act, which is well protected and where all human activities are prohibited unless permitted. Protected forests are an area notified under the provisions of Indian/State Forest Act, which has limited protection—all activities permitted unless prohibited. Unclassified forests are the area does not come under the provisions of reserves or protected forests. Nearly 64 per cent of the total geographical area of northeast (2,55,000 km$^2$) is having forest cover, of which only 35 per cent of forest are under the control of Government and rest 65 per cent are under the control of District Council, Village Communities and Private Ownership. At community level we can establish linkage for procurement and marketing of non-timber forest products, promote environmental education at all levels within and beyond the communities. Strengthening of intra-state and inter-state commercial nodes along with marketing networks is essential to improve the micro- and macro-economic related to products of biodiversity. This will boost the conservation strategy. We have also to understand the geographical complexities of the region. All policy have integrated forest and hill region conservation agency may be created, if exists the proper result could be verified by preparing publication. We have also to recognize hill region as ecologically fragile and sensitive pockets and provide adequate incentives in terms of cash or kind to the locals. The safe opportunities can be provided for ecotourism involving integrated understanding of ecological diversity, biodiversity and cultural diversity of the region. The habitat conservation and local community development should aim at enhancing the co-existence of indigenous people and wildlife. This may be in the form of micro-credit loans, environmental education and dissemination of alternative farming technique, human safety awareness and habitat conservation. We can expect result in the form of better economy of locals and lesser pressure on forests etc. community-based natural resource schemes provides the co-existence of ecotourism industry and hunting concessions. These schemes entail a system of returning benefits to rural communities in order to motivate them to protect wildlife outside protected areas and discourage poaching. Conservation education for local populations, practice such as farm field schools, building local capacity for conservation and understanding would contribute towards conservation, help in ecosystem functioning and its ethical and economic value as well as recreational and aesthetic importance. Awareness programmes such as seminars and workshops should be held in schools and colleges and even for the local folks. Public displays in the form of billboards and handing out pamphlets with about the importance of biodiversity and the need of its conservation are needed. Better sharing of income from tourism can be done since biodiversity is a generator for income through tourism and in many developing countries it is one of the most significant sources of national revenue generations. The tourism industry can increase employment within local communities by creating additional job opportunities. This approach would compensate the cost of maintaining wildlife and contribute to the changing local people's negative perception of conservation. The most sustainable approach should be to ensure the development of local economy based on biodiversity and revenue collection from natural ecosystems as well as a reduction in the dependence on farming in the forest patch (jhum). The conservation of biodiversity should be based on sound scientific knowledge, practical local indigenous knowledge and collaboration. It is time for concerned authorities to take up the necessary actions to conserve this rich biodiversity, before it is too late.

## REFERENCES


1. Berkes, F., 1999, *Sacred Ecology: Traditional Ecological Knowledge and Resource Management,* Taylor and Francis, Philadelphia, PA.
2. Gadgil, Madhav and Ramchandra Guha, 1992, *This Fissured Land,* Oxford University Press, Delhi.
3. Ghosh, A. K. and Tiwari, K. K. (1984), Faunal Resources of Northeast India, in Tripathi, R. S. (ed.) Resource Potential of Northeast India, Vol. II (Living Resources), Meghalaya Science Society, Shillong, Meghalaya.
4. Multilateral, 1993, Convention on Biological diversity, Article 8 (j).
5. Ramakrishnan, P.S. "Sustainable Mountain Development. The Himalayan Tragedy, *Current Science,* Vol. 92, No. 3, 10 February 2007.

6. Ramakantha, V.; Gupta, A.K.; Kumar, Ajith, "Biodiversity of Northeast India: An overview", *Wildlife*. 4. 1. 2003. 1-24.

7. Ramakrishnan, P. S, 1992. *Shifting Agriculture and Sustainable Development: An Interdisciplinary Study from North-eastern India*, UNESCO-MAB series, Paris, Parthenon Publ, Carnforth, Lamcs, UK, p. 424.

8. Sponsel, Leslie E. and Poranee, N., 1991, *Nonviolent Ecology: The Possibilities of Buddhism,* pp 139±50.

9. State Forest Report, 1999, Forest Survey of India, MoEF, Govt. of India.

# Floristic Diversity of Northeast India and its Conservation

— Mr. Krishna Upadhaya, Mr. Hiranjit Choudhury & Mr. Nripemo Odyuo*

## Introduction

India is one of the 12 mega-biodiversity countries of the world having three hotspots—the Western Ghats, the Himalayas and Indo-Burma (Myer *et al.*, 2000). The northeast India, which is comprised of the states of Arunachal Pradesh, Assam, Manipur, Meghalaya, Mizoram, Nagaland, Tripura and Sikkim is a part of two biodiversity hotspots *i.e.*, the Himalaya and the Indo-Burma. The former includes the Darjeeling district of West Bengal, Sikkim, Assam, and Arunachal Pradesh of northeast India. The latter includes the state of Manipur, Meghalaya, Mizoram, Nagaland and Tripura. The northeastern region occupies 7.7 per cent of India's total geographical area and supports 50 per cent (ca. 8000 species) of the flora (Rao and Hajra, 1986; Rao 1994), with high concentration of endemism (Chatterjee, 1940, Nayar, 1996). It represents the transitional zone between the Indian, Indo-Burma–Malaysian and Indo-Chinese regions. It is also a part of the Vavilovian centre of biodiversity and origin of many important cultivated plant species and some domesticated animals (Agarwal, 1996). The northeast India by virtue of its geographical position, climatic conditions and altitudinal variations supports a variety of ecosystems ranging from

* We are thankful to the Head, Department of Basic Sciences and Social Sciences, North-Eastern Hill University, Shillong for providing necessary facilities. N. Odyuo is thankful to the Director, Botanical Survey of India for facilities.

mixed wet evergreen, dry evergreen and deciduous forests at low altitude to subtropical broadleaved forests along the foothills to temperate broadleaved forests in the mid hills, mixed conifer and conifer forests in the higher hills, and alpine meadows above the tree line. The region shows high concentration of primitive flowering plants as well as diversified angiosperms and this led Takhtajan (1969) to describe the region as the 'cradle of flowering plants'.

The region is also the abode of approximately 225 tribes out of the total of 450 in the country. These tribes of the region are dependent on forest for fuelwood, fodder, fibre, timber, medicines etc., and shifting cultivation is the major form of agricultural practice in this hilly region. Shifting agriculture or *Jhum* in the entire northeast India is a socio-economic problem involving the tribal societies (Rao and Hajra, 1986). Next to shifting cultivation, fuelwood extraction is another major form of forest destruction as majority of the people from the region still depends on firewood. Thus, extraction of forest product for maintenance of day to day life and shifting cultivation has resulted in large scale deforestation (Ramakrishnan, 1987). The other factors for loss of forest cover are industrialization, urbanization and activities such as construction of dams etc. Because of these activities many of the plant species are threatened in the region.

## Forest cover

The northeastern region covers an area of 2,62,179 sq.km (8 per cent of the country) and has 1,73,316 sq.km of forest cover which is about 66 per cent

**Table 5.1: Forest cover in different states of northeast India**

| States | Geographical area | Forest Cover | | | | Percentage of geographical area |
|---|---|---|---|---|---|---|
| | | Very dense forest | Moderately dense forest | Open forest | Total forest | |
| Arunachal Pradesh | 83,743 | 14,411 | 37,977 | 15,389 | 67,777 | 80.93 |
| Assam | 78,438 | 1,444 | 11,387 | 14,814 | 27,645 | 35.24 |
| Manipur | 22,327 | 923 | 5,541 | 10,622 | 17,086 | 76.53 |
| Meghalaya | 22,429 | 338 | 6,808 | 9,842 | 16,988 | 75.74 |
| Mizoram | 21,081 | 133 | 6,173 | 12,378 | 18,684 | 88.63 |
| Nagaland | 16,579 | 236 | 5602 | 7,881 | 13,719 | 82.75 |
| Sikkim | 7,096 | 498 | 1912 | 852 | 3,262 | 45.97 |
| Tripura | 10,486 | 61 | 4969 | 3,125 | 8,155 | 77.77 |
| **Total** | **2,62,179** | **18,044** | **80,369** | **74,903** | **1,73,316** | **66.10** |

*Source:* FSI (2005)

of the total geographical area as against the national average of 20.6 per cent (FSI, 2005). Very dense (canopy cover 70-100%), moderately dense (40-70%) and open (10-40%) forest constitute 10.4 per cent, 46.4 per cent and 43.2 per cent of the total forest cover respectively . The highest forest cover has been reported from the state of Mizoram (88.63%) followed by Nagaland (82.75%), Arunachal Pradesh (80.93%) and Tripura (77.77 %) as shown in Table 5.1.

## Vegetation Types

The region supports wide variety of vegetation types ranging from tropical forest to alpine meadows. The vegetation can be broadly classified into- *Tropical vegetation:* These forests are found upto 900 m above sea level with maximum species diversity and very high rainfall. Based on the species composition and the amount of rainfall this forest type may have subtypes such as tropical evergreen (*Castanopsis indica*, *Dipterocarpus* sp., *Dysoxylon* spp., *Duabanga grandiflora*, *Knema angustifolia*, *Mesua ferrea*, *Elaeocarpus* spp., *Terminalia* sp., etc.); tropical semi-evergreen (*Bombax cieba*, *Dillenia* sp., *Eleaocarpus* spp., *Gmelina arborea*, *Lagerstroemia parviflora*, *Terminalia myriocarpa*); and tropical moist deciduous type (*Albizia* spp., *Artocarpus* spp., *Shorea robusta*, *Terminalia myriocarpa*, *Lagerstroemia* spp., etc.).

In the *subtropical zone* (900-1800 m), both subtropical broadleaved forest consisting of tree species like *Castanopsis* spp., *Ficus* spp., *Quercus* sp., *Photonia*, *Schima* etc., and Pine forest (*Pinus kesiya*) occurs. These are basically evergreen and dense in nature.

**Table 5.2: Forest Types in Various States of Northeast India**

| Forest types | States | | | | | | | |
|---|---|---|---|---|---|---|---|---|
| | Arunachal Pradesh | Assam | Manipur | Megha-laya | Mizoram | Nagaland | Sikkim | Tripura |
| Tropical evergreen | + | + | + | + | + | + | – | + |
| Tropical semi evergreen | + | + | + | + | + | + | + | + |
| Tropical deciduous | + | + | + | + | – | + | + | + |
| Subtropical broad leaved | + | + | + | + | + | + | + | – |
| Subtropical Pine | + | + | + | + | + | + | – | – |
| Temperate | + | – | + | + | + | + | + | – |
| Subalpine | + | – | + | – | – | + | + | – |
| Alpine | + | – | – | – | – | – | + | – |
| Grassland | + | + | + | + | – | + | – | + |
| Bamboo | + | + | + | + | + | + | + | + |

**Sources**: Chowdhery 1999, Baishya 1999, Baishya et al 2001, Chauhan 1999, Deb 1999, Haridasan 1999, Singh 1999, Hynniewta 1999, Singh and Chauhan 1999.

*Temperate forests* occur between 1800-3500m altitudes and may be mixed broadleaved (*Acer* spp., *Alnus nepalensis*, *Castanopsis* sp., *Exbucklandia populnea*, *Rhododendron* spp., etc) or Coniferous (*Abies densa*, *Tsuga dumosa*, *Taxus wallichiana*) in nature.

Beyond 3500 m altitude is the *sub-alpine forest* and is characterized by the tree species like *Abies spectabilis*, *Cupressus* sp., *Juniperus* sp., *Larix* sp. and *Rhododendron* spp.

The *Alpine zone* above the altitude of 4000 m remains covered with snow for most part of the year and the vegetation is very scarce.

Besides the above forest types degraded forest, grassland and bamboo forest are very common in the whole of northeast India. The various forest types found in different state is presented in Table 5.2.

## Floristic Diversity

Northeast India is the richest area in terms of biological wealth in the Indian subcontinent. It is the meeting ground of temperate east Himalayan flora, Paleo-artic flora of Tibetan highland, wet evergreen and wet deciduous flora of southeast China and Southeast Asia. It is estimated that of about 17,500 flowering plants species in India approximately 50 per cent (HH 8500) are found in northeast India. State-wise number of species is shown in Table 3. The dominant family of the region includes *Orchidaceae, Fabaceae, Asteraceae, Cyperaceae, Poaceae, Rubiaceae* and *Euphorbiaceae* (Rao and Murti, 1990). The floristic richness of the region can be assessed by the fact that of around 1229 orchid species found in India, 730 (59%) species are found in northeast India (Upadhyaya and Nagaraju, 2006). The maximum concentration of orchid species is observed in Arunachal Pradesh (605 species) followed by Sikkim (496 species). *Bulbophyllum, Calanthe, Cymbidium, Dendrobium, Eria* are some of the dominant genera having maximum species. Many of these orchids are threatened due to various human activities.

**Table 5.3. Estimated number of species in different states of northeast India**

| Number of species | States | | | | | | | |
|---|---|---|---|---|---|---|---|---|
| | Arunachal Pradesh | Assam | Manipur | Meghalaya | Mizoram | Nagaland | Sikkim | Tripura |
| Angiosperms | 4,117 | 3,010 | 2,376 | 3,122 | 2,141 | 2,431 | 4,500 | 1,463 |
| Gymnosperms | 29 | 7 | 5 | 6 | 6 | 9 | 24 | 13 |
| **Total** | **4,146** | **3,017** | **2,381** | **3,128** | **2,147** | **2,440** | **4,524** | **1,476** |

**Source:** Chowdhery 1999; Baishya, 1999; Chauhan, 1999; Deb, 1999; Khan et al, 1997; Singh, 1999; Hynniewta, 1999; Singh and Chauhan, 1999; Mao and Hynniewta, 2000.

About 87 species of rhododendrons are known from the Himalayan region, of which all occur in the northeast India and only 6 are found in the western Himalayas. They are found in altitudes ranging from 800-6000 m, majority of which stretch between 2000-4000 m. Highest diversity of rhododendrons in the northeast has been observed in the state of Arunachal Pradesh which has 75 species alone. Out of the total species recorded from the Himalaya region about 65 per cent (57 species) are either rare or threatened (Sekar and Srivastava, 2010).

The region is also rich in bamboo diversity and out of about 130 species found in India, 65 species are reported from northeast India of which 14 are threatened (Naithani, 2006). Some of the common bamboos of the region are : *Arundinaria callosa*, *Bambusa tulda*, *B. pallida*, *Dendrobium hamiltonii* and *Melocanna baccifera*. The region with 37 species is also rich in palm diversity and majority of them are threatened (Sarmah *et al.*, 2006). The region is also rich in wild plants of horticultural potential and cultivated crops and wild relatives of crop plants (Mao and Hynniewta, 2000). The region is dominated by tribals who use wild plants in their daily life as food plants, fuel, fodder, poison, fibers and also for rites, rituals and religious purpose. The diversity of medicinal plants is also high and it is estimated that about 750 plant species in the region are used as traditional medicine by the local people (Handique, 2009).

Some of the interesting plant of the region includes *Sapria himalayana*— largest root parasite with flowers measuring 35 cm across; *Balanophora dioca*— found in undisturbed forest; *Monotropa uniflora*— a nonchlorophyllous showy plant that grow on thick humus; *Galeola falconeri* (one of the tallest orchid), *Epipogeum roseum*, *Agenitia indica* etc., which live on dead organic matter in dense forests. The region also harbours a number of insectivorous plants— *Nepenthes khasiana* commonly known as pitcher plant is endemic to the state of Meghalaya. The other insectivorous plants include *Aldrovanda vesiculosa*, *Drosera* spp. *Dischidia* sp., and *Utricularia* spp.

## Endemism

The northeastern region is very rich in endemic species. Chatterjee (1940) estimated that out of the total 6850 endemic species in India, 3196 are endemic to the region. However, there is a lack of data on endemic species as many of the species considered to be endemic to the region were collected from other parts of the country and neighbouring countries. The high concentration of endemics in this region could be attributed to the varied micro-climate and micro-habitat created due to high mountains, valleys and rivers. The highest concentration of endemics is found in the state of

Arunachal Pradesh with 240 species restricted entirely to the state followed by Assam (102), Manipur (74) Meghalaya (65), Sikkim (30), Mizoram, (27) and Nagaland (14). The families like *Orchidaceae, Poaceae, Asteraceae, Fabaceae, Rubiaceae* and *Ericaceae* have the largest representation of endemic species. *Rhododendron, Hedychium, Impatiens* and *Begonia* are some of the genera that have high number of endemics (cf. Mudgal and Hajra, 1999a, 1999b).

## Threats to Biodiversity

The major threats to the rich diversity of the region is shifting cultivation or *jhum*, deforestation, mining, developmental activities and urbanization. The region has lost an area of 278 sq km during 2003 to 2005 (FSI, 2005). The decrease in the forest cover of the region was mainly due to the losses observed in the states of Assam, Manipur and Nagaland. These losses were due to illicit felling in insurgency affected areas, shifting cultivation practice and also due to flowering of bamboo (FSI, 2005). However, there has been increase in forest cover in the state of Arunachal Pradesh, Meghalaya, Mizoram and Tripura (Table 5.4). The increase in the forest cover in these states was mainly due to the regrowth in shifting cultivation areas, plantations and protection (FSI, 2005). Thus, one of the major reasons for the loss of forest cover in the region is shifting cultivation as evident from the existing fallow lands other than current fallows that covered an area of 5,400 sqkm and in addition to this the current fallows with an area of 3,380 sqkm (FSI, 2005).

**Table 5.4: Change in forest cover, existing fallow land and current fallow lands in northeast India**

| States | Forest cover (sq km) | | | Fallow land (sq km) | Current fallows (sq km) |
|---|---|---|---|---|---|
| | 2003 | 2005 | Change | | |
| Arunachal Pradesh | 67,692 | 67,777 | 85 | 470 | 300 |
| Assam | 27,735 | 27,645 | –90 | 650 | 1,100 |
| Manipur | 17,259 | 17,086 | –173 | 0 | 0 |
| Meghalaya | 16,925 | 16,988 | 63 | 1,620 | 650 |
| Mizoram | 18,583 | 18,684 | 101 | 1,560 | 360 |
| Nagaland | 14,015 | 13,719 | –296 | 790 | 910 |
| Sikkim | 3,262 | 3,262 | 0 | 300 | 50 |
| Tripura | 8,123 | 8,155 | 32 | 10 | 10 |
| **Total** | **1,73,594** | **1,73,316** | **–278** | **5,400** | **3,380** |

**Source:** FSI (2005).

The increase in population in the northeastern states is very rapid and is above the national decadal growth rate (21.34%) except for the states of Assam and Tripura (Census of India, 2001). Though the land-man ratio is very low in the northeastern states, but the pressure for more agricultural land has threatened the forests of the region. Many of the forested lands are encroached upon for new settlement.

Over-exploitation of several medicinal plants such as *Coptis teeta*, *Nardostachys grandiflora*, *Aconitum* sp., *Panax pseudo-ginseng*, *Paris polyphylla*, *Homalomena aromatica*, many species of Zingibers, collection of ornamental plants (such as orchids) from the wild have depleted the natural resources. Many of the plants considered as common have become rare and threatened in the region. *The Red Data Book of Indian Plants* have listed 623 threatened species, of which 120 are from the northeast

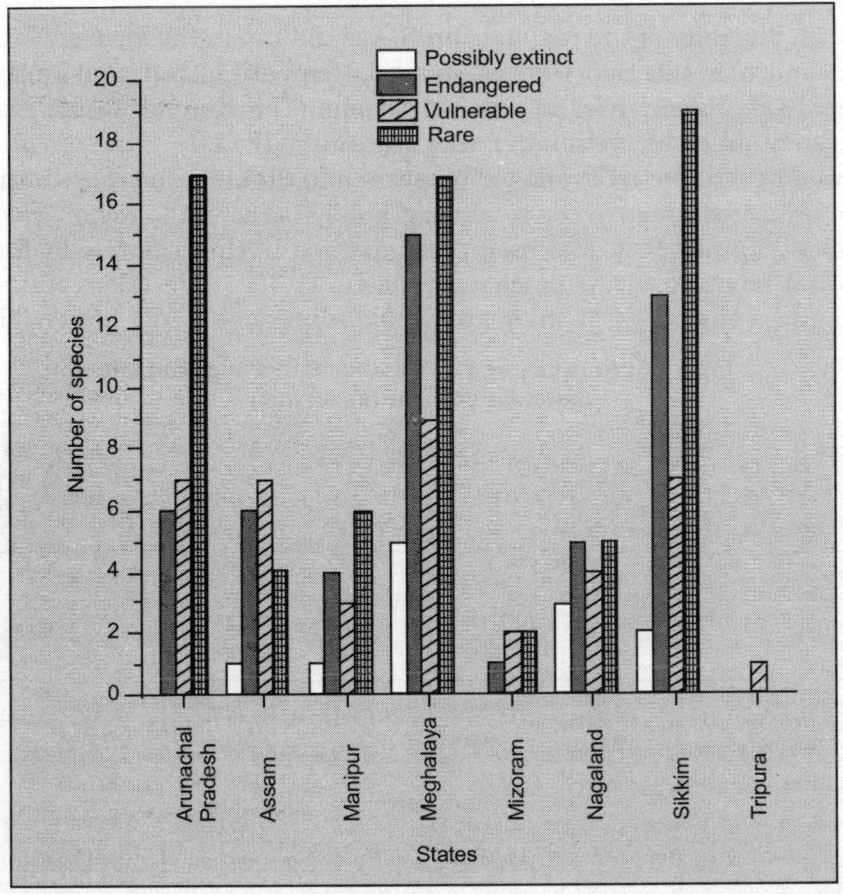


**Fig. 5.1. State-wise distribution of rare and threatemed species**

region falling under the Extinct (11 species), endangered (37), vulnerable (26) and rare (50) category (Nayar and Sastry, 1987, 1988, 1990). State-wise distribution of rare and threatened species is shown in Fig. 5.1. However, the data presented here is an underestimate and many of the plant species viz., *Ilex khasiana, Ilex venulosa, Goniothalamus simonsii* etc. though classified under different threat category by IUCN (IUCN, 2010) have not been listed in the *Red Data Book of Indian plants* (Nayar and Sastry, 1987, 1988, 1990).

Developmental activities such as road construction in forested areas, creation of new township, development of hydroelectric projects etc., leading to habitat loss and fragmentation are responsible for the loss of biodiversity in the region.

## Conservation Status

The rich diversity of the region is protected mainly in the form of National Parks and Wild Life Sanctuaries. In total, there are 17 National Parks and 60 Wild Life Sanctuaries in northeast India. The state of Assam has the highest number of National Parks (5) and Wild Life Sanctuaries (18) followed by Arunachal Pradesh, Mizoram and Sikkim. The contribution of these protected areas to the total geographical area of the region accounts for about 7.3 per cent. Maximum contribution in the region is by Sikkim (30.76%) followed by Arunachal Pradesh (11.7%). The other states are having less than 10% of their area under National Parks and Wild Life

**Table 5.5: Area covered by National Parks and Wild Life Sanctuaries in northeast India**

| States | National Park | | Wild Life Sanctuaryies | | Total area (sq km) | % of geographical area |
|---|---|---|---|---|---|---|
| | Number (s) | Area (sq km) | Number (s) | Area (sq km) | | |
| Arunachal Pradesh | 2 | 2290.82 | 11 | 7487.75 | 9778.57 | 11.7 |
| Assam | 5 | 1977.79 | 18 | 1932.01 | 3450.798 | 4.9 |
| Manipur | 2 | 81 | 6 | 995.10 | 1076.10 | 4.8 |
| Meghalaya | 2 | 267.48 | 3 | 34.20 | 301.68 | 1.3 |
| Mizoram | 2 | 150 | 8 | 1090.75 | 1032.25 | 5.9 |
| Nagaland | 1 | 202.02 | 3 | 20.35 | 222.37 | 1.3 |
| Sikkim | 1 | 1784 | 7 | 399.10 | 2183.10 | 30.76 |
| Tripura | 2 | 36.71 | 4 | 566.93 | 603.64 | 5.7 |
| **Total** | **17** | **7101.54** | **60** | **11765.56** | **18867.28** | **7.3** |

Sanctuaries (Table 5.5). Besides, there are a number of reserved forests and community-based reserved forest in the region. For instance, the sacred groves found in the state of Arunachal Pradesh, Manipur and Meghalaya have also played a major role in conservation of biodiversity and are home to many threatened species of the region (Haridasan and Rao, 1987). However, the sacred groves are exposed to disturbance of different magnitudes and many of the species found in sacred groves are also under severe stress (Upadhaya *et al.*, 2008).

## Conservation strategies

The region is very rich in plant diversity but many of the areas of the region remain still unexplored. Such areas should be explored to known floristic wealth of the region. The existing protected areas should be given further protection. Protected areas in the form of National Parks and Wild Life Sanctuary should be increased and this can be achieved by bringing the forest patches around these areas. The total percentage of the area under the protected category is very less and many inaccessible areas with intact forest can be declared as National Park and Wild Life Sanctuaries, so that the total percentage of geographical area can be increased.

Shifting cultivation is closely associated with the socio-cultural activities of the people of the region and they cannot do away with such traditions that have been practiced for centuries. This practice can be replaced with tree farming system which differs from the traditional shifting cultivation only in a way that the fallow land is not abandoned but is maintained initially for 1-3 years with plantation. Farming of medicinal plants and cash crops could be another alternative to shifting cultivation that should be encouraged, as it gives better livelihood options.

Establishment of botanical gardens, and sanctuaries like the *Nepenthes* sanctuary in Meghalaya, *Rhododendron* sanctuary in Sikkim should be increased so that along with the target species other species are also protected. Multiplication of threatened species through tissue culture and their introduction as well as protection of the natural habitats should be prioritized.

Social- and community-forestry should be encouraged as this will reduce the pressure on forest lands. Growing of bamboos, canes and plants of economic importance should be encouraged near the residences of the people and community land to minimize the stress on the forest and also improve the livelihood of the people Local communities and institutions should be encouraged to take up the conservation initiatives as Tribal Wisdom and Indigenous Knowledge System of the people has always played an important role in biodiversity conservation.

## REFERENCES


1. Agarwal, K.C. (1996), *Biodiversity,* Agra Botanical Publishers, India.
2. Baishya, A.K. (1999), "Assam" in, V. Mudgal and P.K. Hajra (eds) *Floristic diversity and conservation strategies in India*, Botanical Survey of India, Calcutta, Vol. II, pp. 615-662.
3. Baishya, A.K; Haque, S; Bora, P.J. and Kalita, N. (2001), "Flora of Arunachal Pradesh — An overview, *Arunachal Forest News* 19(1&2): 1-25.
4. Chatterjee, D. (1940), "Studies on endemic flora of India and Burma," *Journal of Asiatic Society of Bengal Science* 5: 19-97.
5. Chauhan, A.S. (1999), "Manipur" in V Mudgal and PK Hajra (eds) op. cit. Vol. III, pp. 1153-1182.
6. Chowdhery, H.J. (1999), "Arunachal Pradesh", in V Mudgal and PK Hajra (eds) op. cit. Vol. II, pp. 574-614.
7. Deb, D.B. (1999), "Tripura" in V Mudgal and PK Hajra (eds) op. cit. Vol. III, pp. 1511-1528.
8. FS, (2005), *Forest Survey of India*, Ministry of Environment and Forests, Dehradun.
9. Handique, P.J. (2009), *Medicinal Plants of North East India: Status Diversity Conservation Cultivation and Trade*, Dehradun, p. 314.
10. Haridasan, K. (1999), "Meghalaya" in V Mudgal and PK Hajra (eds) Vol. III, pp. 1183-1216.
11. Haridasan, K. and Rao, R.R. (1987), *Forest Flora of Meghalayam,* Bishen Singh and Mehandra Pal Singh, Dehradun.
12. Hynniewta, T.M. (1999), "Nagaland" in V Mudgal and PK Hajra (eds) Vol. III, pp. 1259-1298.
13. IUCN, (2010) Standards and Petitions Subcommittee 2010. Guidelines for Using the IUCN Red List Categories and Criteria. Version 8.1. Prepared by the Standards and Petitions Subcommittee in March 2010. Downloadable from http://intranet.iucn.org/webfiles/ doc/SSC/ RedList/ RedListGuidelines.pdf.
14. Khan, M.L., Shaily, M. and Bawa, K.S. (1997), "Effectiveness of the protected area network in biodiversity conservation, a case study of Meghalaya state", *Biodiversity and Conservation* 6: 853-868.
15. Mao, A.A. and Hynniewta, T.M. (2000), "Floristic diversity of north east India", *Journal of the Assam Science Society* 41(4): 255-266.
16. Myer, N., Muttermeier, R.A., Muttermeier, C.A., da Fornseca, G.A.B. and Kent, J. (2000), *Nature* 403: 853-858.
17. Naithani, H.B. (2006), "Diversity of bamboo species in north-east Indiam", in: HN Pandey and SK Barik (eds.), *Ecology, Diversity and Conservation of Plants and Ecosystems in India*, Regency Publications, New Delhi, pp. 312-324.
18. Nayar, M.P. (1996), *Hotspots of Endemic Plants of India, Nepal and Bhutan*, SB Press, Trivandrum.

19. Nayar, M.P. and Sastry, A.R.K. (1987, 1988, 1990), *Red Data Book of Indian Plants*. Vols. 1-3. Botanical Survey of India, Howrah (Calcutta), India.

20. Ramakrishnan, P.S. (1987), "Shifting agriculture and rainforest ecosystem management", *Biology International* 15: 17-18.

21. Rao, R.R. (1994), *Biodiversity in India: Floristic Aspects*, Bishen Singh Mahendra Pal Singh, Dehradun.

22. Rao, R.R. and Hajra, P.K. (1986), Floristic Diversity of Eastern Himalaya-in a conservation perspective. Proceedings of Indian Academic Sciences (Animal science/Plant Science) 103-125.

23. Rao R.R. and Murti S.K. (1990), "Northeast India a major centre for plant diversity in India," *Indian Journal of Forestry* 13(3): 214-222.

24. Sarmah, A., Haridasan, K., Hegde, S.N. and Borthakur, S.K. (2006), "Diversity and distribution of palms in north east India and their role in tribal life", in Pandey HN Pandey and SK Barik (eds), op.cit. pp. 243- 257.

25. Sekar, K.C. and Srivastava, S.K. (2010) "Rhododendrons in Indian Himalayan region: Diversity and Conservation", *American Journal of Plant Sciences* 1: 131-137.

26. Singh, K.P. (1999), "Mizoram", in V Mudgal and PK Hajra (eds) Op.cit. Vol. III, pp. 1217-1258.

27. Singh, P. and Chauhan, A.S. (1999), "Sikkim", in V Mudgal and PK Hajra (eds) *ibid.,* pp. 1419-1450. 662.

28. Takhtajan, A. (1969): *Flowering Plants – Origin and Dispersal,* Oliver & Boyd Ltd, Edinburgh.

29. Upadhaya, K., Barik, S.K., Pandey, H.N. and Tripathi, O.P. (2008), "Response of woody species to anthropogenic disturbances in sacred forests of northeast India. International Journal of Ecology and Environmental Sciences 34 (3): 245-257.

30. Upadhyaya, R.C. and Nagaraju, V. (2006), "Orchids scenario in NE region: issues and strategies", in VB Singh, K Akali Sema and P Alila (eds), *Horticulture for Sustainable Income and Environmental Protection.* Vol. I, pp. 317-329.

# Mount Saramati

## *Ideal Site for Biodiversity Conservation and Ecotourism in Nagaland, Northeast India*

— Mr. Nripemo Odyuo, Mr. Krishna Upadhaya & Mr. S.A. Jamir*

## Introduction

The northeast India harbours some of the important remnants of tropical, subtropical, temperate and sub-alpine vegetation. The rich biodiversity are preserved mostly in the form of Biosphere reserves, National Parks, Wild Life Sanctuaries and some remote and inaccessible areas (Rao and Hajra, 1986). The area is hilly and the environmental services in the form of food, water, medicines, energy and cash-generating products provided by the natural assets, form the basis for the physical security of mountain people and ensure the sustainability of their production system into the future. Mountainous regions in most cases are inaccessible, fragile, marginalized by political and economic decision-making and home to one of the poorest people in the world (Messerli and Ives, 1997). The socio-economic conditions of people living in the mountains are far below those of the lowlands due to limited cultivable land resources and livelihood options. Poverty and environmental degradation both go together in the mountains, thus putting a major challenge before the researchers to conserve biodiversity and at the same time improve livelihoods of communities' dependant on natural resources. While steepness, fragility and marginality often remain as constraint, which exposes mountains to pervasive degradation, there are

* We are thankful to the people of Thanamir and the then Deputy Commissioner of Kiphirie, Government of Nagaland and his staff, for their kind help and cooperation. N. Odyuo is thankful to the Director, Botanical Survey of India for facilities.

also several opportunities to be trapped. Given the complexities of development in the mountains, tourism development is often viewed as an obvious alternative and only means for achieving sustainable mountain development. However, all ecotourism destinations are not in the mountains; and only a few have been cited as ecotourisms destinations (Williams *et al.*, 2001).

Shifting agriculture or *jhum* in the entire northeast India is a socio-economic problem involving the tribal societies (Rao and Hajra, 1986). The state of Nagaland in northeast India (Latitude 25°10′ and 27°4′ N and Longitude 93°15′ and 95°15′ E) with an area of 16580 sq.km is known both for its rich biodiversity and cultural diversity. Being a hilly state, shifting cultivation is a major form of agriculture and is posing a serious environmental problem (Ramakrishnan and Tokyo, 1981). An area of about 79,000 ha has been affected by shifting cultivation and in addition to this it has been estimated that the current area under current fallows is 91,000 ha (FSI, 2005). The forest is fast degrading and the state has lost a forest cover of 296 sq. km during the period 2003-2005 (FSI, 2005). For a small state like Nagaland this rate is quite alarming. Mt. Saramati located in the western part of Nagaland (26°7′N and 97°13′E) bordering Myanmar ranks as one of the highest peaks of the Southeast Asia with an altitude of 3841 m above sea level. It represents one of the most unexplored and biodiversity rich areas of the country (Hynniewta, 1994, 1999; Jamir and Rao, 1998). Most of the previous botanical exploration carried out in the state by Clarke (1886), Hooker (1872-97), Kanjilal *et al.,* (1934-40), Bor (1942) and Jamir and Rao (1988) were not able to explore Mt. Saramati due to poor accessibility. Botanical exploration at Mt. Saramati was recently initiated by Hynniewta (1994). The rich floristic diversity of Mt. Saramati is threatened by anthropogenic activities like shifting agriculture, firewood collection and timber extraction for construction purposes that are taking place at a large scale. The present paper focuses on the socio-economic status of the people; natural resources present for effective biodiversity management and promoting tourism. An attempt has also been made regarding future strategies that would help in improving the livelihood of the local tribal people.

## Study Area

Mt. Saramati covers an area of more than 200 sq.km with altitude ranging from 2000 m to 3841 m, a part of which is in Myanmar. It is indeed surprising that Mt. Saramati, one of the most pristine ecosystems of the country has received such a meager attention from researchers. So far only little is known about the flora, fauna and people of the area. The reason for the poor state of knowledge is obvious. The prime reason is the poor accessibility. There is no metalled road except an entry road upto Penkim from where it takes three hours to reach the Thanamir, the only village in close proximity to Mt. Saramati. From Thanamir one has to undergo two days extensive trekking to reach Mt. Saramati. The other reason is inhospi table condition during monsoon. The area can only be visited during dry season extending from November to April. During wet season, accessibility becomes extremely difficult and also the area is infested with wild animals.

## Results and Discussion

### *Village Profile*

The Thanamir village around Mt. Saramati came into existence about 100 years back when Yimchunger tribe from nearby area arrived and founded small settlement taking advantage of the fertile and unexploited land in the mountain for agriculture and hunting of wild animals. This community

**Table 6.1 : Population, Livestock and Infrastructure Status of Thanamir village**

| Village profile | |
|---|---|
| Number of houses | 105 |
| Total Population | 591 |
| Male | 253 |
| Female | 338 |
| Average size of family | 5.6 |
| Landholding/family | 5 sq. km |
| Cultivated land/family | 4 sq. km |
| Forest land/family | 6 sq. km |
| **Live stock component** | |
| Goats | 150 |
| Pigs | 134 |
| Mithun | 211 |
| **Infrastructure** | |
| School | Primary school |
| Health | No facility |
| Electricity | No |
| Drinking water | From forest connected by a pipe line |
| Road | No |
| Post and telegraph | No |
| Hotel/lodges | No |

defined a conservation area to protect their water resources and an area of agricultural and forests for wild animals. Mt. Saramati awes endurance in its pristine state till date due to its inaccessibility that has restrained humans to settle in most of its vistas. Abundance of forest resources around to fulfill the needs of the people has also saved it from obliteration. The total number of households in the village is 105 with a population of 591 individuals that includes 253 males and 338 females (Table 6.1). The primary occupation of the Yimchunger tribe is shifting cultivation and hunting. The people of the village are totally dependent on the forest for *jhum* cultivation and collection of wild leafy vegetables and fruits. Their staple food includes Coix (*Coix lacrymajobi*) commonly known as *jobs tear*. Besides Coix, Colocasia, Maize and Rice are also cultivated. *Alnus nepalensis* is the most preferred tree species that is planted in the abandoned *jhum* lands because of its first growth, coppicing capacity and increasing nitrogen fertility of the soil. The others means of survival includes rearing of a domesticated animals like goats and pigs (Table 6.1). About 50 people are involved as porters for tourist treks if tourists are available; one family is involved in lodging (the headman). Almost every house rear Mithun (*Bros frontalis*) a semi-domesticated wild animal that is found only in the state of Nagaland and Arunachal Pradesh in India.

## Biodiversity Status

Mt. Saramati represents intact forest communities' representing the climax vegetation of the area and is a center of biodiversity due to variety of landscapes and climatic conditions, which range from subtropical to sub-alpine. Based on altitude and floristic composition three major vegetation types have been identified, *i.e.,* subtropical pine forest, temperate forest and sub alpine forests (Table 6.2). Besides rich floristic diversity a number of wildlife such as deer, bear, wild boar, porcupine, wild cat, wild dogs, black squirrel, monkey and birds like tragopan, jungle fowls, hornbills, pigeon, eagle, wood peckers, owl etc., are also found. However, at present most of these species are at risk because of the destruction of primary vegetation in and around the village due to shifting cultivation and hunting. The value of Mt. Saramati is enhanced by the fact that it harbours a number of medicinal (*Aconitum lycoctonum*, *Panax pseudo-gingseng*), economic (*Eleocarpus* sp., *Quercus* spp., *Castanopsis* sp.) and ornamental (a variety of orchids and *Rhododendrons*) plant species and also provides refuge to a number of endemic, rare and endangered species of the region (Hynniewta, 1994). It also serves as home for many rare and threatened animals. A preliminary botanical exploration carried out by Hynniewta (1994) and the present study reveals the presence of a total of 354 (including 23 pteridophytes) species of vascular plants distributed in 241 genera and 98 families (Table 6.3). Though Mt. Saramati covers only 1.21 per cent of the total geographical area of the state it harbours about 14 per cent of the total flora of the state. This reflects the magnitude of species richness. However, the recorded biodiversity may contribute only a portion of the total biodiversity of this area and detailed floristic work need to be carried out. The area is expected to have rich diversity due to its location at the confluence of Indo-Burma region which is one of the biodiversity hotspots (Myer *et al.*, 2000).

**Table 6.2: Life zones, vegetation and animals in Mt. Saramati**

| Climatic Zones | Vegetation | | | Animals | |
|---|---|---|---|---|---|
| | Climax species | Shrubs | Herbs | Mammals | Birds |
| Subtropical pine forests (up to 2000m) | *Pinus kesiya, Acer laevigatum, Lithocarpus dealbata, Schima wallichii, Quercus griffithii, Alnus nepaulensis* | *Eupatorium* sp., *Rubus* sp., *Smilax* sp., *Rosa* sp. | *Viola* sp., *Anaphalis* sp., *Commelina* sp., *Cyanotis vaga, Polygonum* sp. | Black squirrel, Wild dogs, Wolf and Deers. | Jungle fowls, Hornbills and Sparrows |
| Temperate forests (2000-3500m) | *Engelhardtia spicata, Eleacarpus* sp., *Quercus* sp , *Exbucklandia populnea, Betula alnoides, Schima khasinia, Prunus* sp., *Rhododendron* spp. | *Symplocos* sp., *Ardisia* sp., *Berberis asiatica, Mahonia pycnophylla, Gaultheria* sp. | *Impatiens* sp., *Panax pseudo-gienseng* sp., *Arundiniaria* sp., *Carex* sp., *Arisaema* sp., *Begonia* sp. | Bear, Wild Boar, Black squirrel, Clouded leopard, Wild cats Monkey, Fox and Deers | Jungle fowls, Hornbills, Stripped eagle, Wood peckers, tree sparrow |
| Sub-alpine forests (> 3500 m) | *Rhododendron* spp., *Juniperus recurva, Taxus baccata* | *Juniperus recurva, Rhododendron* spp., *Lyonia ovalifolia, Gaultheria fragmen-tissima* | *Impatiens* sp., *Campanula aristata, Deyeuxia* sp., | Clouded leopard, Wild cats, Golden Cat, Procupine | Tragopan, Sunbirds |

**Table 6.3: Plant diversity status of the state of Nagaland and Mt. Saramati**

| Groups | *Nagaland | | | Mt. Saramati | | |
|---|---|---|---|---|---|---|
| | Family | Genera | Species | Family | Genera | Species |
| Angiosperms | 186 | 963 | 2431 | 82 | 217 | 325 |
| Dicot | 158 | 724 | 1688 | 75 | 157 | 241 |
| Monocot | 28 | 239 | 743 | 7 | 60 | 84 |
| Gymnosperms | 5 | 6 | 9 | 3 | 6 | 6 |

**Sources:** *Mao and Hynniewta (2000)

## Ecotourism

The increasing number of visitors to Mt. Saramati began after 1990s due to relaxation in regulations that opened a number of new areas for both foreign and domestic tourists. Being located in a remote, inaccessible and restricted area, Mt. Saramati hosted few foreign tourists (18 only) during the period September 2003–March 2004, (official data for foreign tourists before September 2003 was not available) and 998 local tourists during the period 1998-2003 (Figure 6.1). Local tourists were mostly from the state of Nagaland. Foreign tourist require Restricted Area Permit (RAP) whereas, tourist from other parts of India require Inner Line Permit (ILP) to visit Nagaland. Tourists are coming from different parts of Nagaland and abroad to enjoy the scenic beauty, explore new areas and also the rich cultural heritage. The people of Thanamir are proud of their traditions, socio-political structure, culture and also their distinctiveness as Yimchunger as any other Naga tribes. About 50 per cent of the people still practice their traditional religion, which is full of taboos and beliefs. According to local belief, ascending Mt. Saramati peak is considered an achievement enough for celebration in which the whole village take part. People dress-up in their traditional attire and perform a traditional dance, which is becoming a popular tourist attraction activity in the recent times. The rich culture of Yimchunger tribe, extensive trekking route, scenic beauty, rare and endangered flora (orchids/ rhododendrons/ medicinal plants) preserved for aesthetic and ethical values,

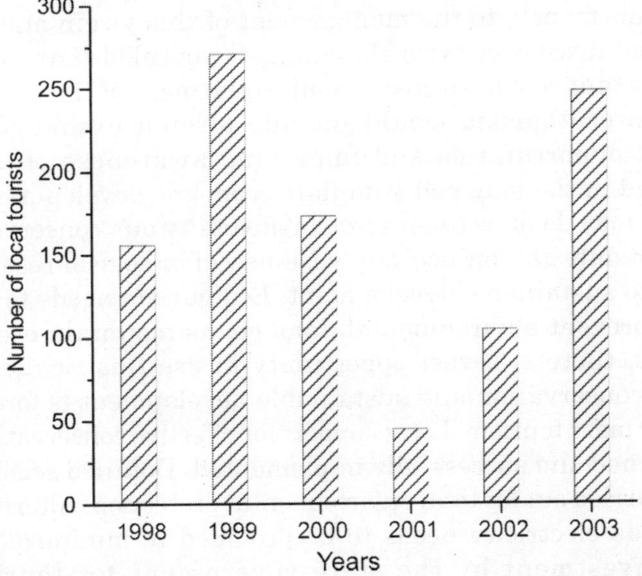


**Fig. 6.1: Inflow of local tourist at Mt. Saramati (1998-2003)**

variety of wildlife, snow covered peaks (during winters) are some of the striking feature making Mt. Saramati interesting for promoting tourism.

Despite the increasing popularity of Mt. Saramati for trekking and nature tourism, self-employment has been low. Thus, most of the tourists visit the area in organized groups and make use of the local services only in the form of porters and guides. The poor infrastructure and the lack of proper road are some of the factors responsible for low inflow of tourists per year. Hotels/lodges, tea stalls, local products etc., could be some of the possibility that need to be strengthened to increase the number of tourists. If properly planned, tourism could link Mt. Saramati directly with global economy. There are hardly any successful models for ecotourism in northeast India where benefits are being returned to local communities to encourage biodiversity protection. Ecotourism provides direct benefit to conservation and or local people who in turn have an incentive for conservation and the ability to be self-sustaining within the context of the natural and cultural habitats in which it takes place (Murphy, 1985). The local communities benefit from biodiversity for subsistence of the people right (utility value). These utility values could also be for enterprise development providing income generation opportunities for poor rural households.

## Future Strategies

The legal protection of Mt. Saramati is a difficult task as it belongs to the local people and government has no control over it. Ecotourism can contribute enormously to the management of this virgin and unexploited area. Detailed discussion with the villagers revealed that tourists would play an important role in socio-economic upliftment of the people. Benefits arising from ecotourism would include foreign exchange, revenues, employment opportunities and improving awareness of conservation objectives and in the long run stimulate economic development. However, market force may do little to conserve biodiversity but 'conservation' should be viewed not only as 'non-use' but 'wise-use' of biological resources, which contributes to sustainable development. Ecotourism needs to be managed properly to prevent environmental damage, as mountain ecosystems are fragile. Thus, there is a vast opportunity to use this richness to ensure biodiversity conservation and sustainable development before the area is opened up for mass tourism. Local support for effective conservation measures must be planned and successfully implemented. Detailed scientific studies needs to be carried out for total environmental protection. Alternative energy source such as electricity needs to be provided to minimize pressure on firewood. Investment by the state government for tourism-related infrastructure to promote tourism would not only add value to raise the state's economy but would be surely of great advantage for economic uplift, job opportunities as well as improving the livelihood of remote area like Saramati (Figure 6.2).

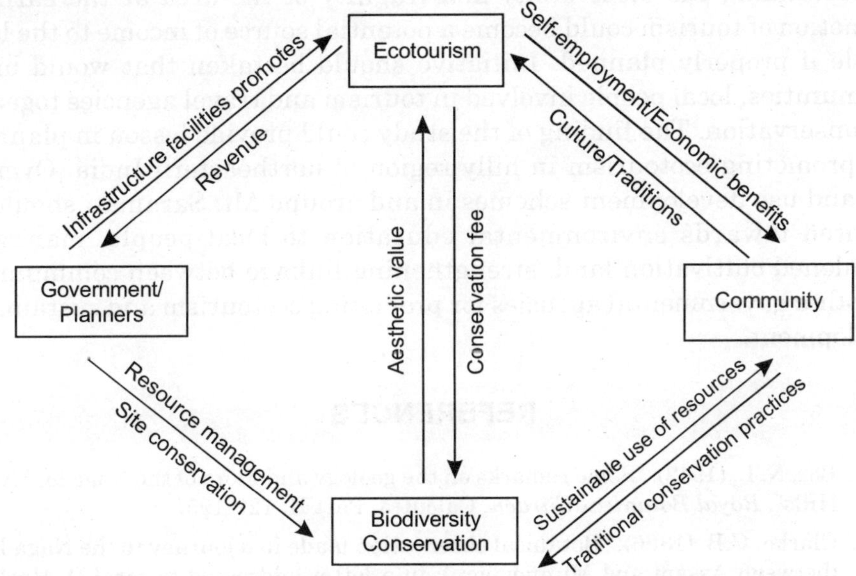


**Fig. 6.2: Linkages between biodiversity conservation and ecotourism**

The indigenous people possess broad knowledge on biodiversity resources and the local environment. They have their own ways of managing resources. However, the low supports of shifting cultivation are forcing the people to encroach primary forest. Local stakeholders need to be trained as nature guides, e.g., birds, animals, forest and plants. Small village resort can also provide economic benefits for the local people. Promotion of vegetables, poultry and local fruits, milk production, traditional food, handicrafts can be attractive to tourist and earn economic benefits for the local communities from tourists. Forest department, Tourism department can also play important role for promoting tourism by establishing rest houses and publishing materials on different aspects such as sites, plants, animals etc. If local communities are taken into consideration and ecotourism is well planned and implemented then biodiversity conservation and ecotourism can prove to be a successful model in Mt. Saramati and northeast India as a whole.

## Conclusions

Mt. Saramati is endowed with rich biodiversity and forest-based resources that are an integral part for the livelihood of the local people. Shifting cultivation is forcing the people to encroach the primary forest for increasing the food production and is posing a serious threat to the forest resources and biodiversity of the area. A detailed research needs to be carried out for understanding the biodiversity and fragility of the area at the earliest. Promotion of tourism could become a potential source of income to the local people if properly planned. Initiative should be taken that would bring communities, local people involved in tourism and travel agencies together for conservation. The finding of the study could provide lesson in planning and promoting ecotourism in hilly region of northeastern India. Overall, the land use development schemes in and around Mt. Saramati should be oriented towards environmental education to local people, managing abandoned cultivation land, strengthening linkage between communities and other governmental agencies for promoting ecotourism and sustainable development.

## REFERENCES

1. Bor, N. L. (1942), "Some remarks on the geology and Flora of the Naga and Khasi Hills", *Royal Botanical Garden*, Calcutta, Part II: 129-195.
2. Clarke, C.B. (1886), "Botanical observation made in a journey to the Naga Hills (between Assam and Munneypore); in a letter addressed to Sir J.D. Hooker," *Journal Linnean Society (Botany)* 22:128-136.
3. FSI, (2005), *Forest Survey of India*, Ministry of Environment and Forest, Government of India, Dehradun.
4. Hooker, J.D. (1872-97), *Flora of British India* Vols. 1-7, London.
5. Hynniewta, T.M. (1994), "Botany of Mt. Saramati and its environs," *Bulletin of Botanical Survey of India* 36: 178-188.
6. Hynniewta, T.M. (1999), "Nagaland" in, Mudgal, V. and Hajra, P.K. (eds) *Floristic diversity and conservation strategies in India*, Botanical Survey of India, Calcutta, Vol. III, pp. 1259-1298.
7. Jamir, N.S. and Rao, R.R. (1988), *Ferns of Nagaland*, Bishen Singh and Mahandra Pal Singh Publications, Dehradun.
8. Kanjilal, U.N.; Kanjilal, P.C., Das, A.; De.; R.N. and Bor, N.L. (1934-40), *Flora of Assam*, Vols. 1-5, Shillong.
9. Mao, A.A. and Hynniewta, T.M. (2000), "Floristic diversity of Northeast India" *Journal of Assam Science Society* 41(4): 255-266.
10. Messerli, B. and Ives, J.D. (1997), *Mountains of the world: A global priority*, Carnforth, Parthenon.
11. Murphy, P.E. (1985), *Tourism: A community approach*, New York, Methuen, pp. 34-36.
12. Myer, N., Muttermeier, R.A., Muttermeier, C.A., da Fornseca, G.A.B. and Kent, J. (2000), *Nature* 403: 853-858.

13. Ramakrishnan, P.S. and Tokyo, O.P. (1981), "Soil nutrient status of hill agro-ecosystems and recovery pattern after slash and burn agriculture (*jhum*) in north eastern India", *Plant and Soil* 60: 41-64.

14. Rao, R.R. and Hajra, P.K. (1986)", "Floristic diversity of the Eastern Himalaya-in a conservation perspective. Proceedings of Indian Academy of Sciences (Animal Science / Plant Science) Suppl. pp. 103-125.

15. Williams, P.W., Singh, T.V. and Schuter, R. (2001), "Mountain ecotourism: Creating a sustainable future", in Weaver D.B. (ed.) *The Encylopidia of Ecotourism*. Oxon, U.K. CAB International, pp. 205-218.

# Tribal Relation with Nature

## *A Case of the Lepchas of West Bengal*

— Dr. Dulal Chandra Roy

## Introduction

Tribes live in a close proximity to nature. Although they may not be absolutely dependent on nature but even today most tribal activities centred around nature. They not only use nature for their survival but they know how to preserve and conserve nature without disturbing her. They respect and worship nature. Before reaching to the modern lifestyle, tribes passed through different stages: nomadic, food-gathering, hunting, shifting and settled cultivation. At each stage tribes accommodate themselves with nature and live in close harmony with nature.

Tribes live peacefully in nature like other animals. Their close association with nature helps them to read, interpret and understand nature correctly than most civil societies of today. For their survival they could learn nature's sights, sounds and smell. Tribes, like most animals, even today can forecast natural happenings well in advance and can save themselves from the danger of natural hazards. They possess the strong sixth sense to smell the wind, to gauge the depth of sea, to anticipate earthquake etc. which the civil society with modern sophisticated equipments and scientific knowledge fail to do correctly. Earthquake is one such natural hazard which the seismologists fail to predict in advance but its effect is havoc and cause huge loss of life and property. Unsuccessful attempts have been made in different developed countries to evolve any method to predict earthquake.

Worldwide century-old folk tales carry the message that some animals like dogs, cats, chickens, horses, toads can feel the earth vibration before humans. Catfish moving violently, chickens stopped laying eggs, bees leaving hives in panic are some common observations before earthquake. Although nothing concrete has been found but in 1975 Chinese officials could save 1,50,000 lives by evacuating Haicheng town just days before 7.3 magnitude quake by observing the behaviour of the animal. Like some animal, the untouched tribes also reach higher ground before tides or leave the sea bed before Tsunami and save them from the natural hazards. Jarawas, Shompens, Sentinelese, Onges, Great Andamanese tribes of Andaman islands were saved from Tsunami that hit the Asian coastline on 26th December 2004. Their strong sixth sense and indigenous knowledge of reading the movement of wind, sea and bird have saved the small communities from the danger of natural calamities. All these show strong correlation between the tribe and the nature.

Tribes not only use the nature but they know how to protect and preserve it. All natural elements are Godly to them. They always like to propitiate natural elements and consider that their happiness and existence depend on nature's satisfaction and blessing. White, L. J. arguably the father of modern ecological movement put it—"popular religion in antiquity was animistic. Every stream, every tree, every mountain contained a guardian spirit who had to be carefully propitiated before one put a mill in a stream, or cut tree, or mined the mountain" (1973, 1205). Tribal belief system is so strong that even in modern days in some way or the other they worship nature. In some cases tribes are found to convert to the mainland religions like Christianity, Hinduism, Muslim and the like but in the core of their heart they remain to the nature worshipper. Even after three or four generations of conversion, tribes are found to practice some of their days-old traditional beliefs and customs which are nature based.

In India, tribal association with nature is long and deep. Even under the changed occupational pattern 91 per cent tribes in India are engaged in primary sector against 73 per cent national average. Only 3 per cent tribes are engaged in manufacturing sector against 11 per cent of national average. In tertiary sector, tribes account for only 5 per cent against 16 per cent national average. Association of the tribes with nature is yet to become a story of the past and they depend heavily on nature for their existence. Some tribes in Andaman and Nicobar islands are still the hunters and food gatherers. In other parts of the country they have compelled to shift from their total dependence on forest to shifting cultivation and then to settled cultivation. Even then forest and tribal life are closely related and in the event of any absurdities they feel comfortable with the forest. In some cases forest is the provider of subsidiary source of income like collecting honey, wood, leaves etc. Realising their association on forest the government of India passed the Scheduled Tribes and Other Traditional Forest Dwellers (Recognition of Forest Rights) Act in 2006 and ensures tribe's right over the land and resources.

## THE LEPCHAS

Lepchas, the autochthonous inhabitants of eastern Himalayas, are found in good numbers in Sikkim, hilly region of Darjeeling, eastern Nepal and western Bhutan. Historically this whole area was under the same political rule and Lepchas were the rulers of their own community. In course of time political shuffling make the Lepchas to be ruled by different communities and are divided and become the citizens of different countries. Anyway, Lepchas are the aboriginals of the eastern Himalayas.

Lepchas are in majority in Sikkim where they constitute 7.51 per cent of total population of the state. Total strength of the Lepchas in Sikkim is 40,586 in 2001. In Darjeeling total Lepcha population is 31,210 in 2001 which comprises 1.94 per cent of the district population. In Nepal, 3,660 Lepchas comprise 0.02 per cent of total population of the country. Political shuffling and immigration of other communities in their homeland make the Lepchas cornered, marginalised and uprooted from their forest and land.

Initially Lepchas were the food-gatherers and hunters. Before Tibetan suzerainty in Sikkim in 1642, Lepchas were the free sons of the soil and used to move from one forest to another in search of food and hunting. "From the forest they obtained fruits of numerous descriptions, edible and otherwise useful; thus all their wants were supplied. They knew no care, but little sorrow, cheerful as the birds, and sturdy as the trees around them, they roamed through the forest inhaling health" (G.B. Mainwaring, 1876, 1985, p. ix). Initially Tibetan rule in undivided Sikkim and their land distribution system and later British rule in Darjeeling and their forest reservation had restricted free movement of the Lepchas in their forest. Now the Lepchas have settled in terrace-based cultivation.

Initially Lepchas were pure nature worshippers. Later during Tibetan rule all Lepchas were converted into Buddhism and later some of them reconverted into Christianity. At present in Darjeeling approximately 60 per cent Lepchas are Buddhist while the rest are Christians. In Sikkim 85.14 per cent Lepchas are Buddhist, 12.76 per cent Christian and 2.10 per cent are Hindu. (State Socio-Economic Survey, Govt. of Sikkim, 2006: 361). Even after conversion, Buddhist Lepchas to a great extent remained the followers of traditional Lepcha culture and call Bongthing and Mun in any ritual. The transition from animistic religion to modern religion has had a profound ecological effect.

## THE LEPCHA-NATURE RELATION

Lepchas call themselves *Mutanchi Rong-Kup Rum-Kup* means 'the Beloved Children of Mother Nature or the Children of God'. Lepchas are perhaps the only tribe who by their name links them with nature. In the outside world, the community is popularised as 'Lepcha'. There are different versions about the origin of their name – Lepcha. One version relates their origin from the Nepali word *Lapchao* which means a type of fish available in Nepal. Here also their name originates from natural elements.

In this section we discuss some aspects of Lepcha inter-connectedness with nature. The degree of inter-connectedness is so high and intrinsic that it affects all aspects of Lepcha life. It creates a unique Lepcha-nature culture which is purely nature based. All Lepcha cultural aspects including their folk tales, folk songs, literature, religion, material culture etc. are nature dependent.

### Lepcha Mythology of Origin

Mythologically "the first and foremost primogenitors of the Lepchas, *Fodongthing* and *Nazaongnyo* were created by God from the pure, virgin snows *Kingtsoomzaongboo Choo's* pinnacles and sent them down to live, prosper and spread all over the fairy land of Mayel Lyang that lies on the lap of *Kingtsoomzaongboo Choo* that is Mount Kanchanjunga" (K.P. Tamsang, 1983: pp. 1, 2). Lepchas strongly believe that they are not only the true sons of the soil but they have originated from the Himalayas. Lepcha is a classless society but they have different clans or *Moo* and they believe that each *moo* originates from different peaks of the eastern Himalayas. Each *moo* has separate *Chu* (Peak), *Daa* (Lake) and *Lyap* (Entrance) which link their origin with the mountain region of the area. They have separate names for each *Chu, Daa* and *Lyap* of the region while the Geological Survey of India recognises the peaks by numbers. Lepchas believe that after death their souls return to their corresponding *Chu* via *Lyap* to meet and take rest with their ancestors. Each Lepchas respect, praise and sentimentally attach with the entire Himalayan range. Their sense of respect creates their obligation in preserving and maintaining the Himalayas without causing any harm to it.

### Lepcha Religious Practice

Traditionally Lepchas were nature worshippers. Mount Kanchanjunga is their divine deity. They worship all other natural elements like peaks, rivers, lakes, streams, cloud, water, soil, tree, rain, sun etc. of the region. Mythologically Lepchas relate them to different natural aspects of the locality. Each Lepcha clan has mythological link with different peaks, lakes of the Himalayan range. In all the three important events of life like *Tungbaong* (Naming Ceremony), *Bri* (Marriage), *Sung-Lyaon* (Death Rites), *Bongthing* and *Mun,* the Lepcha priest and priestess utter the names and offer prayer and offerings to the respective peak, lake and also keep them witness of the occasion.

Lepcha love and respect of nature have been reflected in their invocation in different *Faats* (Prayer). *Faats* are special offerings to different elements of nature. *Muk-Zik-Ding-Rum-Faat* is the offering to Mother Nature for timely and sufficient rain, mist and good climate for habitation and vegetation. The *Faat* is observed during March-April, i.e the period of germination. It is said that in the evening of each *Faat* there is at least one shower of rain. *Chu-Rum-Faat* is the offering to Mount Kanchanjunga and other peaks who are the divine deity of the Lepchas. *Tendong-Lho-Rum-Faat* is the special offering to Tendong peak of Sikkim which is believed to cause deluge in the bygone days. The government of Sikkim has declared 8th of August as state holiday to celebrate the occasion. *Lyaang-Rum-Faat* is the offering and prayer to Mother Earth. *Mut-Rum-Faat* is the offerings to jungle spirit and the Lepchas praise the spirit both before and after hunting.

## Lepcha Medicinal Knowledge

Lepcha health management practice forms a part of their culture, the man-made part of their environment. Lepchas have a close and symbiotic relation with the nature. The Lepcha health management system has two parts: (*a*) propitiation of spirits—good or bad—responsible for causing diseases and (*b*) use of curative medicines prescribed by *Bongthing* or *Mun* from local herbs.

Nature not only provides food and shelter but even today most Lepchas depend on forest for herbal medicine to keep them fit and healthy. Lepchas mostly depend on their *Bongthing* and *Mun,* the local herbalist for their common ailment. The modern medical facilities are yet to reach far-flung hamlets and they are delighted and keep themselves fit and fine with traditional method. For common diseases like cough and cold, indigestion, skin diseases etc. their older folk of the family treat them from the surrounding herbs. The herbalist does treat jaundice, piles, bone fracture, cardiovascular diseases, gynaecological disorder etc. A list (Govt. of Sikkim) on ethno- medicinal plants which are commonly known to the Lepchas is shown in Annexure 7.1.

Most common Lepchas possess working knowledge on herbs but *Maondaok*, the Lepcha medicinal man, is the expert. As per Lepcha folk tale, *Tamsangthing* narrated the knowledge on medicinal plants to *Bongthing* and *Mun* and *Pundim Chu* is the original source of all herbal medicines. *Mun* possesses better knowledge on herbal medicine than *Bongthing*. Each year during *Sugi Rum-Faat*, all *Muns* assemble in a particular place and renew their knowledge on herbs and offer prayer to *Nyoo-Koong Nyoolik*, the first *Mun* for her blessings. Before going for modern medical treatment, even today all Lepchas consult and take permission from the *Bongthing* and *Mun*, the bare-footed doctors of the Lepchas in the villages. There is no evidence of epidemic in Lepcha history and the community possess good health and their health management is purely nature based and environment friendly.

## Lepcha Traditional Ecological Knowledge

Tribal knowledge about nature has been generated from their long experience and observation of nature's behaviour. The elder taught this knowledge to the young who again transmits it to the next generation. The younger generations are taught how to observe and read nature including the behaviour of bird, insects, animals, weather, rain, plants, shrubs etc. and gather knowledge of the environment they live in. This knowledge also reflected in the culture and lifestyle of the tribes. Nature is a non-stop event and changes every moment. Tribal youths are taught for generations 'to wait', 'observe' and 'learn' the happenings of the nature and thereby gather full knowledge of the natural happenings. Lepchas have full patience and keep close watch on all happenings in this part of the country. One meaning of their name, Lepcha, is 'to wait'.

By virtue of their long dependence on nature, the Lepchas know each and very elements of the region. The mountains, rivers, lakes, plains, plants, shrubs, bushes, birds, animals and all natural elements are known and have separate Lepcha names. This besides enriching Lepcha vocabulary also depicts rich knowledge and wisdom of the Lepchas on the natural elements and events.

Lepchas can differentiate edible and non-edible plants and roots of the locality. They know the indigenous technique of freeing poison from some poisonous roots and make them edible. Such roots are very tasty but at the same time can take life if poisons are not taken out carefully. The root poison is used in arrowhead for hunting animals. Lepchas are the born botanists zoologists and expert chemists. It is said that J.D. Hooker gathered botanical knowledge on the region from Lepchas and always keep the Lepchas as his company while moving any part of the Lepcha land. He described Lepchas as "great nature lovers and good entomologists and botanists, and have their own names for every animal, insect and plant, and are, I should think, unequalled anywhere as collectors" (J.C. White, 1909 : Reprint, 2005 : p. 7).

## Lepcha Concept of Balancing Ecology

Lepchas not only use nature for their livelihood but they possess a good sense of preservation and conservation of nature.

Lepcha story of hunting in the forest and fishing in the river show their awareness in balancing the ecology. It is said that they do never hunt animals or catch fish more than their requirement. If more fishes are caught in the net they release them in water and keep only that much which is needed for the day's meal. It is also said that they do not catch either the baby fish or the mother fish carrying eggs.

Lepcha society is intimately linked with bamboo which they call *Po*. They use bamboo in all sphere of life like construction of house, bridge, utensils, carrying containers, hat, agricultural implements etc. Lepcha water carriers, water conduits, drinking vessels, pins and broachers, bows and arrows, quiver and scabbards, thatching of roof—all made from different varieties of bamboo which are available in the forest. It is almost proverbial that Lepchas will remain in this part of country so long bamboo grows here. Use of bamboo than wood has its ecological significance in balancing the environment as bamboo bushes grow much faster than tree. Lepcha life-style is eco-friendly.

Lepcha love and respect of natural elements and its ecological effect has been reflected through their rituals. *Muk-Zik-Ding-Rum-Faat, Chu-Rum-Faat, Tendong-Lho-Rum-Faat, Lyaang-Rum-Faat* are some of the rituals where Lepchas are found to offer prayer and offerings to natural elements for good rain, good vegetation, good weather.

## Lepcha Material Culture

All traditional material culture of the Lepchas is nature based. Lepchas use wood, bamboo and cane in construction of house and bridge utensils, ornaments, agricultural implements, hunting implements, carrying containers, musical instruments and what not. *Doo-Kye-Moo-Lee*, the traditional Lepcha house is constructed of wood, bamboo and thatch. Not a single imported item like nail or screw is used in its construction. The house is earthquake proof, flood proof, landslide proof, warm in winter and cool in summer. Lepcha cane and bamboo bridges are the typical example of Lepcha knowledge of engineering and architectural skill. Musical instruments of the Lepchas are made of bamboo or wood which is nature based. Lepchas use all bio-degradable items which are collected from the nature.

## Lepcha Folktales, Folksongs

Most folktales and folksongs of the Lepchas narrate the nature and its different elements including the animals. Lepcha tale of Earthen Tower and reaching heaven relates to the preparation of pottery which is nature based. The popular love story of Teesta and Rangeet is widely narrated during any marriage and is the story of two rivers of the region. Different animals like bear, tiger, lion, monkey, stork, frog, geese, dog, bird etc. came frequently in any Lepcha tale. None of the animals are neglected but they are used as friend and many times worshipped by the Lepchas. In the tale of *Zolasy Pandi* river Teesta was used as messenger and birds are engaged to carry the message of cropping period for differing vegetables which even today the Lepchas are following. The tale of *Pago Rip* narrates the sad story of *Tambum*, the bumble bee and relates the flowering of *Pago Rip* at mid-night and fade away in the morning. A deep correlation has been established between the animal world and the Lepchas habitation through the folktales.

## Lepcha Literature

Lepcha literature is nature based. Lepchas love and association with nature have been reflected in their poems, songs, stories and novels. In fact-nature and Lepcha literature are inseparable. Lepcha songs and poems are nature-based and are the representation of Lepcha tradition and mythology which are again nature dependent. Lepcha literature is the reflection of their folk tales and folk songs and both are nature-based. All natural elements of the region and the animal world are the source of Lepcha literature. Lepcha dictionary is enriched with the names for different plants, animals, peaks, trees, shrubs and other natural elements of the region. Lepchas are the nature's children and they know all the bird and beast, tree and shrub, flower, fruit and fungi of the region and have their separate names. These natural elements not only enriched their literature but their names have been accepted by all newcomers. Lepcha vocabulary is very typical and most scientifically arranged. Name of all rivers of the region starts with 'R', for example, *Rangeet, Relly, Ra-thaong, Raang Raang, Rung-nyoo, Rum Bee, Rum Maam, Ryaong* etc. Similarly the names of all wild animals starts with 'S', for example, *Sa ka* (deer), *Sa chaak* (leopard), *Sa ngoong* (lizard), *Sa toom* (wolf), *Sa thaong* (tiger), *Sa naa* (means bear), *Sa ryaok* (means jackal), *Sa laoyk* (rhinoceros), *Sa hu* (monkey) etc.

## Lepcha Village Name

A good number of Lepcha dominated villages of the region are named after the typical natural condition or natural elements of the area. Be it tree or animal or shape of land but the place name is the reflection of any of the typical character of the nature. It was perhaps these dominant natural component not only identifies the place but separates it from other places. For example, *Kanki Bong* (*Kanki* is the name of a type of tree), *Po-Chaok* (*Po* means bamboo), *Pa-Zok* (anglised Pashok which originally means jungle), *Sonada* (the bears den), *Pakyong* (a kind of cane).

## Lepcha Personal Names

Like the place name of the region, most personal names of the Lepcha, both male and female, are meaningfully linked with the environment and nature of the region. Although nature is generally feminised but the Lepcha personal names of the males are also linked and taken from the different elements of the nature. In some cases the same natural component is used for naming both the sexes; but the females are separated by using *mit* or *kit* as middle name. Some examples of Lepcha male names which are directly linked with nature are: Somee Lepcha (*Somee* means climate), Soaongfoom Lepcha (*Soaongfoom* means dawn or the first sun light), Sa Aom (*Sa Aom* means light), So Raam Lepcha (*So Raam* means thunder), Lyaangsong Lepcha (*Lyaangsong* means aroma of the earth) etc. Some nature based meaningful Lepcha female names are: Lyaangkit Lepcha (*Lyaang* means earth or soil), Koorsaongmit Lepcha (*Koorsaong* means white orchard), Safyummit Lepcha (*Safyum* means a cool or gentle breeze), Ramhimit Lepcha (*Ramhi* is the name of a river in Lepcha), Namthomit Lepcha (*Namtho* is the ray of sun in Lepcha), Niripmit Lepcha (*Nirip* is a type of flower available in this region), Paril Lepcha (*Paril* is a type of snake) etc.

## Conclusion and Suggestions

Nature, the sum total of all living and non-living things, is very special to human beings in general and to the tribes in particular. Nature is the sole provider of life support system to the tribes. There is close and intimate relation between the tribes and the nature. Because of their close association tribes understand, know, read, judge, assess and interpret nature more correctly and accurately. There is an intrinsic bond between nature and tribe. They are the pure botanist, zoologist, environmentalist and what not. Tribes not only use the nature but they accommodate themselves in the nature without disturbing it. Lepcha livelihood is totally dependent on their Mother Nature—starting from cultivated plants to wild edibles, beverage to local drinks, firewood to light production, fish poisoning to hunting devices, gum yielding techniques to extraction of dyes, fodder to fibre, timber to building construction, incense to worship and lastly ethno-medicine to medico-religious belief. Such a diverse use of natural resources is an age-old practice and could be well considered as a primitive agro-forestry based livelihood option. They worship most elements of nature and this inculcates a sense of preservation of nature. Destruction of nature is considered as sin to them and through nature they try to reach to the God. In a word, nature is Godly to the tribes.

Lepcha culture is nature-culture. They not only live in nature with harmony but there is a high rate of dependentness on nature. Lepchas have accommodated themselves in nature by using and preserving it. This makes a two way inter-connectedness between the Lepchas and the nature. Nature is the provider of life-support system to the Lepchas and in return Lepchas love, respect and worship her as God. Destruction of natural elements is considered as sin and they protest strongly in the construction of Mega Hydro Electrical Power Projects by NHPC in Sikkim. Realising, although late, the value and importance of Lepcha Traditional Ecological Knowledge, the government of Sikkim has scrapped four out of six Mega Projects in Sikkim. The primogenitors of the Lepchas were created out of virgin snow of Mount Kanchanjunga and the melting of ice block from the peak is considered as the beginning of the end of the tribe and human life in the region.

In Lepcha society, religion and nature are linked very closely. They worship almost all natural elements of the region. Nature provides everything for the livelihood of the Lepchas and they took sufficient measures in protecting and preserving all the natural elements. L.A. Waddel as early as 1899 narrated Lepchas as the true lovers of the nature. " ..... a true son of the forest and a born naturalist. He knows the habits of every bird and beast and creeping things: and the properties of every plant" (Reprint, 1978: pp. 77, 78).

Time has changed Lepcha dependence on nature. In contemporary period Lepchas are compelled to settle in terrace based cultivation. Nearly 80 per cent Lepchas are directly involved in settled agriculture and only 5 per cent depend on livestock, forestry, fishing and hunting. The degree of direct and close relationship with nature has decreased with the changed living style of Lepchas. The relation has further been deteriorated with religious conversion and consequent cultural transformation. Religious conversion into Buddhism and Christianity has replaced the role of *Bongthing* and *Mun* by the Lama or Church priest who have nothing to do with traditional Lepcha nature culture. The Buddhist Lepchas, by using *Bongthing* and *Mun* along with the Lama, are the retainers of true Lepcha culture. The peculiar blending of Buddhism and traditional Lepcha religion is called *Jyktenmo*. Today the Buddhist Lepchas are more nearer to the nature than the Christian Lepchas. Traditional Lepcha material culture has been faded away by the modern market system. Synthetic and polythin have replaced all traditional bamboo, wood and cane materials of the Lepchas which were more eco-friendly. Lepchas no longer perform the rituals of fishing and hunting: bow and arrow have become useless: *Doo-Kye-Moo-Lee*, the typical Lepcha house of wood, bamboo and cane is found in the museum at Bhopal. The changed food habit not only detached the Lepchas from nature but they forget their days-old scientific knowledge of separating edibles from non-edible roots, fungus etc. and the wisdom of freeing poison from the poisonous roots.

In the present ecological imbalance in the earth when the development thinkers have started talking about 'sustainable growth', the Lepcha concept of nature can be used as a true model for human survival. The story of catching fish as much as required and worshipping almost all elements of nature in different occasions like *Muk-Zik-Ding Rum Faat, Tendong Lho-Rum Faat, Chu-Rum-Faat, Lyaang-Rum-Faat*, etc. are some of the evidences of Lepcha accommodation and coexistence in nature. Lepcha culture is not only a tribal culture but it is Lepcha-nature culture which is eco-friendly. Lepchas were not aware about the present day ecological crisis but by following their nature culture they remained safe and free from the modern hazards. The exogenous factors have affected the ecology of the region and the Lepcha nature culture may be considered as the model of solution. The modern world has many things to learn from the Lepcha treasure of knowledge and their love, respect, worship, association, accommodation and relatedness with nature is most important. Referring to the importance on tribal knowledge Her Excellency, the President of India, Shrimati Pratibha Devi Singh Patil, on the occasion of the national level Tribal Festival 'Prakriti' held at New Delhi on 16th March 2011, has rightly said "'Prakriti', the name of the festival, suggests the intimate relationship between the tribes and the nature. The tribes of India are the custodians of a large volume of our indigenous knowledge and traditional practices, much of it based on a deep understanding of natural products and nature cycles. They are the inheritors of the age-old practice, which constitute the heritage of the country. All efforts should be made to preserve and document this vast knowledge in a proper manner."

## ANNEXURE 7.1

### Lepcha Ethnobotanical Plants

| Botanical Name | Family | Lepcha Name | Parts used | Purpose |
|---|---|---|---|---|
| 1 | 2 | 3 | 4 | 5 |
| *Actinidia callosa* Lindley | Actinidaceae | ***Tuk-syik-rik*** | Fruit | Edible |
| *Actinidia strigosa* Hook. F. & Thomson | Actinidaceae | ***Tuk-syik rik*** | Fruit | Edible |
| *Aesandra butyraceae (*Roxb.) Baeheni | Sapotaceae | ***Yet-paot*** | Fruit | Edible |
| *Apium graveolens* L. | Apiaceae | ***Sung-zaam-be*** | Leaf stalk | Edible |
| *Brassica juncea* L. | Brassicaceae | ***Kundaong-be*** | Leaf | Edible |
| *Castanopsis echinocarpa* Miq. | Fagaceae | ***Sa-rika-syoo-koong*** | Fruit | Edible |
| *Chirita urticifolia* Buch. Ham. Ex. D. Don | Gesneriaceae | ***Yung-shut Koong*** | Leaf | Edible |
| *Diplagium esculentum* (Retz.) Sw. | Athryiaceae | ***Sa-maa-kua-daong tung-kroak*** | Tender shoot tip | Edible |
| *Edgaria darjeelingsis* C.B. Clarke | Cucurbitaceae | ***Sa-mo-be*** | Young shoot | Edible |
| *Elaeocarpus sikkimensis* Masters | Elaeocarpaceae | ***Syaapko-koong*** | Fruit | Edible |
| *Eriobotrya benghalensis* (Roxb.) Hook. F. | Rosaceae | ***Ber-koong*** | Fruit | Edible |
| *Fagopyrum dibotrys* (D. Don) Hara | Polygonaceae | ***Pa-laop-be*** | Leaf and flower | Edible |
| *Fagopyrum esculentum* Moench | Polygonaceae | ***Ka-hro-klyaam*** | Leaf and mature seed | Edible |
| *Ficus hispida* L. | Moraceae | ***Sung-saot-koong*** | Fruit | Edible |
| *Ficus oligocodon* Miq. | Moraceae | ***Ta-shong-Te-Koong*** | Fruit | Edible |
| *Ficus semicordata* Buch. Ham. & J.E. Smith | Moraceae | ***Tung-syi-koong*** | Fruit | Edible |
| *Garcinia stipulata* T. Anderson | Clusiaceae | ***Saa-maa-kaa-daaum-koong*** | Fruit | Edible |
| *Garcinia xanthochymus* Hook. F., | Clusiaceae | ***Yuk-saal-koong*** | Flower & fruit | Edible |
| *Holboellia latifolia* Wallich | Lardizabalaceae | ***Praong-chaa-rik*** | Young shoot & seeds | Edible |
| *Manihot esculentum* Crantz. | Euphorbiaceae | ***Thung-la-boon*** | Tuber | Edible |

| 1 | 2 | 3 | 4 | 5 |
|---|---|---|---|---|
| *Melia dubia* Cav. | Meliaceae | ***Sa-laot-koong*** | Fruit | Edible |
| *Morus laevigaa* Miq. | Moraceae | ***Tsum-tao-koong*** | Fruit | Edible |
| *Nephrolepis cordifolia* (L.) Presl. | Nephrolepidaceae | ***Panianewala*** | Tuber | Edible |
| *Oroxylum indicum* (L.) Kurz | Bignonoaceae | ***Pa-go-rip*** | Flower | Edible |
| *Persia fructifera* Kostermans | Lauraceae | ***Foam-koong*** | Fruit | Edible |
| *Phytolacca acinosa* Roxb. | Phytolaceae | ***Shaot-rip*** | Tender shoot and leaf | Edible |
| *Prunus persica* (L.) Batsch | Rosaceae | ***Tuk-po-koong*** | Fruit | Edible |
| *Schisandra grandiflora* (Wallich) Hook. F. & Thomson | Schisandraceae | ***Tuk-syil-rik*** | Fruit | Edible |
| *Tupistra nutans* Wallich | Liliaceae | ***Perfek*** | Inflorescence | Edible |
| *Vernicia cordata* (Thungerg) Airyshaw | Euphorbiaceae | ***Koox-tyo-koong*** | Fruit | Lighting |
| *Eurya serasifolia* Kobuski | Theaceae | ***Tuk-tsaong-koong / Flaop-tung-chaoong-kung*** | Branches | Rubbed for producing fire |
| *Polygala arillata* Buch. Ham.ex D. Don | Polygalaceae | — | Branches | Rubbed for producing fire |
| *Bidens biternata* our.) Merr. & Sherff. | Asteraceae | ***Kuro-mukh*** | Mature leaves | Tea leaf substitute |
| *Hypericum hookerianum* Wight & Arn. | Hyperiaceae' | ***Danna-am chaew-rip*** | Mature leaves | Tea leaf substitute |
| *Lonicera magnebracteata* Nayar & Giri | Caprifoliaceae | ***Pemu-mukh*** | Mature leaves | Tea leaf substitute |
| *Juglans regia* L. | Juglandaceae | ***Ka-ol-koong*** | Rind of the fruits | Fish poisoning |
| *Milletia extensa* (Benth.) Baker | Fabaceae | ***Bru-koong*** | Bark and young shoot | Fish poisoning |
| *Xeromphis spinosa* (Thunb.) Keay | Rubiaceae | ***Rung-gaong-koong*** | Unripe fruits | Fish poisoning |
| *Calamus inermis* T. Anderson | Arecaceae | ***Ru-broo*** | | Making arrows for hunting |

| 1 | 2 | 3 | 4 | 5 |
|---|---|---|---|---|
| *Cephalostachyum capitatum* Munro | Poaceae | ***Pa-yaang-po*** | Culms | Making arrows for hunting |
| *Cleidon spiciflorum* (Brum. F.) Merr. | Euphorbiaceae | ***Pa-laak-koong-daam-saa*** | Leaves and twigs | Extraction of gum |
| *Ostodes paniculata* Blume | Euphorbiaceae | ***Pa-loak-koong-hlo-saa*** | Fruits | Extraction of gum |
| *Bridelia retusa* (L.) Spreng. | Euphorbiaceae | ***Paizu koong*** | Bark | Making dye |
| *Rheum nobile* Hook. F. & Thom. | Polygonaceae | ***Canshafea*** | Rhizome | Making dye |
| *Rumex nepalensis* Spregngel | Polygonaceae | ***Pallu*** | Rhizome | Making dye |
| *Bauhinia vahlii* (Wight & Arn.) Benth. | Caesalpiniaceae | ***Ka-chuk-mukh*** | Bark | Fibre |
| *Boehmeria macrophylla D. Don* | Urticaceae | ***Paliong-mukh*** | Bark | Fibre |
| *Debregeasia longifolia* (Brum. F.) Wedd | Urticaceae | ***Ongylop*** | Bark | Fibre |
| *Edgeworthiagardneri* (D. Don) Wallich | Thymelaeaceae | ***Oregeli-mukh*** | Bark | Fibre |
| *Kydia calicina* Roxb. | Malvaceae | ***Kududi-koong*** | Bark | Fibre |
| *Laportia terminalis* Wight | Urticaceae | ***Patley-sisnoo*** | Bark | Fibre |
| *Stephania glabra* Roxb. | Menispermaceae | ***Burkil-kunthek-rik*** | Bark | Fibre |
| *Cinnamomum glaucescens* (Nees) Drury. | Lauraceae | ***Saam-dim-koong*** | Bark and wood | Aromatic odour/incense |
| *Juniperus recurva* D. Don. | Cupressaceae | ***Syoi-po-kung*** | Wood | Aromatic odour/incense |
| *Juniperus squamata* D. Don. | Cupressaceae | ***Syoi-po-kung*** | Wood | Aromatic odour/incense |
| *Listea cubeba* (Lour.) Persoon | Lauraceae | ***Taang-hyercher-koong*** | Leaf | Aromatic odour/incense |
| *Micromelum integerrimum* (Colebr.) Roem. | Rutaceae | ***Taam-soong-koong*** | Leaf | Aromatic odour/incense |

| 1 | 2 | 3 | 4 | 5 |
|---|---|---|---|---|
| *Artemisia indica* Willd. | Asteraceae | ***Tuk-ryil-kung*** | Twigs | Treatment |
| *Artemisia indica* Willd. | Asteraceae | ***Tuk-ryil-kung*** | Leaves | Rituals |
| *Calotropis gigantea* (L.) R. Br. | Asclepiadaceae | ***Angot*** | Roots | Treatment |
| *Hedychium coronarium* Koeing. | Zingiberaceae | ***Phachengfea*** | Roots | Religious belief |
| *Leea macrophylla* Roxb. Ex. Ham. | Leeaceae | ***Daam-paal-taom-koong*** | Seeds | Treatment |
| *Mirabilis jalapa* L. | Nyctaginaceae | ***Gulabhar-rip*** | Roots | Religious belief |
| *Persea duthiei* (King ex Hook. F.) | Lauraceae | ***Kaulo-koong*** | Flowering twigs | Treatment |
| *Artemisia nilagirica* C. B. Clarke | Asteraceae | ***Tuk-ril-koong*** | Twigs | Worship |
| *Lycopodium japonicum* Thunb. | Lycopodiaceae | ***Nagbeli*** | Plant | Worship |
| *Thysanolaena maxima* (Roxb.) Kurz. | Poaceae | ***Pusore*** | Leaf (teeth marked) | Worship |
| *Acer laevigatum* Wallich | Aceraceae | ***Tung-nyok*** | Leaves and young shoots | Fodder |
| *Alstonia scholaris* (L.) R. Br. | Apocynaceae | ***Pur-vok-koong*** | Leaves and young shoots | Fodder |
| *Artocarpos lacucha* Buch. Ham. | Moraceae | ***Bodhar-koong*** | Leaves and young shoots | Fodder |
| *Boehmeria scabrella* (Roxb.) Graud. | Urticaceae | ***Paliong-mukh*** | Leaves and young shoots | Fodder |
| *Brassaiopsis mitis* C.B. Clarke | Araliaceae | ***Chuletro*** | Leaves and young shoots | Fodder |
| *Elatostema sessile* J.R. & G. Forst. | Urticaceae | ***Kunchel-bee*** | Leaves and young shoots | Fodder |
| *Exbucklandia populnea* (R. Br. Ex Griffith) R.W. Brown | Hamamelidaceae | ***Pipley-koong*** | Leaves and young shoots | Fodder |
| *Ficus hookeriana* Corner. | Moraceae | ***Kabra-koong*** | Leaves and young shoots | Fodder |
| *Saurauia nepalensis* DC. | Saurauiaceae | ***Gogun-paot*** | Leaves and young shoots | Fodder |

| 1 | 2 | 3 | 4 | 5 |
|---|---|---|---|---|
| *Alnus nepalensis* D.Don | Betulaceae | ***Sungroo-koong*** | Trunk | Furniture and building construction |
| *Calamus acanthospathus* Griffith | Areacaceae | ***Rle*** | Trunk | Furniture and building construction |
| *Castanopsis hystrix* Miq. | Fagaceae | ***Dalney-katus*** | Trunk | Furniture and building construction |
| *Chukrasis villutina* Roem | Meliaceae | ***Chikrasi-koong*** | Trunk | Furniture and building construction |
| *Cinnamomum ciciodaphne* Meissn. | Lauraceae | ***Saam-Derin-koong*** | Trunk | Furniture and building construction |
| *Duabanga grandiflora* (Roxb. ex.DC) Walp. | Sonneratiaceae | ***Dur-koong*** | Trunk | Furniture and building construction |
| *Juglans regia* L. | Juglandaceae | ***Kaol-koong*** | Trunk | Furniture and building construction |
| *Michelia doltsopa* Buch. Ham. ex. DC | Magnoliaceae | ***Ranichap/Swetochap*** | Trunk | Furniture and building construction |
| *Nyssa javanica* (Blume) Wng. | Cornaceae | ***Saam-braong-koong*** | Trunk | Furniture and building construction |
| *Terminalia myriocarpa* Heurek & Muell. - Arg | Combretaceae | | Trunk | Furniture and building construction |

| 1 | 2 | 3 | 4 | 5 |
|---|---|---|---|---|
| *Ampelocissus barbata* (Wallich) Planch | Vitaceae | ***Mei-hroom-rik*** | Whole plant | Juice of the plant used for sores in mouth and tongue of small milk sucking baby |
| *Artimisia indica* Willd. | Astderaceae | ***Tuk-ril-koong*** | Flower, Leaf | Vermifuge tonic, in making asinthe |
| *Bauhinia variegata L.* | Caesalpiniaceae | ***Ka-chuk-koong*** | Bark, Root | Ulcer, bleeding, piles, dysentry |
| *Bischofia javanica* Blume | Bischofiaceae | ***Sa-naong-koong*** | Bark | Diarrhea |
| *Calamus macracenthus* T. Anderson | Arecaceae | ***Re-be-Rip*** | Rhizome and Leaf | Cataract and other eye diseases |
| *Celastrus paniculatus* Willd. | Calastraceae | ***Ruk-lim-koong*** | Seed, Leaf, Fruit | Rheumatism, paralysis, lumbago |
| *Centella asiatica* (L.) Urb. | Apiaceae | ***Mongu-tafa/makch-mukh*** | Whole plant | Urinary disorder |
| *Cinnamomum tamala* (Buch.) Ham. Nees. & Eberm. | Lauraceae | ***Naap-soar-koong*** | Bark leaf | Chronic diarrohoea, gonorrhoea |
| *Costus speciosus* (Koenig) Smith. | Costaceae | ***Hik-bo-rik-loap*** | Rhizome | Scabies, itches, stomach trouble |

| 1 | 2 | 3 | 4 | 5 |
|---|---|---|---|---|
| *Dichroa febrifuga* Lour. | Hydrangeaceae | ***Gye-boo-khaa-noak*** | Fruits | Purgative |
| *Entada pursaetha ssp. sinohimalensis* Grierson & Long | Mimosaceae | ***Ka-look-paot*** | Fruit cotyledon | Skin diseases, mumps |
| *Ficus hirta* Vahl | Moraceae | ***De-chyoo-koong*** | Root | Antidote |
| *Gouania tiliaefolia* Lam | Rhamnaceae | ***Tung-chaong-maon-rik*** | Leaf | Used to make poultice for sores |
| *Holarrhena antidysenterica* Wallich | Apocynaceae | ***Faodjyi-rip*** | Bark, leaf, latex | Acute dysentery |
| *Morus australis* poiret | Moraceae | ***Num-byaong-koong*** | Bark, root, fruit | Purgative, also in hoarse voice, inflammation of the vocal cord. |
| *Mucuna marcrrocarpa* Wallich | Fabaceae | ***Ta-kryup-poat*** | Seed | Vermifuge |
| *Mussaenda frondosa* L. | Rubiaceae | ***Tum-baar-koong*** | Root, leaf, flower | Asthma and cough |
| *Oroxylum indicum* (L.) Kurz | Bignoniaceae | ***Pa-go-kong/rip*** | Papery seed, bark | Pneumonia, chronic sores |
| *Paederiascandens* Merrill | Rubiaceae | ***Tuk-fit-rik*** | Fruit | Toothache and pyorrhea |
| *Prunus cerasoides* D. Don | Rosaceae | ***Kaon-ke-koong*** | Bark | Pounded bark applied for healing fractured bones |
| *Rhododendron arboretum* Smith | Ericaceae | ***Al-etok-koong*** | Petals | Dysentery and diarrohoea |

| 1 | 2 | 3 | 4 | 5 |
|---|---|---|---|---|
| *Rhus chinensis* Mill. | Anacardiaceae | ***Tung-haer-koong*** | Leaf | Chronic rheumatism, syphilis, sciatica |
| *Stephania japonica* (Thunberg) Miers. | Menispermaceae | ***Kuntek-rip*** | Bulbous root | Fever and diarrohoea |
| *Stephania japonica* (Thunberg) Miers. | Menispermaceae | ***Kuntek-rip*** | Young shoot | Urinary diseases and dyspepsia |
| *Viscum album* L. | Loranthaceae | ***Saam-fey-pro*** | Leafy shoot | Fracture and body ache |

## REFERENCES


1. Govt of Sikkim, (2009), "Report on the Status of the Lepchas of Sikkim". unpublished government Document.
2. Hooker, J.D., (1854), *Himalayan Journal. Notes of a Naturalist* Vol.1, Dehradun: Natraj Publishers.
3. Jana, S.K. and A.S. Chauhan, (2000), 'Ethnobotanical studies on Lepchas of Dzongu, North Sikkim, India', *Annals of Forestry*, 8 (1) pp. 131-144.
4. Mainwaring, G.B., (1876), *A Grammar of Rong (Lepcha) Language*, Reprint (1985), Daya Publishing House, New Delhi.
5. Roy, D.C., (2005), *Dynamics of Social Formation among the Lepchas*, Akansha Publishing House, Delhi.
6. Roy, D.C., (2010), *Status of Women among the Lepchas*, Akansha Publishing House, Delhi.
7. Roy, D.C., (2011), *Lepchas: Past and Present*, N.L.Publishers, Siliguri, West Bengal.
8. Stocks,C.De.B., (1925) "Folk-lore And Customs of the Lap-chas of Sikhim". *Journal of the Asiatic Society of Bengal.* New Series, Vol. XXI, No. 4, Reprint (2001) Asian Educational Services, New Delhi.
9. Tamsang, K.P., (1983), *The Unknown And Untold Realities of the Lepchas*, Luen Sun Offset Printing Co. Ltd., Hong Kong, Reprint, 1998, Mani Printing Press. Kalimpong.
10. Tamsang, L.S., (2008), *Lepcha Folk Lore and Folk Sons*, Sahitya Academy, Kolkata.
11. Waddel, L.A., (1899), *Among the Himalayas*, Constable, London, Reprint (1978) Ratna Pustak Bhandar, Kathmandu, Nepal.
12. White, Jr, L., (1973), "The Historical Roots of Our Ecological Crisis", in Tan Barbour (ed). *Western Man and Environmental Crisis*, Addison-Wesley Publishing Co.
13. White, J.C., (1909), *Sikkim and Bhutan; Twenty Years on the North East Frontier-1887–1908*, Reprint (2005), Pilgrim Publishing, Venarasi.

# Indigenous People, Traditional Knowledge in Respect of Ownership Issues in Biodiversity

— Dr. Bindu Vijay, Mr. Vivek Dubey & Mr. Amartya Saha


**ABSTRACT**

*Biodiversity is generally defined as the sum of genetic and phenotypic differences existing in living organisms at the molecular, individual, population, and ecosystem levels. Biodiversity is closely associated with cultural diversity and Traditional Knowledge (TK). Traditional knowledge refers to knowledge, innovations, and practices of indigenous people, and is orally transmitted from generation to generation. Today there is a growing concern for the protection of TK as it is not only important for people who depend on it for food, shelter, clothing, but also for the industries and agriculture. Recent years have seen threat to biological diversity. This extinction is irreversible and given our dependence on food crops, medicines and other biological resources, pose a threat to our own well being. The loss of biodiversity often reduces the productivity of ecosystem thereby shrinking nature's basket of goods and services.*

*Until the 1970s, biodiversity was considered to be part of the "common heritage of humankind". The common heritage principle has also been used in the development of international and national gene banks, which still operate in the spirit of this principle. The Convention on Biological Diversity (CBD) was signed in 1992 and came into force in 1993. The objectives of this convention are the conservation of biological diversity, the sustainable use of components of biological diversity, the fair and equitable sharing of benefits arising out of the use of genetic resources, and appropriate transfer of relevant technology. It is under the Article 8 (j) of CBD that the need to protect TK has gained an international foothold.*

*The last three decades have seen a significant change in the regime governing access to biodiversity. From a common heritage of mankind, biodiversity is evolving into a resource under the sovereignty of nation states and is subject to intellectual property rights (IPRs). This change is not without controversy.*

*The various negotiations at international and national level for the protection of TK and for the conservation of biological resources are now carried out on various issues of implementing the Convention on Biological Diversity (CBD), 1992. India being a party to the Convention is the first to implement it by enacting the Biological Diversity Act, 2002 with a three tire institutional mechanism established thereunder. However, the Act still needs some clarifications on the issues of implementation like benefit sharing. Thus, this paper examines all these issues related to indigenous people and their TK. How their ownership issues are affected by the growing destruction of natural resources and how intellectual property right law can be instrumental to provide protection to them.*

***Keywords:*** *Traditional Knowledge, indigenous people, biodiversity, benefit sharing*

## Introduction

Biodiversity is the abbreviated form of biological diversity. The concept of diversity is important in many areas of biology. The term biodiversity emerged in the 1980s as a result of changing understanding of the role of diversity in natural processes. The term biodiversity comes to us from conservation biology. The word biodiversity is widely used these days, not only by scientific communities but also by general public, environmental groups, policy-makers, industrialist and economists. It is also most debated terminology in national and international politics.

Biodiversity is generally defined as the sum of genetic and phenotypic differences existing in living organisms at the molecular, individual, population, and ecosystem levels. However there exist numerous definitions for this word, of which Jutro (1993) at least identified 14. Two among these are widely used, quoted and officialised since they have been approved by several countries based on worldwide negotiations, agreements and strategies. The first most used definition is included in Article 2 of Convention on Biodiversity (CBD). According to this "Biological diversity" means the variability among living organisms from all sources including inter alia, terrestrial marine and other aquatic ecosystem and the ecological complexes of which they are a part; this includes diversity within species, between species and of ecosystem.

The second most used definition of biodiversity is sponsored by Global biological diversity strategy (WRI, IUCN and UNEP, 1992) which says that "the totality of genes, species and ecosystem in a region".

## BIODIVERSITY AND TRADITIONAL KNOWLEDGE

This rich resource is the gift of nature and is important for all life form including human beings, and for the functioning of ecosystem. Biodiversity is closely associated with cultural diversity and traditional knowledge (TK). Traditional knowledge is now widely recognized as having played and still playing crucial roles in economic social and cultural life and development not only in traditional societies but also in modern societies, because it concerns all aspects of life (food, health, housing, communications, etc.) and the environment ( relations between biodiversity and ecological factors, identification criteria of biodiversity elements etc.). The local/indigenous peoples have been custodians of diversity so far. Traditional knowledge refers to knowledge, innovations, and practices of indigenous people, and is orally transmitted from generation to generation. Today there is a growing concern for the protection of TK as it is not only important for people who depend on it for food, shelter, clothing, but also for the industries and agriculture. Recent years have seen threat to biological diversity. This extinction is irreversible and given our dependence on food crops, medicines and other biological resources, pose a threat to our own well being. The loss of biodiversity often reduces the productivity of ecosystem thereby shrinking nature's basket of goods and services and this loss has direct effect/ threat on traditional knowledge. Biodiversity generates economic value in different ways. It primarily benefits the local communities living in close proximity to biological systems such as forests farmlands, coastal habitats, etc. However urban population, global economy all is benefited by the rich biological diversity. New technology especially the modern biotechnology is making it possible to transfer genes across species and kingdoms. This is revolutionalizing agriculture and opening up new opportunities in pharmacetucal industry. In fact-biodiversity is one important reason for the impressive growth for pharmaceutical chemical and agro-industry in this century. All these are making biodiversity a valuable asset of the present century, leading to issues of biopiracy. One of the classical case of biopiracy is that of "Madagascar periwinkle". Western companies developed powerful medicines from African natural resources, the rosy periwinkle (*Catharanthus roseus*, belonging to family Apocyanaceae) from Madagascar, indicated for leukemia. Benefits from the commercial use of this plant have largely been enjoyed by companies and research institutes that developed marketable products and obtained patent. But neither the local first informants nor the country of origin received a share of these benefits.

## Value of Traditional Knowledge

Traditional knowledge makes valuable contribution to the two main aspects of sustainable development, environment and fulfillment of human needs. Traditional knowledge has contributed to the general knowledge on sound environmental principle and management, such as in forest conservation, soil conservation, agricultural practices, crop improvement etc. the contributions of traditional knowledge to human development, especially in food productions and health care are widely recognized. Even today majority of the world population depend on traditional knowledge and practices for food and medicines. For much kind of diseases, like jaundice, many people still prefer going to traditional healer.

## Treats to Traditional Knowledge

TK is facing a lot of threat. A significant part of land, forest habitat of local people and indigenous people and local communities in many countries is being affected by a combination of deforestation, logging, construction and dam project, mining and urban development etc. Traditional knowledge in agriculture has also been affected in many countries by the conversion from biodiversity based farming system to monocultures promoted through green revolutions. In some countries rural to urban migration is also taking place. This transfer of especially young people, results in the erosion of traditional knowledge. Modern technology is also one important reason for dwindling of the traditional knowledge. In the absence of technology, especially in villages people use to gather around and transmit the inherited knowledge, but these days the oral transfer of traditional knowledge has come to stand still.

## CBD CONVENTION AND SHARING OF RESOURCES

Today genetic resources are no longer the common heritage of human kind and they cannot be treated as freely accessible commodities. Prior to the commencement of the Convention on Biological Diversity (CBD) in 1992, access to genetic resources and associated traditional knowledge was free for all mankind. Genetic resources and knowledge were often taken from communities and countries by organisations, food, pharmaceautical, perfume and other industries and individuals who monopolised the benefits. The Convention on Biological Diversity (CBD) is one of the most important treaties in the history of humanity as it deals with the infinitely complex but fragile diversity of life on earth.

The Convention on Biological Diversity (CBD) was signed in 1992 and came into force in 1993. The objectives of this convention are the conservation of biological diversity, the sustainable use of components of biological diversity, the fair and equitable sharing of benefits arising out of the use of genetic resources, and appropriate transfer of relevant technology. It is under the Article 8(j) of CBD that the need to protect TK has gained an international foothold. It is widely accepted that the sustainability of the global ecosystem in general, and of agricultural in particular, is dependent on the preservation, enhancement, and exploitation of biological diversity.

Indigenous peoples, local communities and smallholder peasant farmers, through traditional knowledge, innovations, and practices, have developed and nurtured plant species for agriculture and medicine over millennia, contributing to both biological and cultural diversity. Traditional knowledge is constantly evolving to support lives and livelihoods. It supports food security and food sovereignty for peoples and communities across the world and it is the very foundation of our food supply. For the indigenous and traditional peoples nature is not a commodity to be bought and sold, patented or preserved apart from society, precisely because nature is what defines humanity. The earth is their (our) mother and cannot be compromised, sold or monopolised. Thus there is an inextricable link between nature, society and culture.

Biodiversity and traditional knowledge are threatened as a result of privatisation and monopoly rights that corporations want to impose. Traditional knowledge often cannot constitute the intellectual property of an individual, as it is generally inherited and so is related to lineage. Thus it is rather the property of one or more communities. Intellectual property rights ( IPR) are private rights. As an incentive for innovation, they grant their holder the ability to exclude others from certain activities, such as using a product or process, for a defined period of time. The control afforded by IP protection thus enables the right holders to limit who can use the resource, and so claim the benefits of commercialisation with little competition. India is one of the richest countries in terms of biodiversity and the associated traditional knowledge. However, the Indian experience in this regard is not promising. India enacted the Biological Diversity Act in 2002, mainly to regulate access to biodiversity and facilitate benefit-sharing. Benefits of biodiversity among its stakeholders are minimal. Closely related to the CBD's provisions on access and benefit sharing are those regarding the preservation of and respect for the knowledge, innovation and practices of indigenous and local communities. This "traditional knowledge" has often been conserved by indigenous and local communities through informal, collective processes extending across generations.

## Exploration of Traditional Knowledge of Kani Tribe

The widely publicized case of the 'Jeevani drug' (from plant *Trichopus zeylanicus travancoricus*) based on the traditional knowledge of the Kani tribe in Kerala is hailed as the first ever example of benefit-sharing with an indigenous community. 'Jeevani' is a herbal medicine developed by the scientists of the Tropical Botanic Garden and Research Institute (TBGRI) as a restorative, immuno-enhancing, anti-stress and anti-fatigue agent based on the knowledge of the Kani tribe. Jeevani acts on the human system in the following ways:

- Activates the body's natural defenses
- Activates delayed type hypersensitivity reactions and antibody synthesis
- Increases the number of polymorphonuclear granulongtes
- Activates the cellular immune system
- Exhibits hepato-protective and cholorectic activities
- Jeevani has adaptogenic properties as evidenced by anti-peptic ulcer and anti-fatigue effects.

Though Kani case is considered to be a success story of benefit sharing case, it is also hailed as failed concept of benefit-sharing. The reason being, there are those members of the Kani tribe who benefited directly from the collaboration as well as those who may not have benefited so far, but are likely to do so in the future. Finally the miracle plant Arogya pacha is endemic to many parts of Western Ghat. If benefit-sharing is done, then it should have reached every member of the community who has nurtured the plant.

# IMPLEMENTATION OF CBD IN INDIA

## Nodal Implementing Agency in India

The Union Ministry of Environment and Forests (MoEF) is the nodal agency for implementing the CBD. In fact, it serves as the nodal agency in the country for the United Nations Environment Programme (UNEP), including biodiversity-related Global Conventions like the CBD and Ramsar Convention and for the follow-up of the United Nations Conference on Environment and Development (UNCED). The Ministry is also entrusted with the issues relating to multilateral bodies such as the Commission on Sustainable Development (CSD) and the Global Environment Facility (GEF).

## National Reports

India has been regularly submitting its reports to the CBD Secretariat on the progress of implementation of the decisions taken by successive COP meetings. The first national report focused on Article 6, the general measures for conservation and sustainable use that urged the Contracting Parties to develop national strategies, plans or programme for the conservation and sustainable use of biological diversity and also integrate the conservation and sustainable use into relevant sectoral and cross-sectoral plans, programme and policies. A comprehensive third National Report was submitted in November 2005 (prior to the COP8 Meeting in Curitiba, Brazil) while the fourth report is to be submitted by 30 March 2009 before the COP9 meeting.

## AN OVERVIEW OF THE STATUS AND TRENDS OF CONSERVING BIOLOGICAL DIVERSITY IN INDIA

India is one of the 17 mega biodiversity countries. With only 2.4% of the land area, India already accounts for 7-8% of the recorded species of the world. India is equally rich in traditional and indigenous knowledge.

## Strategies

India's strategies for conservation and sustainable utilization of biodiversity in the past have comprised of providing special status and protection to biodiversity rich areas by declaring them as National Parks, Wildlife Sanctuaries, Biosphere Reserves, Ecologically Fragile and Sensitive Areas. Efforts have been made towards off-loading the pressure reserve forests through alternative measures of meeting the fuelwood and fodder needs such as afforestation of degraded forest areas and wastelands. National facilities for *ex situ* conservation, like botanical gardens and gene banks, have also been developed and upgraded to provide backup to *in situ* conservation.

Special efforts are now being devoted to conservation of endangered, endemic, and economically important plants and animals. Efforts have also been initiated towards documentation of microbial diversity by strengthening the institutional capabilities and setting up of well-equipped repositories for this purpose.

## Survey and Documentation

Systematic surveys of flora and fauna of the country covering all the ecosystems began with the establishment of the Botanical Survey of India

(BSI) in 1890 and the Zoological Survey (ZSI) of India in 1916. Nearly 70 per cent of the country's land area has been surveyed and over 45,000 species of plants and micro-organisms and about 89,000 species of animals have been described till date. It has been estimated that an additional 400,000 species may still be awaiting documentation (NR3).

## Capacity Building

An All-India Coordinated Project for Capacity Building in Taxonomy, launched in 1999 and now operating in 82 units, provides for establishment of Centres for Research in identifying priority gap areas (e.g., virus, bacteria, micro Lepidoptera, etc.) in the field of taxonomy, education, and training and also strengthening the BSI and ZSI for their coordinating and monitoring roles. The project has set up specialized groups drawn from universities, botanical and zoological surveys of India to take up taxonomic work in gap areas including animal viruses, bacteria and archaea, algae, fungi, lichens, bryophytes, pteridophytes, gymnosperms, palms, grasses, bamboos, orchids, helminthes and nematodes, micro-lepidoptera, and mollusca.

## In Situ Conservation

India's strategy for conservation of biological diversity of different habitats, ecosystems, and biomes is based primarily on protecting biodiversity-rich areas and designating them as National Parks, Wildlife Sanctuaries, Biosphere Reserves, and Ecologically Fragile and Sensitive areas. The National Forest Policy, 1981, lays down that one-third of the geographical area of the country should be under forest/tree cover. The 10th Five-Year Plan mandate is to increase the forest and tree cover in the country to 33 per cent of the geographical area by 2012 as against the present area of 23 per cent. Approximately 4.6 per cent area of the total geographical area is already under extensive *in situ* conservation of habitats and ecosystems.

There are 92 national parks and 500 wildlife sanctuaries in the country covering an area of 15.67 million hectares. This development process is being continued for an additional 278 national parks and sanctuaries in 26 states including the northeastern states. Provisions for declaring important biodiversity areas, as 'Biodiversity Heritage Sites' have been made through the recently enacted Biological Diversity Act, 2002. New legal categories of protected areas have been proposed, namely 'Conservation Reserves' and 'Community Reserves' with a view to include some adjacent habitats and corridors with the designated Protected Areas.

Biosphere reserves and internationally recognized areas of terrestrial and coastal ecosystems have been given special attention by launching schemes to facilitate conservation of representative landscapes and their immense biological diversity and cultural heritage. Fourteen biosphere reserves have been designated so far in the country, out of which four biosphere reserves namely Sunderbans, Gulf of Mannar, Nilgiri, and Nanda Devi have been included in the World Network of Biosphere Reserves. Efforts are on for getting the remaining biosphere reserves also included in the global network.

Establishment of important areas with respect to agricultural biodiversity has been undertaken such as the Citrus Gene Sanctuary in Meghalaya and 14 more such sites are under study. A conservation centre exclusively devoted to agriculturally important micro-organisms is being developed. Important crop diversity areas, that are traditionally rich in gene pools of cultivated plants and their wild relatives, are being considered for recognition as national heritage sites.

## Forests

Extensive programme for afforestation of degraded forest land, waste lands, etc. are in progress for increase of forest and tree cover from the present level of 23 per cent of the country's land area to 33 per cent in 2012. These programmes include integrated forest protection schemes, National Afforestation and Eco-development Board, Joint Forest Management, etc. wherein use of ecofriendly bioinoculants inclusive of mycorrhizal technologies, is being practiced in the country.

On account of the richness and uniqueness of biodiversity elements and wide ranging indigenous knowledge systems on use of bioresources coupled with increasing scale of degradation of bioresources, at least two mountain areas (the Himalaya and Western Ghats) in the country have emerged as global conservation priorities. In response to this recognition, the government of India, under its Protected Area (PA) programme, has made significant contribution. As such, the coverage under designated PAs is approximately 9.6 per cent of geographical area in the Himalayas and 10.1 per cent in the Western Ghats. This is higher than the national average (4.7%) and corresponds well with the acceptable global realistic target of 10 per cent coverage under PAs. An international cooperative programme supported by GEF is operative on Belowground Biodiversity which is coordinated by the Jawaharlal Nehru University, New Delhi.

## Coastal Areas

The Coastal Regulation Zone includes coastal stretches of seas, bays, estuaries, cricks, rivers, and back waters which are influenced by tidal action (on the landward side), upto 500 m from the high tide line including the inter-tidal zone. Restrictions have been imposed on the setting up and expansion of industries and operations or process, etc. in the coastal regulation zone via a government notification. A national and 13 state level coastal zone management authorities have been constituted and Coastal zone management plans have been prepared demarcating ecologically sensitive areas. Integrated coastal zone management plans have also been prepared for Andaman and Nicobar and Lakshadeep Islands through scientific institutions. Microbial consortia are also used for revegetation of degraded sites.

India is home to some of the best mangroves in the world. The mangrove conservation programme was launched in 1987 and so far 35 mangrove areas have been identified for intensive conservation and management. New and additional mangrove conservation areas are being identified continuously in consultation with state governments. The National Committee on Mangroves and Coral Reefs has recommended intensive conservation and management of corals in four areas, namely, Andaman and Nicobar Islands, Lakshadweep Island, Gulf of Kachh, and Gulf of Mannar. This will also help in conserving their microbial symbionts gene pools.

## Rivers and Wetlands

The National River Conservation Directorate of the MoEF is engaged in implementing the river action plan under the National River Conservation Plan (NRCP). At present, it covers a total of 31 rivers in the country spread over 18 states. Under the National Lake Conservation Plan (NLCP), a programme for conservation and management of lakes and other similar water bodies, 28 lakes have been taken up so far. National Wetland Conservation Programme (NWCP) has been initiated for 66 wetlands across 21 states.

## Policy Support

Targets for conservation of different ecosystems have been defined in various ways directly or indirectly in relevant national plans, programme, and strategies, some of which are listed below:

- National Environment Policy, 2006

- National Policy and Macro-level Action Strategy on Biodiversity, 1999
- National Biodiversity Strategy and Action Plan (NBSAP) (under finalization)
- National Forest Policy amended in 1988
- National Conservation Strategy and Policy Statement for Environment and Sustainable Development
- National Agricultural Policy
- National Land Use Policy
- National Fisheries Policy
- National Wildlife Action Plan
- Environmental Action Plan
- National Forestry Action Programme
- National Seeds Policy
- National Biotechnology Development Strategy (under finalization)
- 10th Five Year Plan
- National Programme on Cattle and Buffalo Breeding (NPCBB)
- Conservation Programme for Livestock Breeds

Technical Report of the UNDP-funded National Biodiversity Strategy and Action Plan Project on various components of biodiversity has been prepared, based on a wide participation of stakeholders, and its inputs are being used in developing the National Biodiversity Action Plan. In addition to these planned programmes, participatory processes are being developed with local communities for the ecosystem conservation and management. Rural communities in India have ancient traditions of conservation of natural ecosystems and species and many of these practices still survive with outstanding success. This includes sacred groves (sites) providing protection to patches of forests (sacred groves), water bodies (sacred ponds, lakes, etc.) and entire landscapes for cultural and religious practices. Several diverse areas are also under community protection, commonly referred to as the community conserved areas.

Article 37 of the Biodiversity Act, 2002, indicates that areas of biodiversity importance would be notified as biodiversity heritage sites. Ecologically sensitive zones have been identified under the Environment (Protection) Act, 1986, to impose restriction on the industries, operations, processes, and other developmental activities in the region that have detrimental effect on the environment, to provide for restoration of denuded areas, management of catchment areas, watershed management, etc., for a planned development. India Eco-development Project, a World Bank assisted project has been undertaken to improve the capacity of protected area management to conserve biodiversity and obtain active involvement of the local people. Forest Conservation Act (1980) provides regulations prohibiting diversion of forest areas for other uses.

## Promoting Conservation of Species Diversity

Species-oriented special programme, such as Project Tiger and Project Elephant were launched in 1973 and 1992 respectively. Their effectiveness is being monitored and reviewed regularly. The Botanical Survey of India has come out with the following publications on threatened plant species:

1. *Red Data Book of Indian Plants,* Vol. I (1987), Vol. II (1988), Vol. III (1989)
2. *Conservation Status of Endemic Plants in Peninsular India - An Evaluation*
3. *Threatened and Endemic Orchids of Sikkim and North-Eastern India* (1984)

The Zoological Survey of India has also come out with publications on threatened animal species including the *Red Data Book on Indian Animals* (Part-I) and *Status Survey of Endangered Species*.

A planned breeding programme has been initiated for the Red Panda at the Padmaja Naidu Himalaya Geological Park, Darjeeling. The Centre for Cellular and Molecular Biology (CCMB), Department of Biotechnology, Government of India, Council for Scientific and Industrial Research, and the State Government of Andhra Pradesh are establishing a facility called Laboratory for Conservation of Endangered Species. Efforts to identify suitable alternative homes for single isolated populations of species such as Jerdon's Courser, Asiatic Lion, Manipur Deer, Wroughton's Free Tailed Bat and the like, and manage the same as Protected Areas effectively have been in progress since 2002. A large number of zoological parks, botanical gardens, and captive breeding programme supplement the on-going conservation activities.

## Promoting Conservation of Genetic Diversity

In the context of domesticated biodiversity for important animal breeds, conservation programme have been undertaken such as on the Spiti horse, Nilli-Ravi buffaloes, Pandharpuri buffaloes, Bhadawari and Toda buffaloes, Krishna Valley cattle, Sahiwal cattle, Tharparkar cattle, Kodi adu goats, Jamnapuri goats, Beetle goats, Barbari goat and Double-humped camels.

National Bureau of Plant Genetic Resources (NBPGR) has been continuously engaged since 1976 in documenting the large number of varieties grown traditionally by farmers under diverse agricultural systems in addition to about 2,300 varieties developed by breeders and released at the central and state levels for general cultivation.

The National Gene Bank, developed by the NBPGR at New Delhi with more than 40 Active Germplasm Sites located in different agro-ecosystem conditions across the country, currently holds over 300,000 seed samples and propagules under the long-term conservation strategy. Another gene bank, established at the National Bureau of Animal Genetic Resources, Karnal, promotes *ex situ* conservation of livestock germplasm in the form of semen, embryo, somatic cells, and DNA. Livestock farms are also being developed for various native breeds of cattle, buffalo, sheep, goats, poultry, camel, horses, yak, mithun, and pig. A comprehensive National Livestock Database is also underway. The National Bureau of Fish Genetic Resources is engaged in documentation, characterization, and conservation of fish genetic diversity. The National Bureau of Agriculturally Important Micro-organisms has been established at Mau to conserve the microbial gene pool relevant to dairying and agriculture.

## Facing Threats from Invasive Alien Species

At the central level, there are two relevant departments in the Ministry of Agriculture—the Department of Agriculture and Cooperation (DAC) and Department of Agricultural Research and Education (DARE)—which are concerned with plant protection outreach and research, respectively. Through Indian Council for Agricultural Research, nearly 90 Institutes and more than 100 universities in the country have programme on various invasive alien species. Guidelines on Quarantine and Strategic Plan for exotic introduction has been published. In addition, the threat of invasive pest species gaining entry into India through imported plant/planting material is taken care of under the Plant Quarantine (Regulation of Import into India) Order, 2003. In addition, CITES regulations are implemented and IMO guidelines for Ballast Water introduction are in place.

The taxa causing the most damage in India include insects, mites, molluscs, weeds, and pathogens. Union Ministry of Agriculture organizes discussions with all concerned departments at regular intervals to advance strategies and programmes to address serious pest problems, including invasive alien species. Priorities for management of pest species are decided on the basis of criteria including the crop, pest species, areas affected, economic importance, available technology, and feasibility of management approaches. A national committee has also been set up to take decisions on introduction of exotic fish species where desirable. This is to safeguard against illegal introduction of banned exotic fish species from neighbour countries.

## Reducing Pollution and its Impacts on Biodiversity

A National River Conservation Directorate has been set up to reduce pollution in rivers under the National River Conservation Plan. The Ganga Action Plan and Yamuna Action Plan are being implemented. Several other rivers are under active consideration of the NRCP for this purpose. National Lake Conservation Programme has also taken up lakes such as Powai, Ooty, and Kodaikanal for conservation. Six ecologically sensitive areas (ESAs) have been established in the country for not allowing any pollution from industrial sources and also for conserving the biological diversity in these areas from the sustainability point of view.

## Livelihoods, Local Food Security and Health Care

Local level governance has been strengthened through the 'Panchayat' (village council) system and building supportive bodies such as Biodiversity Management Committees and Watershed Committees duly supported through national and state level legislations. Special attention has been paid to tribal areas by declaring Scheduled Areas by providing special facilities for livelihoods, local food security, and health care. Joint Forest Management Committees have created opportunities for sustainable livelihoods based on natural resources. This initiative has been a successful approach and it has been incorporated in the programme of the State Forest Departments. Network of Medicinal Plant Conservation Areas (MPCAs) has been established in various parts of the country for *in situ* as well as *ex situ* conservation of medicinal plants.

## Protecting Traditional Knowledge, Innovations, and Practices

An institutional mechanism has been created by establishing the National Biodiversity Authority (NBA) to build a national database, create an information and documentation system for biological resources and associated traditional knowledge, and regulate access to genetic resources with a view to implement the three objectives of CBD. Through the Biological Diversity Act, 2002, a provision of preparing People's Biodiversity Register at the village/ panchayat level has been made. This document will contain information on local species diversity and also the associated traditional knowledge along with details of holders of traditional knowledge like *vaids* (local healers). A Traditional Knowledge Digital Library (TKDL) is being prepared for the protection of traditional knowledge of medicine in India such as Ayurveda, etc. TKDL will help by controlling the misappropriation of traditional knowledge of medicine from patenting. National Innovation Foundation has also been established to record the traditional knowledge, innovations, and practices at the grassroot level for the purpose of product development and appropriation.

Section 41 of the Biological Diversity Act, 2002, makes the provision of Biodiversity Management Committees (BMCs) at the panchayat level in the country. The main function of these BMCs is to document People's Biodiversity Register (PBR), a document of local species diversity and the associated traditional knowledge along with the details of holders of traditional knowledge like *vaids*. This will be used to create a Biodiversity Information System and thus recognizing the ownership and rights over traditional knowledge, innovations, and practices. This effort will be overviewed by the NBA and the State Biodiversity Boards linked to NBA. NBA will be responsible for protecting the rights and ownership of not only the local people but all citizens of the country over traditional knowledge, innovations, and practices. It is also responsible for developing a benefit-sharing mechanism if the traditional knowledge is utilized for developing commercial products.

Programme for the sustainable utilization of biological diversity by involving local communities across India have been undertaken under the National Afforestation and Eco-development Board. Joint Forest Management has spread all over India covering more than 17 million hectares of forests in which local communities are engaged in sustainable utilization of biological diversity for meeting daily needs. Local norms of starting dates for the harvesting of non-timber forest produce have been formulated keeping in view the sustainability of prioritized tree species.

Through community initiatives, Kitchen Herbal Gardens have been established in several states in India. A mission-mode project on Household Food and Nutritional Security was initiated in 2000, and completed in 2005. The project focused on tribal areas and local communities in 10 states of India. All-India Coordinated Research Project on Under-Utilized and Under-Exploited Plants of Local Importance was initiated in 1982, with the primary objective of generating improved technology and developing high yielding varieties in selected crops of local importance.

## Ensuring Fair and Equitable Sharing of Benefits

Biological Diversity Act, 2002, has provided various checks and balances while considering access to genetic resources. Through this Act, National Biodiversity Authority (NBA) at the national level, State Biodiversity Boards at the state level and Community Biodiversity Committees at the grassroot level have been set up.

NBA will decide upon requests for access to genetic resources based on material transfer agreement subject to prior informed consent and mutually agreed terms. The NBA is also empowered to impose conditions for sharing of benefits while granting access to genetic resources. Prior approval of NBA will also be essential before seeking any form of IRRs for any product developed from biological resources obtained from India. Protection of Plant Varieties and Farmers' Rights Act, 2000, is also fully supportive of this objective..

### Enhancing Financial Capacity to Implement the Convention

MoEF is the operational nodal point for GEF in India. Sixteen projects are under implementation, out of which three have been completed. Eleven projects have been improved in principle under GEF and are in the preparatory phase. UNDP/GEF small grant programme has supported 90 projects in India since 1992 to support activities that demonstrate community based approaches. Additional financial resources have been accessed from India Canada Environment Facility (ICEF) through the Institutional Strengthening Project.

## INDIAN INITIATIVE FOR PROTECTION OF OWNERSHIP ISSUES IN RESPECT OF INDIGENOUS PEOPLE

To conserve the biodiversity and counter the problem of bio piracy and to protect the ownership issue of indigenous people, India made a maiden effort in the world by enacting the magnificent three legislation in the parliament:

1. Protection of Plant Varieties and Farmers' Rights Act, 2001
2. Biological Diversity Act, 2002
3. Patents Amendment Act, 2005

### Protection of Plant Varieties and Farmers' Rights Act, 2001

India is the original home for many crops like rice, little and kodo millets, moth bean, jutes, pepper etc. These plants were identified form the wild, selected and cultivated by Indian farmers over hundreds of years. The present wealth of varieties in India includes both crops that have originated in the country and those introduced from other countries in the past. The foreign crops include sorghum, pearl, millet, ragi, groundnut, tea, rubber etc. Recently, few crops like sunflower, oilpalm and kiwi fruit were also introduced here. Indian farmers have evolved a rich diversity out of these introduced crops. In the long process of selection, conservation and cultivation, farmers have gained extensive knowledge of these diversity.

This traditional knowledge (TK) includes suitability of variety for specific growing seasons, resistance to different diseases, pests and other natural vagaries, suitability to different soils and quality of the produce. Its availability with farmers is as highly valuable to modern scientific improvement as the genetic diversity of crop plants. This makes the contribution of farmers to plant genetic diversity as important as the contribution scientists make in developing modern plant varieties. Therefore, when scientists are given the right to own new varieties created by them, this right concurrently recognizes the right of the farmers on their varieties. The Protection of Plant Varieties and Farmers' Rights Act, 2001 (PPVFR Act) therefore, seeks to protect the rights of farmers and breeders on plant varieties. The Act recognizes the individual and community roles played by farmers in the improvement and conservation of varieties. Under this Act, Plant Breeders Right (PBR) on a plant variety is established by registration of the society. By registering a plant variety, the person becomes PBR holder. The PBR holder can be one person, a group or community or an institution. The PBR holder alone has the exclusive right to sell, market, produce or distribute the seeds or planting material of that variety. Other important features of the PPVFR Act are provisions with regard to researcher's rights, benefit-sharing between breeders and farming or tribal communities who have contributed to genetic diversity used by the breeder and establishment of a national gene fund to promote conservation.

## Biological Diversity Act, 2002

The CBD states that a member country should facilitate access to its genetic resources by other parties on mutually agreed terms, but that access requires a PIC of the country providing the resources. It also provides for an equitable sharing of any benefits arising from the commercial use of these resources, or any TK associated with the biological resources subject to domestic legislations. In response to its obligation under the CBD, after 10 years of negotiations and discussions with all the stakeholders, India has enacted the Biological Diversity Act in 2002. The Act mainly deals with access to genetic resources by foreign companies, individuals or organization. The National Biodiversity Authority (NBA) was set up under Section 8 of the Act to deal with requests for access to genetic resources by foreigners and to manage requests to transfer the results of any related research out of India and to determine benefit-sharing arising from the commercialization. The salient features of the Act are to:

- regulate access to biological resources of the country with the purpose of securing equitable share in benefits arising out of the use of biological resources; and knowledge relating to biological resources.

- conserve and sustainable use of the biological diversity
- respect and protect knowledge of local communities related to biodiversity
- secure sharing of benefits with local people as conservers of biological resources and holders of knowledge and information relating to the use of biological resources
- conserve and develop areas of importance from the standpoint of biological diversity by declaring them as biological diversity heritage sites.
- protect and rehabile threatened species
- involve institutions of State Governments in the broad scheme of the implementation of the Act through constitution of committees.

The Act prescribes some special provisions for the protection of TK. Among them Chapter II of the Act regulates access to biological diversity. The Act prohibits 'certain persons' from obtaining any biological resources occurring in India or knowledge associated there to for research or for commercial utilization or for monetary consideration or otherwise to such certain persons without previous approval of the NBA (Article 3, 4). Section 6 of the Act, is the key provision dealing with IPRs on biological resources and associated knowledge.

According to this provision, no person shall apply for any IPR, by whatever name called, in or outside India for any invention based on any research or information on a biological resource obtained from India without obtaining the previous approval of the NBA.

The procedures for the access and other purposes mentioned in the Act are provided to ensure effective, efficient and transparent access procedures through written agreements and applications in prescribed formats. The NBA, through appropriate consultation mechanisms shall dispose of the application and communicate its direction to grant access or otherwise to the applicant within a period of 6 months from the date of receipt of the application. The authority is required to communicate the grant of access to the applicant in the form of a written agreement duly signed by an authorized official. The Rule 14 of the Biodiversity Rules, 2004 also prescribes the Authority to provide reasons in writing in case of rejection of an application and give reasonable opportunity to the applicant for appeal. The Authority shall publicize the approval granted through print or electronic media and also shall monitor the compliance of the conditions agreed by the party and the applicant when approval for grant for access was accorded. The access procedures are only regulatory in nature, but are not prohibitive in any manner to any applicant irrespective of their nationalities, affiliations, origin, etc.

The Act also provides for revocation of the approvals granted to an applicant only on the basis of any complaint or *suo moto* under the following conditions:

1. Violation of the provisions of the Act or conditions on which the approval was granted, or
2. Non-compliance of the terms of the agreement, or
3. Failure to comply with any of the condition of access granted, or
4. On account of overriding public interest or for protection of environment and conservation of biodiversity (Rule 15(1))

After having withdrawn the access permit, the Authority is required to send an order of revocation to the concerned Biodiversity Management Committee and the State Biodiversity Board to prohibit the access and the access the damage, if any, caused, and steps to recover the damages (Rule 15(2)).

## Criteria for Benefit Sharing

While the NBA gives Indian nationals/researchers permission to access biological resources, simultaneously it would also lay down some conditions as to how many benefits that arise should be shared with local communities. The Act provides benefit-sharing may include monetary payment, technology transfer or joint ownership of Intellectual Property Rights, but this is not an exhaustive list. The Act, subject to Section 21 and Rule 20 of the Biodiversity Rules, insists upon including appropriate benefit-sharing provisions in the access agreement on mutually agreed terms related to access and transfer of biological resources or knowledge occurring in or obtained from India for commercial use, bio-survey, bio-utilization or any other develop guidelines and shall notify the specific details of benefit-sharing formula in an official gazette on a case-to-case basis. The suggested benefit- sharing measures may include 'monetary benefits', such as royalty, joint ventures, technology transfer, product development, and 'non-monetary benefits' such as education and awareness raising activites, institutional capacity building, venture capital fund etc. The time frame and quantum of benefits to be shared shall be decided on concerned case applicant, authority, local bodies, and other relevant stakeholders, including local and indigenous communities. One of the suggested mechanisms for benefits sharing includes direct payment to persons or group of individuals through district administration, if the biological material or knowledge was accessed from specific individuals or organization could not be identified, the monetary benefits may be paid to the National Biodiversity Fund. Five per cent of the benefits may be earmarked for the authority or State Biodiversity Board towards administrative service charges.

With the assistance of NBA, 18 State Biodiversity Boards (SBBs) have been formed by their respective state governments. Several biodiversity management committees have also been constituted by SBBs. The main function of the Biodiversity Management Committee (BMC) constituted under Rule 22(1-11) of Biodiversity Rules, 2004, is to prepare People's Biodiversity Registers, which shall contain comprehensive information on the availability and knowledge of local biological resources and medicinal or any other TK associated with them. Other important functions of the BMC are to advise the SBB and the NBA on matters for granting approval, maintain data about the local *vaids* and practitioners using the biological resources, besides maintaining a register containing information on access to biological resources and knowledge granted, details of collection fee received and details of benefit-sharing deprived along with the mode of sharing. NBA has set up eight expert committees to prepare guidelines on different issues. The guidelines for the collaborative research projects have been approved and published in the government's official gazette, however, guidelines on issues like normally traded commodities, intellectual property rights, traditional and tribal knowledge, microbial diversity, etc. are in the line for approval.

## Conclusion

The last three decades have seen a significant change in the regime governing access to biodiversity. From a common heritage of mankind, biodiversity is evolving into a resource under the sovereignty of nation states and is subject to intellectual property rights (IPRs). This change is not without controversy. Will the current IPR-driven regime for biodiversity primarily benefit the most powerful actors in the debate, i.e. transnational pharmaceutical and biotechnology companies and their respective governments, or will both sides benefit? If the former is true, what can be done do develop a more even playing field that will take into account not only biodiversity and the TK associated with it, but also the rights of indigenous and local people and their efforts to conserve them? Traditional knowledge generally does not fit the requirements for a patent application, which requires novelty, an inventive step and the capacity for industrial application, because it is the knowledge generally inherited and so is related to lineage. We require a system which can protect the rights of indigenous people who are custodians of the traditional knowledge.

## REFERENCES


1. Stewart Lockie, David Carpenter, 2010, *Agriculture, biodiversity and markets: livelihoods and agroecology in comparative perspective.*
2. Biological Diversity Act, 2002. No. 18 of the Gazette of India Extraordinary, 5 February 2003; Ministry of Law and Justice (Legislative Department), Government of India.
3. Martin Khor. Intellectual property, biodiversity, and sustainable development: Resolving the difficult issues. Zed Books and Third World Network.
4. Paul Gepts. Who Owns Biodiversity, and How Should the Owners Be Compensated? *Plant Physiol,* 2004 April; 134(4): 1295-1307.
5. What is biodiversity? By James Maclaurin, Kim Sterelny. 2008. The University of Chicago Press.
6. Biodiversity and Intellectual Property Rights: Reviewing Intellectual Property Rights in Light of the Objectives of the Convention on Biological Diversity, Catherine Monagle CIEL and WWF International, joint discussion Paper.
7. Rabodo Andriantsiferana. "Traditional knowledge protection in the African region". Biodiversity and the Law Intellectual property, biotechnology and traditional knowledge in Charles R. MCmanis (ed.) 2007.
8. http://assets.wwfindia.org/downloads/mea_handbook_cel.pdf
9. http://ebookbrowse.com/jipr-13-4-344-350-pdf-d62563036
10. http://www.ciel.org/Publications/PriorArt_ManuelRuiz_Oct02.pdf
11. http://www.enablingchange.com.au/Enabling_EcoAction.pdf
12. http://www.ielrc.org/content/w0105.pdf
13. http://www.iprcommission.org/papers/pdfs/final_report/Ch4final.pdf
14. http://www.quno.org/geneva/pdf/economic/Discussion/Traditional-Knowledge-IP-english.pdf

# Aquatic Organisms as Bio-indicators

— Vinod Kumar Verma and Amita saxena

*Bioindicators* are species or chemicals used to monitor the health of an environment or ecosystem. They are any biological species or group of species whose function, population, or status can be used to determine ecosystem or environmental integrity. An example of such a group are the copepods and other small water crustaceans present in many water bodies. Such organisms are monitored for changes (chemical, physiological, or behavioural) that may indicate a problem within their ecosystem.

A bioindicator is an anthropogenically-induced response in biomolecular, biochemical, or physiological parameters that has been causally linked to biological effects at one or more of the organism, population, community, or ecosystem levels of biological organization. (definition modified from McCarty and Munkittrick, 1996).

Depending on the organism selected and their use, there are three types of bioindicators:

1. Plant indicators
2. Animal indicators

***Plant Indicators:*** The presence or absence of certain plant or other vegetative life in an ecosystem can provide important clues about the health of the environment-(environmental preservation).

*Lichens* (not a plant), found on rocks and tree trunks, are organisms comprising both fungi and algae. They respond to environmental changes in forests, including changes in forest structure (conservation biology), air quality, and climate. The disappearance of lichens in a forest may indicate environmental stresses, such as high level of sulfur dioxide, sulfur-based pollutants, and nitrogen-oxides. The composition and total biomass of algal species in aquatic systems serves as an important metric for organic pollution and nutrient loading such as nitrogen and phosphorus.

***Animal Indicators:*** An increase or decrease in an animal population may indicate damage to the ecosystem caused by pollution. For example, if pollution causes the depletion of important food sources, animal species dependent upon these food sources will also be reduced in number-population decline. Overpopulation, can be the result of opportunistic species growth. In addition to monitoring the size and number of certain species, other mechanisms of animal indication include monitoring the concentration of toxins in animal tissues, or monitoring the rate at which deformities arise in animal populations.

***Microbial Indicators:*** Micro-organisms can be used as indicators of aquatic or terrestrial ecosystem health. Found in large quantities, micro-organisms are easier to sample than other organisms. Some micro-organisms will produce new proteins, called stress proteins, when exposed to contaminants like cadmium and benzene. These stress proteins can be used as an early warning system to detect low levels of pollution.

## Tiniest Bioindicators

### *Water Fleas (Cladocera)*

The water flea, or *Daphnia*, is a tiny, flat, transparent aquatic organism that looks very similar to a tiny flea but it is not an insect. It grows to the size of a grain of sand. Daphnia has two sets of antennae, and uses one set to propel itself up and down through the water. A filter feeder, it sucks in water to filter out particles of food. Its transparent body allows its organs and even developing embryos to be clearly viewed through a strong magnifying glass. Daphnia are present in most freshwater ecosystems of North America and are an important food source for fish and predacious aquatic insects. Daphnia, an important part of the food web in lakes and slow-flowing rivers such as the Upper Connecticut, is considered a particularly important bio-indicator species—an indicator of ecosystem health. Scientists at Dartmouth along with researchers from around the world have formed the Daphnia Genomics Consortium to generate a gene encyclopedia for Daphnia, similar to the recently completed human genome project. Genetic information obtained from this research will help scientists determine how Daphnia respond to environmental agents such as mercury and PCBs, with a goal of identifying ecosystem exposure and response to pollution.

## Marine/Tidal Bioindicators

As with freshwater systems, biological life in marine and estuarine waters can indicate the quality of a waterbody. Benthic macro-invertebrates (e.g., polychaetes) are good indicators of water quality in marine environments as their response to pollutants is comparable to those in freshwater systems. Polychaetes (commonly known as worms) are one of the most tolerant marine organisms to stressors (e.g., low oxygen, organic contamination of sediment, and sewage pollution) so they are typically used as biological indicators. In addition, macro-invertebrates also have limited mobility and a long enough lifespan to both avoid pollutants and accurately assess environmental stressors. Typically it is much harder to assess marine/estuarine conditions as it is often difficult to evaluate reference conditions in these ecosystems.

Typical marine/estuarine indicators include:

- Phytoplankton – indicators of water quality, specifically nutrients (e.g., nitrogen and phosphorus)
- Zooplankton – sensitive to changes in water quality (e.g., toxic pollution, excess nutrients, and low oxygen) and are useful for future fisheries health assessment as they serve as a food source for animals higher up in the food chain
- Benthos – also susceptible to stresses associated with toxic pollution, excess nutrients, and low oxygen
- Submerged Aquatic Vegetation – serve as good indicators of water conditions
- Fish

There are various biological resources that can be used as bioindicator. for example, juvenile fish, crabs, diving ducks, and herons are used as indicators of restoration success in shallow water habitats such as bay grasses and wetlands, as all are susceptible to excess nutrients and turbidity. In tidal areas (e.g., aquatic reefs) adult fish, shellfish beds/reefs, and waterfowl are used as indicators of restoration success as they are susceptible to excess nutrients, turbidity, and sedimentation.

## Coral Reef Indicators

Corals are anthozoans, the largest class of organisms within the phylum Cnidaria. Comprising over 6,000 known species, anthozoans also include sea fans, sea pansies and anemones. **Stony corals** (scleractinians) make up the largest order of anthozoans, and **are the group** primarily responsible for laying the foundations of, and building up, reef structures. For the most part, scleractinians are colonial organisms composed of hundreds to hundreds of thousands of individuals, called polyps. The basic taxonomic classification of corals is given below:

### *Phylum*

Cnidaria—All organisms belonging to this phylum are characterized by the presence of: tentacles, nematocysts (stinging cells), central digestive cavity, radial symmetry

### *Class*

Hydrozoa—Portuguese-man-of-war, Fire Coral, Hydroids, Siphonophores

Schvphozoa—Jelly fish (medusea)

*Anthozoa—Sea anemones and corals*

### *Subclass*

Octocorallia—Sea whips, Sea feathers, Sea plumes, Other gorgonians

*Zoantharia*

### *Order*

Actinaria—anemones

Zooanthiniaria—carpet anemones

*Scleractina—true stony corals*

## Scleractinian Coral Bioindicators (true stony corals)

- Percentage hard coral cover, diversity indices, and vitality indices
- Growth rate (measurement of coral growth rates as an indication of water quality)
- Productivity and calcification profiles (measurement of productivity and calcification profiles as an indication of water quality)
- Coral fecundity and recruitment
- Zooxanthellae loss (quantifying the occurrence and extent of coral bleaching as a general bioassay of environmental stress on corals)
- Coral diseases and cyanobacterial blooms (frequency and severity of occurrences of coral diseases and cyanobacterial blooms)
- Bioaccumulation of metals, phosphorus in coral skeletons
- Physical damage

## Non-Coral Bioindicators

- Butterflyfish (for those species of butterflyfish which are obligate corallivores, a decline in the health of a reef, manifested by decreasing food quality of the stressed coral polyps, will result in a decrease in the abundance and diversity of these species and an increase in territory size, feeding rate and agonistic encounters as mated pairs attempt to maintain their nutritional intake by expanding their territories to include more coral colonies)
- Ectoparasites on coral reef fishes (incidence of ectoparasitism on reef fishes should increase with deteriorating water quality)
- Larval assemblages of fish and other reef taxa (sensitivity of larval fishes, along with their position in the pelagic food web, make them excellent indicators of environmental perturbations)
- Indicators of Fishing/Shell Collecting
- Organic contaminants and the development of fishes (occurrence of developmental defects in a demersal spawning fish as a bioindicator of pollution effects)
- Bioaccumulation in molluscs and macrophytes
- Sessile reef organisms (sponges, gorgonians)
- Heterotrophic macro-invertebrates (stressed reefs undergo an "ecosystem shift" from those dominated by coral-algal symbionts towards those dominated by heterotrophic macro-invertebrates, especially scavengers, filter feeders, and internal bioeroders.)
- Internal bioeroders (rubble, or live coral colonies, invaded by bioeroding sponges and bivalves)
- Coelobites (reef cavity-dwellers)
- Foraminifers (used as community response to gradually increasing nutrient flux, whether natural or anthropogenic)
- Stomatopod crustaceans (stomatopod abundance, diversity, and recruitment are strongly negatively correlated with various pollution measures.)
- Amphipods (are more sensitive than other species of invertebrates (decapods, polychaetes, molluscs, and asteroids) to a variety of contaminants.)
- Gastropod imposex (imposition of male sexual characters on females is extremely sensitive indicator of exposure to tributyl tin)
- Corallivores (specifically abundance of corallivores such as crown-of-thorns starfish (Acanthaster planci) and Drupella gastropods)

## REFERENCES

1. *Coral Reef, Function Role of Biodiversity: A Global Perspective*, John Wiley & Sons Ltd., 293-429.
2. Dahl, A.L., 1981, *Coral Reef Monitoring Handbook,* South Pacific Commisson, Noumea, New Caledonia, 22pp.
3. Done, T.D., Kenchington, R.A. and Zell, L.D., 1982, *Rapid, Large area, Reef Resource Survey using a Manta board.* Proceedings of the 4th Int. Coral Reef Sympsium, Manila, II: 597-600.
4. Done, T., Ogden, J.C., Wiebe W.J. and Rosen, B.R., 1996, Biodiversity and Echosystem Function of Weinz Walz GmbH, 1998. Underwater Fluorometer : Diving-Pam, Handbook of Operation.
5. Jones, B.O., 1986, *The Great Barrier Reef Science and Management, Oceans,* 4-6.
6. Kayane, H., 1992, Deposition of Calcium Carbonate into Holecene Reefs and its Relation to Sea-level Rise and Atmospheric $CO_2$. Proceedings of 7th Int. Coral Reef Symposium, Guam: 50-55.
7. Okamoto, M., 1998. Fundamental Study for Quantitative Measurement of Coral Biomass. *J. Rech. Oceanographique,* 23, 2: 57-65.
8. Report of the UNEP-IOC-ASPEI-UICN Global Task Team on the implication of Climite Change on Coral Reefs. IUCN, Gland, Switzerland.
9. Saxena Amita, 2002, "Biological Indicators of Pollution", in G. Tripathi (ed.) *Aquatic Bio Resources*, CBH Publisher, New Delhi, pp. 34-43.
10. Sea Grant HAWAII, 1997. *Status of Coral Reefs in the Pacific*, University of Hawaii.
11. Wilkinson, C. & Buddemeirr, R., 1994. *Global Climate Change. Implications for People and Reefs.*

# E-Waste—A Major Threat to Environment

— Ms. Kamlesh Agrawal, Ms. Sai Prasanna
Ms. J. Saujanya

## Introduction

"It is hard to believe but experts say that e-waste contain many toxic materials, and is fast emerging as a major health and environment hazard in India."

The term "e-waste" is often loosely applied to consumer and business electronic equipment that is near or at the end of its useful life. Outdated computers, televisions, VCRs, stereos, copiers, and fax appliances are common examples of electronic wastes.

### *Objectives*

- To examine the concept of e-waste, its source, implications, problems caused by e-waste.
- To identify a broad range of solutions, its management and recycling.

### *Methodology*

This study is based on secondary data, and collected from Infotrek Systems Ltd., (engaged in electronic equipment recycling) and different journals, articles, newspapers and already published information.

## Definition

**Source:** Copine, solving e-waste problems, Aug. 2007.

Electronic waste can be defined as "electrically powered electronic equipments or products which have been removed one way or the other from their normal cycle of use either by becoming obsolete, abandoned or impairment beyond further use".

## E-waste: Its Implications

Electronic products often contain hazardous and toxic materials that pose environmental risks if they are land filled. If the landfill's liner fails, the groundwater supply may become contaminated. Televisions, video and computer monitors use cathode ray tubes (CRTs), which have significant amounts of lead. Printed circuit boards contain primarily plastic and copper, and most have small amounts of chromium, lead solder, nickel, and zinc.

**Table 10.1 : List of Toxic Metals and their Effects**

| Element | Use in Wireless Technology | Harmful Effects |
|---|---|---|
| Lead | Used primarily in soldering of circuit boards and other device components. | Extremely harmful to the human body; damages both the central and peripheral nervous systems; can cause seizures, retardation, high blood pressure, damage to the kidneys and liver; adversely affects child development. |
| Beryllium | Forms significant portions of electrical connectors and battery contacts. | Long term exposure can be carcinogenic, especially for the lungs. Extreme exposure can lead to a potentially fatal condition known as Acute Beryllium Disease. |
| Arsenic | Used in some integrated circuits and semiconductors. | Arsenic is a notoriously potent poison; causes severe damage to the digestive tract. |
| Mercury | Can be found to a degree in batteries and circuit boards. | Attacks the central nervous and endocrine systems; harmful to mouth, teeth and gums; poses risk in the neurological development of unborn fetuses. |
| Antimony | Used in production of diodes and batteries. Pure form usedin semiconductor production. | Toxic to humans in ways similar to arsenic; fatal in large doses. |
| Cadmium | Used in soldering, semiconductors and chip resistors. | Potentially carcinogenic; Repeated exposure can damage the lungs, kidneys and liver. |

**Source**: www.recyclingforcharities.com

The items shown in Table 10.1, when burnt not only effects workers health, but also nearby residential areas.

Who is Responsible?

- Manufacturers (Eg. Dell, Intel, HP)
- Companies (IT, Microsoft, Infosys, Wipro)
- Users (Corporates, Private Households)
- Others ?

## E-waste Generation

There is a phenomenal growth of IT industry which is one of the reason for increase of e-waste. The average lifespan of PCs in the IT industry is three years, resulting in a high obsolescence rate. In a study conducted by Infotrek Systems Ltd. it was found that in USA alone:

**Table 10.2 : Country-wise Appliances counted in e-waste**

| Country | Total e-waste generated in tones | Items | Year |
|---|---|---|---|
| Switzerland | 66,042 | Office and telecommunications equipment, consumer entertainment, electronics, large and small, domestic appliances, refrigerators, fractions | 2003 |
| Germany | 1,100,000 | Office and telecommunications equipment, consumer entertainment electronics, large and small domestic appliances, refrigerators, fractions | 2005 |
| UK | 915,000 | Office and telecommunications equipment, consumer entertainment electronics, large and small domestic appliances, refrigerators, fractions | 1998 |
| USA | 2,158,490 | Video products, audio products, computers and telecommunications equipment | 2000 |
| Taiwan | 14,036 | Computers, home electrical appliances (TVs, washing machines, air conditioners, refrigerators) | 2003 |
| Thailand | 60,000 | Refrigerator, air conditioners, televisions, washing machines, computers | 2003 |
| Denmark | 118,000 | Electronic and electrical appliances including Refrigerators | 1997 |
| Canada | 67,000 | Computer equipment (computers, printers etc) and consumer electronics (TVs) | 2005 |

(**Source:** http://www.ewaste.ch/facts_and_figures/statistical/quantities/)

- Between 1997 and 2007, nearly 500 million personal computers became obsolete—almost two computers for each person.

- 15,000,000 PCs become obsolete every year.
- 7,000,000 computers will end up stockpiled for at least 3 years.
- 750,000 computers will end up in landfills in 2007 alone.

According to a survey by IRG Systems, South Asia, the total waste generated by obsolete or broken-down electronic and electrical equipment in India has been estimated to be 1,46,180 tons per year based on select EEE tracer items. According to the study unveiled by MAIT e-waste is expected to touch 4.7 lakh tones in India by 2011, the apex body representing India's IT hardware, training and R&D services sectors, together with GTZ, the German Technical Cooperation Agency.*

**Table 10.3 : Waste Piling up in India**
**(As on 21st July 2009)**

| City | Waste |
|---|---|
| Mumbai | 19,000 tones |
| Delhi | 9,730 tones |
| Bangalore | 4,648 tones |
| Chennai | 4,132 tones |
| Kolkata | 4,025 tones |
| Ahmedabad | 3,287 tones |
| Hyderabad | 2,833 tones |
| Pune | 2,584 tones |
| Surat | 1,836 tones |

**Source** : environmentchange.comindia

- Mumbai at present tops the list
- Bangalore has more than 100 illegal dump pits for e-waste
- Import of e-waste, mainly from the US, under the garb of donations is adding to our woes. They basically dump obsolete computers in India.

## E-waste Management

The emerging area of electronic waste (e-waste) recovery is attracting increasing attention as governments of several developed countries issue directives to address the environmental hazards posed by existing methods to dispose waste electrical and electronic equipment (WEEE) as conventional methods, such as disposal in landfills, informal recycling and incineration, potentially damaging to the environment.

---

**Source:** Toxic Link, a nongovernmental organization in New Delhi

## E-waste Management in India

- E-waste processing in developing nations has only recently emerged as an important issue, thus relevant research remains scarce. Recycling technology advances and new material development is the key to the successful e-waste recovery.
- As a measure to reduce e-waste, e-waste agency (EWA), a Bangalore-based NGO, supported by Indo-German Swiss e-waste initiative, has already put forward a proposal before the Ministry of Environment and Forests (MoEF) to enact legislation on the issue of e-waste.
- There are some interesting projects like E-Parisara Pvt. Ltd. in Bangalore, the local firm which has pioneered e-waste recycling technology in the country and recycles about a tone of e-waste every day, also seeks an e-waste policy.
- Greenpeace India demands complete ban on import of e-waste in India.

  Wipro goes green as India's e-waste mounts. India's Wipro has introduced new PCs that are compliant with the European Restriction of Hazardous Substances (RoHS) directive to manage e-waste. Wipro is the first Indian computer maker to offer products that are RoHS compliant.
- National level working group has been started in India to organize national level workshop and seminars in collaboration with NGOs, producers both formal and informal to identify, plan and implement all issues related to e-waste in India and to develop environmental sound recycling facilities and to control import of e-waste coming in the country in the name of donation /charity.

## Some International Responses to E-waste

- *United States*: In September 2003,California passed the "Electronic Waste Recycling Act of 2003" (SB20), USA's first comprehensive electronics recycling law, establishing a funding system for the collection and recycling of certain electronic wastes. The National Safety Council estimates that the United States will be awash in 500 million defunct computers and monitors by 2007.
- *European Union:* On January 27, 2003, the EU Parliament passed a directive that requires producers of electronics to take responsibility, financial and otherwise, for recovery and recycling of e-waste (Waste from Electrical and Electronic Equipment (WEEE). Electronics

manufacturers to pay for collection and recycling of most obsolete electronics products, from hair dryers to PCs, at the end of their useful lives.

- ***Japan:*** Japan, home of the highest-ranking electronics manufacturers, passed a law in April 2001 requiring manufacturers to recycle appliances, televisions, refrigerators, and air conditioners. Under a new law, manufacturers would charge a recycling fee to consumers.
- ***OECD:*** The OECD has developed international guidelines on the "environmentally sound management" (ESM) of used and scrap personal computers.
- ***China:*** The Standing Committee of the 9th NPC promulgated a law in 2002, requiring compulsory retrieval of used industrial products. They restricted the import of second-hand electronic also.
- *Netherlands:* In 1998, Netherland passed, "The Disposal of White and Brown Goods Decree." It requires manufacturers and importers of electrical and electronic equipment sold in the country to take back their end-of-life products.
- *Austria:* Recycle-IT! Austria (RITA) is an initiative to collect used computers from manufacturers and other companies, upgrade and repair the computers, and then sell them at reasonable prices to low-income households or schools.
- *California and Massachusetts* ban the disposal of cathode ray tube monitors and TVs in landfills because of their lead content. Several states and municipalities are considering similar legislation. University of California signed an agreement not to send electronic equipment overseas or to state prisons to be dismantled or recycled. It also agreed to purchase only "green computers", those that are manufactured without hazardous materials.
- *San Francisco* has taken a series of steps to promote electronics recycling. The city began a pilot program under which consumers and small businesses can drop off equipment at computer dealers or at HMR, an Australian recycling company with a facility near China Basin. The city even paid $100,000 to help HMR defray the cost of a machine capable of crushing 300 CRTs an hour.
- Sustained campaigns by environmental groups have already persuaded industry titans such as Hewlett-Packard, Dell, LG Electronics, Samsung, Sony, Sony Ericsson and Nokia to eliminate most hazardous materials from their products.

## Some Companies Responses to E-waste

- IBM and HP began fee-based programs that let consumers send in unwanted computing gear to be refurbished and donated or recycled. Under HP's Web-based program, for example, charges range from \$13 to \$34 per item.
- According to a report each month, HP's worldwide recycling centers process over 6.5 million pounds of computer-related products that have been returned by customers or generated by HP's own operations.
- Dell and Gateway have also created donation and trade-in programs, while Sony is collecting and recycling its own products free in Minnesota only. Dell offers recycle of unwanted Dell-branded products for free. Plus, if consumers buy a new Dell desktop or notebook and select the free recycling option at the time of purchase, Dell will recycle their old PC and monitor at no cost (even if it isn't a Dell-branded product.)
- IBM released one computer model, the IntelliStation E Pro, in which all plastics are made of recycled resins.
- Wipro Ltd., an IT behemoth listed on the New York Stock Exchange, is the first Indian electronics company to announce it will eliminate heavy metals from its products by June 2007.
- Hewlett-Packard, Dell and IBM, take back old computer equipment for disposal with little or no cost to consumers. Hewlett-Packard has its own recycling program and will pick up any computer product of any brand for a fee ranging from \$14 to \$34. The service includes a coupon for future purchases.
- Apple recycling program: Purchase any qualifying Apple computer or monitor and receive free recycling of your old computer and monitor regardless of manufacturer. They are working to ensure that electronic equipment is properly disposed of at the end of its useful life.

## Recommendations for Action or Guidelines for Future Work on E waste

### *Government's responsibilities**

- E-waste policy and legislation.
- Encourage organized system of recycling.
- Collecting fee from manufacturers/consumers for the disposal of toxic materials.

*Source: e-Parisaraa

- Should subsidies recycling and disposal industries.
- Incentive schemes for garbage collectors and general public for collecting and handing over e-waste.
- Awareness programmers on e-waste for school children and general public.

Apart from these the government should insist on electronic producers to follow one of the below mentioned measures to reduce e-waste.

### Redesign

The focus should be on the reduction of negative consequences of electrical and electronic appliances throughout their entire life cycle. There should be up-gradation of skills and processes of recyclers and establish a collection and disposal system for large and small consumers to return all their e-waste safely. The device must be designed to ensure clear, safe, and efficient mechanisms for recovering its raw materials.

### Reuse and donations

The focus should be on the development of sustainable, transmissible principles and standards for the reuse of EEE. There are many groups that can benefit from the donation of used electronics, including charities to schools and non-profit organisations for developmental and educational purpose.

#### Benefits

- Reduces demand for new products which in turn reduces requirement for raw material.
- Reduces need for water and energy.
- Less packaging per unit.
- Saves landfill space.

### Recycling

The objective by recycling is to improve infrastructures, systems and technologies to realize a sustainable recycling on a global level.

### Repair, refurnish or upgrade

If the equipment is not too old and is still in working condition instead of purchasing a new, one should consider upgrading the software, buying new memory, repairing, replacing certain parts of old one to save money and to avoid creating unnecessary waste. For example, Repairing and upgrading used electrical equipment. (adding memory to a computer and upgrading the use of software).

### *Sale or Trade*

consider selling the electronics at lower price to some one too poor to afford a new PC or find a manufacturer who will give you credit towards a new purchase for turning in your old one.

### *Dispose*

The least preferred option is to landfill electronic waste. This should only be the last option but care to consult state regulations on disposal of any hazardous waste.

## Suggestion to Customer

### *Things to Consider When Buying Electronics*

When shopping for electronics, the following points can be considered:

- ***Products with reduced toxics content***

  Electronics made with reduced lead, mercury and other heavy metals are safer for the environment.

- ***Refurbished or remanufactured products or those with recycled content or made from remanufactured materials***

  Buying remanufactured items or those made with remanufactured parts and other recycled content, uses less energy, conserves natural resources and closes the recycling loop.

- ***Products with longer life expectancy and ease of upgradeability***

  Extend the life of your electronics by purchasing items that are easily upgradeable. Instead of buying new items, install new software, update programs and upgrade memory.

- ***Electronics that can be leased***

  Leased items are returned to the vendor after a specified period of time. Consumers leasing electronics are able to obtain the most up-to-date products, and at the same time have a built-in take-back program to ensure that products are responsibly disposed of at the end of the lease.

- ***Products with less packaging***

  Excess packaging means added waste. Pick up your product instead of having it shipped, and ask for on-line manuals instead of heavy paper volumes.

## *Public Awareness Campaign*

- Manufacturers and suppliers to set goals for reducing electronic waste.
- Encourage them to buy back old electronic products from consumers.
- Disposing bulk e-waste only through authorized recyclers.
- Send non-tradable e-waste to authorized private developers for final disposal.

## Conclusion

"The times are over, when the responsibility of a company for their products ended at the gate of the factory. Once the product leaves the gate of the manufacturer his responsibility, liability and accountability does not end, it just starts."

Hence to deal with e-waste, a major threat to environment, the manufacturers must produce equipment which is easier to upgrade, so that users can keep in use longer even as technology upgrades. Now the major electronics companies need to come forward and commit to greener electronics.

## REFERENCES

1. www.recyclingforcharities.com
2. www.ewaste.ch/facts_and_figures/statistical/quantities
3. Toxic Link, a nongovernmental organization in New Delhi
4. e-parisara
5. Infrotrek System Ltd.
6. Copine, solving E waste problems, Aug 2007.

# An Introduction to Ecotaxation and Environmental Levy

— Dr. Md. Samsur Jaman

## Introduction

Any economic activity generates several types of pressures on the environment. Broadly these pressures can be classified into three categories: (*i*) input demands (e.g., materials, energy, intermediate products); (*ii*) pollution/ waste flows; and (*iii*) ecosystem modifications (e.g., by spatial claims for roads or dams or inter-linking of rivers etc.). These pressures are normally buffered by absorptive capacity, i.e., ability to assimilate waste, absorb pollution, resilience of ecosystem to disturbance, etc. and regenerative processes in the environment. If these pressures exceed the buffering capacities, it leads to environmental change; if the change leads to a reduced capacity of the environment to satisfy the human needs, then one can speak of the environmental degradation. This degradation may lead to policy responses in terms of measures aimed either at reducing environmental pressure or enhancing environmental buffering capacities.

Environmental policy uses a range of instruments that induces behavioural change of economic agents so as to actualise these objectives. Taxes on inputs or outputs, also known as Eco-taxes, is one such instrument that can signal the costs of using the environmental resources and thus internalises the negative externalities in decision-making by producers and consumers. An Eco-tax is a price-like instrument, which assigns a price to the 'unpaid factor' of production, thus translating the polluter pays principle in practice.

Though eco-tax is a policy instrument that attempts to internalise the negative externality, it is quite possible that the existing tax policies may itself encourage inefficient use of environment resources. For instance, investment tax credits in Brazil encouraged exploitation of environmentally weak areas. Similarly, in Haiti, a raised export tax on coffee caused coffee trees to be replaced with staple crops such as corn. This led to increase in erosion of steep lands. In a similar vein, income tax exemptions also impact environmental management. Since in a number of countries including India, agricultural income is exempt from income tax, this has resulted in increase in demand for land and thus contributing to a rapid increase in the conversion of forest to agriculture uses.

## Types of Ecotaxes

In general, a number of ways, i.e., eco-tax schemes exist through which one can internalise the externality. These include input taxes, output or product taxes, export taxes, import tariffs, tax differentiation, royalties and resource taxes, land-use taxes and investment tax credits. For example, tax differentiation involves a positive charge being levied on a polluting product and a negative charge, or subsidy, on a cleaner alternative. The most common example of this tax differential is in the context of transport so to discourage consumer purchases of polluting vehicles or fuels. Less tax on compressed natural gas (CNG) vis-à-vis petrol in Delhi is one such example. Differential taxation of leaded and unleaded gasoline across the Europe and some of the developing countries is another example.

Taxes on polluting inputs are generally suggested when there is a clear linkage between input use and environmental damages. An interesting example of the above tax is 'forestry tax' charged in Brazil, Colombia and Venezuela for wood consumption if there is no reforestation activity. A nice and promising feature of such taxes is that it alleviates the need for (costly) monitoring. However, it needs to be noted that taxes on polluting inputs generally do not yield equimarginal abatement costs. Since one of the benefits of economic instruments (EIs) often cited in the literature is their cost effectiveness, as they equate marginal abatement costs across individuals. This implies input taxes are not always cost-effective.

The most important application of input taxes can be in non-point source of pollution (NPSP) setting such as taxes on fertilizers in agriculture so as to reduce nutrient loading of water-bodies or taxes on gasoline to reduce vehicular pollution. However, a high tax on either may have high undesirable distributional consequences. This is because a high tax on fertilizers tends to penalise grain farmers with generally lower nutrient leakage. Thus, it is not the least-costly policy option. However, in this case by combining recent nitrogen tax with a certain per cent of cash crop requirement may yield the desired reductions in nitrogen leakage, as has been done in the Netherlands.

The choice of taxing in an input or output is not arbitrary. The suitable option depends on the pollutant in question. This can be easily demonstrated using $CO_2$ and $SO_2$ as an illustration.

The current policy could be either no control (e.g., on fertilisers or pesticides), or some technology standards (e.g., mandatory use of catalytic converters) or some emission standards (e.g., EURO II norms for cars). The move to control pollution will be from current policy to input/output/ emission taxes. The taxes levied can be at optimal or at sub/non-optimal rates. The sub-optimal taxes are not by choice, but due to the near impossibility of valuing the future environmental damage caused by the pollutant. The Love Canal in US where the impact of dumping toxic waste got detected only after two decades when the dumping had already ceased is a clear reflection of difficulties in valuing the environmental damages. On the other hand, optimal tax rates mean that the damage is adequately assessed and the pollution is optimally controlled, or in other words, the environment receives the 'right' amount of help.

## Criteria for Selecting a Policy Option

Broadly speaking, there are four criteria that dictate the move from current policy to eco-taxation. However, the application of these criteria depends on the pollutant. First, it must be known that emissions cause environmental condition. In the case of $SO_2$ and $CO_2$, the local damage caused by $SO_2$ has been known for decades, though its long distance damage in the form of acid-rain / deposition is fairly recent. On the other hand, the impact of $CO_2$ on climate change is still controversial. Second, the emissions must be controllable. In terms of control of emissions, pollutants can be classified into two broad types: *Type 1* are those that are an unwanted byproduct of a production process, and *Type 2,* where the marketed output of a production process is or becomes a pollutant. Traditional pollutants like $SO_2$, particulate matters etc. fall in the former category. However, $CO_2$ from fossil fuels, Chlorofluorocarbons (CFCs) etc. are in the second group. For pollutants of type 2, there is no control technology, and the goal of the environmental policy must be to reduce or eliminate the usage of the product. Incidentally, in the case of CFCs, this has been achieved in the developed world as well as in India, but in the case of fossil fuels, no alternatives are available immediately, at least on a sufficiently large scale. However, technologies to control pollutants of type 1 are commercially available such as tall stacks to disperse and dilute the emissions or flue gas sulphurisation to reduce total emissions.

The third criteria is that it must be affordable for the government or agency to monitor the results of its policy; whereas the fourth and the last criteria is that there must be 'political will' to impose the costs of control on polluting firms (and their customers). At the moment, there exist huge differences in monitoring costs between $SO_2$ and $CO_2$ as shown below in Table 11.1:

**Table 11.1 : Proportion of $SO_2$ and $CO_2$ in terms of total emission**

| Pollutant | Proportion (%) of total emission coming from | |
|---|---|---|
| | Non-point sources (Housing, Commerce, Transport and Agriculture) | Point sources (Power stations, refineries and other industries) |
| $SO_2$ | 11 | 89 |
| $CO_2$ | 44 | 56 |

**Source:** Park and Pezzy (1998: 168)

Since 44 per cent of $CO_2$ emissions come from small and often mobile emitters, i.e., NPSPs, it makes prohibitively expensive to monitor a large majority of individual emissions. Moreover, beyond a threshold, it is extremely difficult to increase the energy efficiency of most existing equipment, it clearly reflects in little political will to set efficiency standards for existing $CO_2$ technologies. The $CO_2$ efficiency standards thus apply to only new equipments. Even if technologically it is possible to reduce $CO_2$ emissions, they hardly give any incentive to find alternative means of control and provide no direct control over the level of emissions. This implies it is preferable to have emission standards than the technology standards. Emission standards should ideally be set in terms of the total emissions from a site or industrial estate or region, often known as 'bubble policy' in the US, rather than in terms of emissions from one stack or emissions concentrations. The equivalent indirect move for $CO_2$ would be to move from setting standards to fixing the amount of carbon energy actually sold (since $CO_2$ emissions are directly in proportion of this), which is rather incredibly costly. But this paves the idea of moving from (indirect) technology standards for $CO_2$ to control it by a tax called as Carbon Tax. A carbon tax will create a pervasive incentive to reduce $CO_2$ emissions in the most cost-effective way, without specifying which users are to reduce emissions, by how much, or with which technologies. Since direct monitoring of $CO_2$ emissions is very costly and as almost all carbon fuel used is burned, the tax incentive is applied to carbon inputs instead.

## Effectiveness of Ecotaxation

### *Effectiveness*

Taxes might be called effective if they do what they are intended to do. In theory, environmental taxation should attempt to improve the market efficiency of the environmental goods and services by imposing a price on such goods equal to the marginal costs of their use (i.e., the marginal environmental damage costs). If policy-makers can calculate these costs, environmental taxation is inherently effective, provided no other major imperfections distort the relevant markets. However, finding the marginal environmental damage costs is rather difficult. The UK landfill tax introduced in 1996 is considered to be the only example, which is explicitly based on an estimate of these costs.

*The environmental taxes can have different functions:* (*a*) cost covering; (*b*) incentive effects; and (*c*) revenue rising. In order to assess the effect of taxes, two criteria are generally used that also encompasses these functions. These are:

1. *Environmental Effect :* The effect of the tax on environmental pollution or the use of scarce resources.
2. *Incentive Effect :* A comparison of the tax rate with the marginal pollution abatement costs, or as a proxy, average abatement costs of measure taken by the polluters.

Together they indicate the 'overall effectiveness'. Both the criteria, however, can be used to assess a similar impact in different ways. The first criterion directly attempts to trace the contribution of the tax to the monitored pollution reduction, while the second criterion endeavours to establish incentives for taxpayers to change their behaviour in a way more favourable to the environment by adopting suitable measures or by saving on scarce resources.

The main function of fiscal or revenue raising environmental taxes is raising income for government expenditures. Environmental effects are a side-effect. However, positive environmental impact may be expected because of the price effect on behaviour. Consequently, evaluating the environmental effectiveness of this type of tax involves examining the environmental effects, e.g., in terms of pollution reduction. Similarly, incentive taxes are designed to achieve a specific environmental impact. So the evaluation of environmental effectiveness includes comparing pollution reduction targets. It also involves measuring the incentive effect by comparing the differential between the tax rate and the cost of pollution reduction.

On the other hand, cost-covering charges are designed primarily to raise funds for financing specific environmental systems, measures or programs. Two types of cost-covering charges are : (*i*) user charge; and (*ii*) earmarked charge. In both cases, funds raised from the major objective, so effectiveness evaluation involves assessing the money available for carrying out the environmental measures or programs. However, the cost-covering charges may also have an incentive impact if charge rates for cost-recovery reach substantial levels, e.g., in the case of Dutch water pollution charge. Incentive effects are sometimes aimed for cases where formerly fixed rates for certain environmental services were differentiated according to the level of the service rendered. Variable charge rates for household garbage collection in the form of 'pay-per bag' scheme or 'effluent treatment charges' based on the quantity and/or quality of effluent are two such examples where rates are differentiated according to the services rendered.

### *Effectiveness of Taxes/charges—Evidence*

As mentioned, the effectiveness of charges/taxes can be assessed based on environmental effectiveness and incentive effectiveness.

At some places actual environmental effectiveness of green taxes could not be ascertained due to non-availability of ex-post policy evaluation studies. OECD in a study has concluded that there is little tradition in ex-post policy evaluation. A practical reason for non-evaluation studies is the complexity. These studies have to cope up with difficult methodological problems as well as the problems of data availability. Both these problems however can be minimised if the evaluation is built into the process of designing and implementing stage itself. The OECD has considered this question in somewhat deep.

The taxes on inputs or outputs are second-best, and are frequently applied on the energy source or chemical that is generating the pollution. Ideally the pollution charge should be imposed on the emissions. But in practice, this is rather impossible. Taxing the source of the pollution rather than the pollution itself does not allow for (a) the possibility that mitigation measures can be undertaken at the 'end of the pipe'; and (b) the fact that the impacts in terms of damages vary spatially, so that a general tax overtaxes use in a place where there is no environmental problem, and undertaxes it in places where the problem is very serious. The first issue can be tackled rather easily by giving rebates for payments when the polluter makes such an investment in an end-of-pipe clean-up.

However, the problem of spatial variation is difficult to address. The problem can be circumvented if we have different rates of taxation depending upon where the inputs are used, which is practically difficult to implement even at a crude level. Moreover if input or output taxes are varied across regions, this would result in trade leakages between regions (provided the input or output permit prices exceed the transport costs between regions), which would dilute the impact. Still, the other big advantage of using taxes on polluting inputs and outputs is that they can be a major source of revenue, which can generate resources for environmental protection, and even facilitate shifting the structure of taxation away from taxing 'goods' such as consumption and employment to taxing 'bads' such as pollution.

## Economic Instruments providing the Greatest Environmental Benefits

There are a wide range of economic instruments that can be used. Economic instruments can be applied at every level from the micro to the macro. The comments that follow relate to their use at the macro-level or their additive effect at the macro-level (many responsiveness boosting measures need to be applied at the micro-level even though in many cases it is their aggregate (macro) effect that is the key concern. The instruments principally discussed are environmental levies or eco-taxation.

From the basic ideas discussed above, an ecologically sustainable economy would:

- use dramatically less raw material and energy.
- not use fossil fuels / use renewable energy.
- have a closed cycle structure where material resources (apart from energy) were fully recycled (largely through the economy rather than nature)—waste dumps would only be used for temporary storage.
- be designed to eliminate the use of toxic substances.
- be spacially compact to leave ample room for nature.
- be premised on a stable population.
- be built around the sale of service flows rather than the sale of goods.

Economic instruments (taxes, user charges, tradeable permits, deposits, insurance premiums, etc.) and responsiveness promoting measures should be introduced as a suite to drive the economy to a sustainable structure (in relation to all environmental issues) otherwise perverse incentives will be created and illogical environmental outcomes will be generated.

Often it is not the absolute price effect generated by economic instruments that counts (provided that there is a strategic application of responsiveness boosting measures) but rather it is the level of certainty and predicability and the financial trajectory that counts. When economic growth is occurring, environmental levies and other economic instruments intended to have macro effects should increase in perpetuity—indexed to the growth of the economy—unless the regulated activity is replaced at some point by better alternatives.

If these conditions are met then economic instruments and their accompanying responsiveness-boosting measures can register with decision makers as meaningful strategic drivers to factor into a wide variety of organisational management spheres (e.g. corporate planning, investment policy, product development and marketing, R&D, production and distribution, education and training, recruitment, performance criteria, etc.).

## Conclusion

The economic instruments, especially environmental levies send signals that cost-reactors can understand; they demonstrate government commitment and intention and reduce the risk for business decision-makers for targeting sustainability and they create a revenue stream to fund responsiveness-boosting projects.

1. At the micro-level, which economic instrument or combination of instruments is best has to be decided in the context of the specific circumstances. General rules at this level are usually not terribly useful.
2. At the macro-level there is a strong case that *environmental* levies or eco-taxes combined in some cases with tradeable permits can play an important part in creating useful price and policy signals and can provide the revenue streams needed for responsiveness-boosting measures that ensure that the economy is sensitised and able to respond to the price signals.

The case for using input/output taxes (or charges) as an economic instrument for environmental protection, and as part of the programme to move to sustainable development, is strong but requires qualification. For a number of applications such as NPSPs, taxes on inputs are the only way to deal with the issue. This however, does not solve the problem of 'hot spots' or local concentrations of pollutant, for which direct controls of some kind are mandatory. Thus an optimal mix of policy instruments is going to be one that combines economic instruments with direct controls. Another argument in favour of input/output taxes is that they are easier to collect. Since emission charges can be extremely difficult to collect and spatial variation may be impossible for them, the case for moving to input taxes/ charges gets further support. Lastly, eco-taxation and environmental levies can be a part of a broader tax reform so as to set the markets/common property right. Thus, from the point of view of reducing /controlling the environmental degradation and pollution and to sustain development, introduction of eco-taxation and environmental levies is need of the hour.

## REFERENCES


1. OECD (1997), *Evaluating Instruments for Environmental Policy*, OECD Paris.
2. OECD (1999), *Environmental Taxes and Green Tax Reform, Background Paper*, Oslo, 30-31 August, 1999.
3. Park, A. and J.C.V. Pezzy (1998) "Variations on the Wrong Themes? A Structured Review of the Double Dividend Debate", in Thomas Sterner, Edward Elgar, Cheltenham and Massachusetts *The Market and the Environment*, (ed.), pp. 181-203.
4. Ribeiro, M.B., K. Schlegelmilch and D. Gee (1998) "Environmental Taxes seem to be effective instruments for the Environment", in Thomas Sterner, Edward Elgar, Cheltenham and Massachusetts (ed.), *ibid.*
5. Robert N., Stavins, "Experience with Market based Environmental Policy Instruments", Discussion Paper No 01-58, Nov. 2001, Resource for the Future, 1616 P Street, NW.
6. http://coe.mse.ac.in/pdfs/coebreifs/Eco-taxes.pdf

# Biodiversity: A Threat Perception to Sustainable Development in Arunachal Pradesh of India

— Dr. Ram Krishna Mandal

## Introduction

When it is very clear that removing atmospheric carbon and storing it in the terrestrial biosphere is one of the viable options to compensate green-house gas emissions, the agro-ecosystems could be the potential sink and could absorb large quantities of C, if trees are judiciously managed in this system along with agricultural crops and/or animals in an integrated manner. Nonetheless, afforestation/reforestation is yet another viable option to increase carbon stock, but may fail to address the issues of diversity and livelihood security directly. Thus, traditional agro-forests need to be explored and given wider consideration for propagation as a socio-cultural enterprise that can sustain livelihood requirements and also restore the environmental condition in the longer run by mitigating the ill-effects of global warming, and shall have economic value to contribute to over all social development in the country.

When the whole world is crying for the mercy to get rid of current state of environmental degradation in the form of depletion of ozone layer, global warming and climate change, Gandhiji's very notion of development appears as a savior to the world community. Sustainability is the core to his developmental process which appears to be a best viable alternative model of development in the recent years. Long before the "World Commission on Environment and Development", coined and defined the concept sustainable development, Gandhi talked about the philosophy of the concept but in a different term. Today from United Nations to Government of India, everybody is talking about a form of development which will balance the fulfillment of human needs with the protection of the natural environment so that these needs can be met not only in the present, but in the indefinite future. Now the concept of sustainable development becomes indispensable to the development of the human civilization because of the limited nature of the world's resources. Knowing this inherent limitation of mother earth Gandhi warned the human society not to exploit beyond its capacity to withstand the exploitation of natural resources for our development. Rather Gandhi advocated for the "optimal utilization" of our natural resources. For him using anything extra is a stealing. Depicting this Gandhian thought very brilliantly Satish Kumar in his article "Five Elements of Ecology" writes "the crisis of environment comes out of a utilitarian, materialistic, non-sacred, non-spiritual worldview—the Earth is there for us to use, for our comfort, for our convenience." As a consequence we have taken from nature without knowing its limits. When we have a sense of reverence, we shall take from nature only what meets our vital needs. And when we take something, we thank, we show gratitude like we take milk from the mother's breast; the mother is very happy to give her milk in the same way as the Earth is happy to give its fruits as long as we take only what we need. When the baby is full, he or she stops sucking and does not go on sucking. Well, unfortunately we humans go on sucking the Earth.

The environment assumed a central role in India, to a large extent, as a result of the first major international conference on the environment, namely, the United Nations Conference on the Human Environment (UNCHE) held in Stockholm in 1972. In preparation for this meeting, each member country was asked to prepare a report on the state of the environment. India set up a committee on the human environment under the chairmanship of Pitambar Pant, a Planning Commission member. The outcome was three reports, one on the state of the environment, one on the problems of human settlement and one on the possible strategies to manage resources. Environmental goals were subsequently incorporated in the Fifth Five-Year Plan onwards. Legislations such as Wildlife Protection Act, 1972 and the Water (Prevention and Control of Pollution) Act, 1974 were passed soon after as well (Menon, 2006).

## What is Biodiversity?

Nature has varied forms of creation (plants and vegetation, fauna, insects, birds and micro-organism etc.) if all these survive, living would be smooth for all the species on the earth. Thus, biodiversity would mean that there is need for diverse biological varieties to co-exist without the threat of extinction. Thus, biodiversity would simply mean "varieties of species right to existence" it would also mean that no one has the right to threaten a species right to existence. Man, being the homo sapiens, should restrain from actions that would erode species but do everything to protect them from extinction. This will not only protect the environment but also enable smooth human survival as well. Thus, all species are equally important for the sustenance for all human and sub-human species. Hence, there is an urgent need to strengthen the food chain of all living creatures with sustainable and judicious use. Thus, the mantra of the century should naturally be to "protect species from perish". This would call for truly holistic concerns. In the nature's scheme of things, all species play complementary and supplementary role for the survival of all living entities. One life supports the other, which is an unalterable law of nature, thus all species have dual role; (a) every species depends on other species and (b) every species adds to the food basket of other species as well. In this sense, all species on this planet could be deduced as food basket. Planet earth is unique in many ways, which is the only one shelter of innumerable species to coexist, though at the same time, each of them is feeding or nourishing one another. Without these diverse varieties putting up together, a few sacrificing in favour of several others, living would have come to a naught. It is for man's smooth existence that he should strive for the maintenance for bio-diversity order. The unlimited greed of man is threatening the healthy and diverse biological order that needs immediate correction. He is exploiting both biological and other precious natural resource beyond the replacement levels, besides polluting them badly thereby posing greater danger to the future generation's smooth survival. In an effort to save erosion of natural resources, several threatened regions are declared as bio-diversity hotspots which includes the Western Ghats and the Eastern Himalayan that are treasure houses for several flora and fauna. It is time to make man realise the negative impact of nature on 'biodiversity' and make him act as a 'trustee' or 'conservator' of nature in true sense. Otherwise, a day may not be far off when our future generation would be compelled to face several risks including shortage of food and other requirements. The time is most appropriate to realise importance for biodiversity conservation for the good of all species. It also calls for a well planned strategy to adequately compensate people involved in biodiversity conservation by foregoing benefits of opportunity costs accruing from commercial crops or exploitation of natural resources.

Forest is the most important resource in Arunachal Pradesh. This can also be called 'primary source' in the words of Norman Myers, the famous ecologist. This resource is the mother of unique culture and traditions of local tribes and is also at the root of abundance of water, biodiversity and soil formation. Forestry is a multi-faceted business and the Department of Environment and Forest is committed to managing forestry resources in a balanced way so that a full range of benefits (economic, social and environmental) are delivered not only today but for generations to come.

Environment conservation and sustainable development are closely interlinked such that one cannot be achieved at the expense of the other. The preservation of natural resources is one of the important components of environmental conservation in the hilly areas. Forests are the most important natural resources in the hilly state and they play an important role in the economic life of the indigenous people in the state. At the same time forest represent a complex economic resource. In addition to their timber value, they are a valuable source of biodiversity, as a carbon store and in reducing the severity of floods.

The broad aim of this paper is to analyze and discuss the factors and issues that are associated with effective operations in degradation of forest and searching the ways for its conservation with the changes of traditional institutions and customary laws that may exist in managing natural resources in a self governed tribal society of Arunachal Pradesh. However, the specific objectives are:

- To examine the real causes of deforestation and its impact in the state including institutional failures.
- To search the possible ways to conserve the forest in the state for sustainable development.

Therefore, this paper is divided into two sections. The section I seeks to an in-depth study to identify the causes of degradation of biodiversity while section II tries to find out the possible ways to conserve the biodiversity under sustainable development and conclusion flows.

## SECTION-I

## CAUSES OF DEFORESTATION AND ITS IMPACT

In Arunachal Pradesh we are destroying a good percentage of forest area every year. Now the question arises what factors are responsible for deforestation. Among the factors we may mention is poverty, inequality in the distribution of land, low agricultural productivity, lack of infrastructural facilities, low level of economic development, industrialization, urbanization and rapid growth of population. Major causes of forest degradation are legal and illegal land-use changes; use pressure from villages inside and outside the reserve in the form of fuelwood collection and grazing of livestock and institutions that fail to manage the forests. The grabbing of common land by the individual has been observed to a significant extent. In consequence, average distance to be covered by a household to collect CPR products has increased significantly. The size of human and livestock population, scarcity of resources (emergence of new-rich class with commercial interests), distance of the reserve area from the residential area and the quality of the management etc. are some of the important factors that determine the extent of degradation. Market close to the villages cause more severe degradation of forest resources, i.e. market plays the promotional role of forest degradation. Scarcity of commons in relation to population leads to its degradation. Though the imposition of a ban on the extraction of forest and forest products by the Supreme Court in 1996 has formally checked the illegal felling of trees, the emerging neo-merchant class are taking the advantages of local power to exploit the forest resources, and in consequence, the state ownership and management have failed to prevent the conservation and degradation of many forests.

A brief analysis of the causes of natural resource degradation and depletion in the region shows that various factors, from a long time, have resulted to the worsening of the situation causing various socio-economic hazards. By this we mean the distribution of total land area among different uses. The pattern of land use, which is a complex phenomenon, in general is the result of the action and interaction of factors like physical characteristics of land, supply of resources like labour and capital, the framework of socio-economic institutions etc. There is virtually no planning in the field of land utilization. The existing pattern of land utilization has evolved over the past few centuries under the pressure of increasing population. So far land use is concerned the north-eastern region, like other parts of the country, seems to have no planning virtually in this field and a good portion of land is lying as cultivable waste. In the north-east India even though agriculture is the only source of livelihood to the majority of people, the rational land utilization was not possible because of difficult terrain. Being agricultural backward economy, the productive forces have been arrested by retrogressive agrarian land relations. As a result, more and more area has been brought under cultivation by clearing forests, which meant damage to the ecological balance. In the first place, those who caused this damage were not aware of the repercussions of their actions. There are some major factors which are responsible for destruction of forest and thereby flora and fauna in the state discussed below.

Presently some of the major issues facing the resource managers, researchers, policy-makers, international institutions, and some NGOs are: (*i*) loss of biodiversity with its yet unknown potential consequences, (*ii*) increased rate of deforestation and fragmentation, (*iii*) inadequate knowledge of ecological functioning and complex relationships between and within biotic and abiotic components of the forest biome, (*iv*) adverse impact on indigenous communities and forest dwellers, (*v*) inadequate public awareness and lack of transparency resources exploitation (*vi*) adverse changes in soil, water and climate due to deforestation.

***Shifting Cultivation:*** However, the problem of natural resources degradation particularly forests in northeast India appeared to be very serious even during the regime of New Forest Policy explained which envisages that this strategy might have not been implemented with its true spirit. One of the assumptions of the new forest policy was that the forest dependent poor tribal communities are responsible for depletion of these resources as they not only over-exploit but also practice shifting cultivation which needs clearing of forests and hence leads to deforestation. Shifting cultivation directly reduces available forest resources and indirectly enhances soil erosion, increases silting of rivers, streams and dams, and causes an imbalance in environmental factors. More specifically, it is argued that the practice of *jhum* cultivation is the principal factor of deforestation/degradation although a generalized cause and effect relationship between loss of forest and shifting cultivation is misleading because deforestation is a complex socio-economic, cultural and political phenomenon. Moreover, the degradation caused to forests as a result of shifting cultivation depends on the habits and beliefs of the people, the area available, development index, land-man ratio, the population density and the proximity to the market. The forest resources of a specified area may be degraded due to a variety of reasons including government policy of issuing timber permits, market penetration, economic development, and practice of subsistence agriculture and so on. So far management of natural assets is concerned; the question of property rights plays an important role. Most of these resources are treated as open access due to absence or undefined property rights. But unlike other tribal regions, in northeast India communities and private individuals in most cases enjoy the rights of ownership of forest lands. As a result it seems that the new Bill on forest rights will have little impact on forest condition. Hence the real problem with respect to the management has to be analyzed in the context of socio-economic, cultural, and political set-up of the tribal communities in this remote and isolated part of the country. It is argued that the traditional institutional arrangements of tribal communities were effective in sustainable management of local resources for a long time and most likely their breakdown in recent times with the introduction of market economy and development has been behind the present situation of rapid degradation of forest and other natural resources.

The practice of shifting cultivation, cropping of forest areas for a year or two, then clearing another area leaving the first one fallow to revert to scrub forests is widely practiced by tribal communities in the hilly mountainous forest regions. The fallow periods have been gradually shortened with increase in population. If the pressure on land increases, the soil has no chance to regenerate and wider and wider tracts of otherwise productive forests get destroyed. It is noticed that the land under shifting cultivation is still increasing in the north-eastern region causing several imbalances in the ecology of the region.

Agriculture is an important and major occupation of the people of the state. According to 2001 census, about 79.66 per cent of the state's population is living in rural areas and 58.44 per cent of the total workers are cultivators. Due to scarcity of plain land in the state, the rural people have to practice shifting cultivation, i.e., *jhum* cultivation in order to fulfill their minimum requirement for food. The shifting cultivation is called slush and burn method of cultivation. It is labour-intensive process of farming with extensive use of land. The technology being primitive, the level of production and income is very low. It occupies a distinct place in the socio-economic fabric of tribal economy of this state. The man who practices *jhum* cultivation, i.e., shifting cultivation is called *jhumia*. The *jhumia* selects the field on the slope of the hill on rotation basis. Due to deterioration in fertility of soil the jhumia is compelled to shift his cultivation on another plot. He keeps the land fallow for a number of years for regeneration of forests. Again he uses the same land after a number of years. That is why, this process is also called shifting cultivation. This practice is not only done in Arunachal Pradesh but also in all north-eastern states due to lack of sufficient plain land. The area under shifting cultivation and number of families are engaged are shown in Table 12.1 in context of north-east states.

Not also are the *jhumias* facing serious economic problem because the forests in their traditional economic role are unable to sustain them, but society as a whole also has to pay a price for the extensive deforestation in the state in the form of soil erosion, floods and droughts. Therefore, any well-designed forest policy will have to divert the *jhumias* from *jhuming* by providing them with alternative occupations in the long run while in the short run, it will have to ensure that the *jhumias* can derive a higher income from their forest based occupations. Both the long- and the short-term measures have two-fold aim to protect the forests and to improve the economic condition of the *jhumias*. The two aims are complementary because forests cannot be saved without improving the standard of living of the forest-dwellers and vice-versa. Any policy to be successfully implemented has to be acceptable to the people for whom it is designed. So an exercise is to be

**Table 12.1: Shifting cultivation in the North-East Region**

| State | Annual area under shifting cultivation (sq.kms) | Fallow period (in years) | Minimum area under shifting cultivation one time or other (sq.kms) | No. of families practicing shifting cultivation |
|---|---|---|---|---|
| Arunachal Pradesh | 700 | 3–10 | 2,100 | 54,000 |
| Assam | 696 | 2–10 | 1,392 | 58,000 |
| Manipur | 900 | 4–7 | 3,600 | 70,000 |
| Meghalaya | 530 | 5–7 | 2,650 | 52,290 |
| Mizoram | 630 | 3–4 | 1,890 | 50,000 |
| Nagaland | 190 | 5–8 | 1,913 | 1,16,046 |
| Tripura | 223 | 5–9 | 1,115 | 43,000 |
| **Total** | **3869** | | **14,660** | **4,43,336** |

**Sources:** The Task Force Report on Shifting Cultivation, Ministry of Agriculture, 1983.

carried out in the course of the study on shifting cultivation in Arunachal Pradesh to find out the opinion of the *jhumias* themselves regarding their preferred occupation. It is found that although the *jhumias* are aware of the problems of *jhum* cultivation and the low economic returns derived from this occupation, the majority of them are not willing to give it up at least in the short run. The other forest-based occupations like plantations of coffee and rubber can prove to be very attractive as a source of earning a living for the *jhumias*. Social forestry and other reforestation schemes will reduce the dependence of the *jhumias* on the traditional use of forest. These measures, if successfully carried out, will regenerate the economic life of the *jhumias* as well as the forests of the state.

Deforestation, due to practice of shifting cultivation, is considered world's most pressing land use problem. The effects of deforestation on ecology are too well known. The role of forest in maintaining ground water level, preventing soil erosion and land slide, controlling flood in plains, reducing air pollution have been discussed at length in several publications. The extent of deforestation of tropical forest has caused worldwide alarm as tropical forests provide more than 50 per cent of modern medicine. Tropical forests are living museums and laboratories that have yielded only a tiny fraction of their treasures to scientific study. In course of shifting cultivation remarkable varieties of flora and fauna are disappearing, which need immediate attention for extensive and intensive studies.

The type of vegetations destroyed depends upon the length of *jhum* cycle. A dense forest of long cycle has more tree species than grasses, whereas a forest of short cycle has more number of grasses. All the forest resources are disappearing and become rare due to deforestation and illegal felling of trees. The ecological balance favouring the complete hydrological cycle has been seriously upset over the vast areas due to ignorance or lack of appreciation of methods of conserving and managing natural vegetation (whether a forest, grass land or mixed type) and of clearing the vegetation for cultivation. This misuse and destruction of plants cover combined with great increase in human and livestock population has created intense competition for natural resources. In the continued absence of conservation and correctly integrated land use system, overall habitat deterioration has become very widespread.

***Forest Grazing:*** The practice of indiscriminate livestock grazing leads to forest degradation. The excessive and uncontrolled grazing brings about a physical damage to the vegetation and cause erosion of soil, spread of disease, pests and weeds. The unlimited and continuous grazing in the forest interferes with the productive and protective functions of the forest.

***Forest Fires for Shifting Cultivation:*** Forest fires bring widespread damage to the productive capacity and the protective value of forest, destroy wildlife and damage the recreational and the scenic value. The causes may be natural, accidental or intentional etc. The preservation of forest ecosystem demands the elimination of the frequency and severity of the fires. In the months of March and April, the *jhumia* generally uses fires in the forest for *jhum* cultivation. It is generally seen everywhere in the state even in the surrounding areas of capital city, Itanagar. The government machinery becomes fails to stop it. After much hullabaloo over the burning of forest in the Capital Complex that led to the formation of an action plan and appeals from Governor Gen. (Retd.) J.J. Singh and Chief Minister Dorjee Khandu, forest burning continues, mocking at the 'action plan' (*Arunachal Front*, March 21, 2009).

***Land Tenure System in Tribal Areas:*** Communal system of landownership is most suitable for shifting cultivations. Unless there is private ownership of land or cooperative farming, permanent cultivation in the existing economic order is difficult under communal ownership.

***Law of Inheritance:*** It makes reparation from joint family early. As there is not much immovable property to inherit, no adult member is required to cling to the family property. Because of the free gift of labour under shifting cultivation, a married young man is assisted by the co-villagers to construct separate dwelling house. Villagers also give a young couple some share in the *jhum* land for cultivation.

**Religion Belief:** Many religions, customs, ceremonies and festivals amongst the tribal people are linked with shifting cultivation. There are special ceremonies at the time of clearance of *jhum* land, harvesting of products; even in case of illness spirit gods are to satisfied in jhum fields. When *jhumming* is replaced the rural people must have some alternative mass pooealing ceremonies. It is noticeable amongst the Goros converted to Christianity, that although they have changed their religion, their habits associated with *jhumming* still prevails.

***Hill top Dwelling:*** Because of their age-old preference to have dwelling house on the hill tops, it will be difficult to have such suitable hill top near the valley area suitable for permanent cultivation.

***Mixed cropping:*** Mixed cropping gives the jhumias their daily requirements of food grains and vegetables. If only one crop is grown under settled farming, the *jhumias* will have to depend for their requirements on outsiders. But in the absence of marketing facilities it will be difficult for the jhumias to get their requirements easily.

***Food Habits:*** *Jhumias* have special attachment to the rice varieties and vegetable grown in *jhum* land. Encouraging permanent cultivation will have to be associated with change of taste.

***Crop Production:*** As *jhum* cultivation is undertaken by whole village in a compact plot of land and as each homestead gets its requirement within the compact block, it becomes easier in the consolidated field to product crop from wild animals (eg. Elephant, monkey, boars, wild buffaloes) and fires compared to scattered permanent plots in hilly terrain.

***Capital Investment:*** *Jhuming* requires very little capital. If land and human labour is available, cultivation is possible. In permanent cultivation, a pair of bullocks, irrigation, land preparation by manual labour become essential.

In spirit of all these favourable factors for *jhum* cultivation, because of the pressure of population and progressive deterioration of soil in the hill slopes, it has become invariably difficult to get suitable *jhum* land on hill slopes. Extension of *jhum* cultivation in steep slopes will aggravate the problems of soil erosion and the agricultural prospect in hill and plains wil be jeopardized. Hence, *jhuming* as practiced now connot continue owing mainly to the absence of suitable land. Some alternative to *jhuming* either by field rotation or improved system of *jhuming* or by combinations of both settled farming and *jhuming* must be found out.

## Impact of Current Development on Forest

***Urbanization:*** The north-eastern states in general and Arunachal Pradesh in particular are proceeding towards the path of development though the progress is slow and uneven. Because of rapidly growing job facilities, business activities, there is a change of interest from agricultural activities to modern enterprises, government jobs, etc. which leads to the speeding up of cities and towns. Those who migrate to cities or towns are in reality pushed out of villages due to economic and social pressures. Generally the immediate outcome of urbanization is that the urban areas become over crowded which leads to congestion. For dwelling of large number of people, for opening and widening of business establishment, forests are destroyed / cleared. Finally, overall pollution (air, water, soil, noise) takes place, which are not only responsible for degradation of natural resources but also of environment. Till 1961 census the state of Arunachal Pradesh was entirely rural. There was no urban centre in the State. Census wise trend in urbanization is shown in Table 12.2.

**Table 12.2 : Censuswise Urban Centres**

| Census | No. of census Towns | Name of the census Towns |
|---|---|---|
| 1961 | NIL | - |
| 1971 | 4 | Bomdila, Along, Pasighat and Tezu |
| 1981 | 6 | Bomdila, Along, Pasighat, Tezu, Nharlagun and Itanagar. |
| 1991 | 10 | Bomdila, Along, Pasighat, Tezu, Nharlagun, Itanagar, Ziro, Roing, Namsai and Khonsa. |
| 2001 | 17 | Bomdila, Along, Pasighat, Tezu, Narlagun, Itanagar, Ziro, Roing, Namsai, Khonsa, Tawang, Seppa, Daporijo, Basar, Changlang, Jairampur and Deomali. |

**Source**: Various census report.

All these towns are administrative centres in most cases. Before the establishment of administrative centres, *these places were full of forest.* According to 1991 census 12.80 per cent people live in ten urban areas while as per 2001 census 20.41 people live in seventeen urban areas. The decennial urban growth rate in the state has been recorded as 139.63 in 1971-81, 167.04 in 1981-91 and 101.24 in 1991-2001.

***Rapid Population Growth:*** Rapidly increasing population in Arunachal Pradesh caused not only by large scale influx of people from Bangladesh and Nepal, but also by natural growth has put immense pressure on the supply of land for various purposes like housing, industrial and other development projects and also for agricultural production and grazing of animals etc. As the available land in the state is insufficient for these myriad purpose, additional land had to be procured by illegal encroachment upon the forest lands, first in the unclassified forest, then in the reserved forest also.

Rapid population growth is one of the major factors of the depletion of natural resources in north-east states in general and in Arunachal Pradesh in particular. Though it is true that population growth is welcome as it initiates and helps in the growth process of any region or country, but it is up to a certain limit beyond which it works adversely. The north-east region is witnessing excessive pressure of population, which acts as one of the causes of natural degradation. Growing population creates extra demand in terms of basic physical requirement of shelter, fuelwood, food; etc. that makes it necessary to exploit forest and other resources directly accelerating the deforestation. The direct impact of the increasing pressure of population has been in terms of absolute declinc in the area under forest as forest land that has been converted to agricultural land to meet the growing demand of growing population.

Increasing population coupled with widespread poverty has generated pressure on our natural resources and led to a degradation of agricultural land and forest. The forest resources are threatened due to overgrazing, commercial household needs, encroachment, unsustainable practices like unscientific cultivation (shifting cultivation, burn cultivation etc.) and development activities. Excessive fuelwood removal, indiscriminate felling of trees for timber needs, inadequate natural regeneration have also threatened to the rich biological diversity of 1,67,486 sq.km forest cover of north-east India with widest variety of biomass.

The human population census was conducted for the first time in Arunachal Pradesh in 1961. Population increases in 2001 by 326.23 per cent in comparison to the population of 1961. The growth of population and density of population censuswise are shown in Table 12.3.

**Table 12.3: Population Growth and Population Density Since 1961**

| Census | Persons | Population Density |
|---|---|---|
| 1961 | 3,36,558 | 4 |
| 1971 | 4,67,511 | 6 (5.58) |
| 1981 | 6,28,050 | 8 (7.50) |
| 1991 | 8,64,558 | 10 (10.32) |
| 2001 | 10,97,968 | 13 (13.03) |

**Source:** Census Report, Arunachal Pradesh, 1971, 1981, 1991 and 2001.

**Note:** (i) Figures in the parentheses show actual values.

(ii) Population Density = Total Population ÷ Area in sq. km.

The decennial population growth rate since 1961 in the state has been recorded as 38.91 per cent in 1961-71, 35.15 per cent in 1971-81, 36.83 per cent in 1981-91 and 26.21 per cent in 1991-2001. It is more than all India average.

We have observed a high trend of growth of population in Arunachal Pradesh. To see the trend of population in the state in future, we can fit a mathematical equation by the method of Least Square. Let us now construct the necessary table and make necessary computation where we take $Y$ as population and $X$ as year. We take 1981 census year as origin shown in Table 12.4.

**Table 12.4 : Calculations for Population Projection through Least Square Method**

| Census Year | $Y$(Population) | $X$(Year) | $X^2$ | $XY$ |
|---|---|---|---|---|
| 1961 | 3,36,558 | –2 | 4 | – 6,73,116 |
| 1971 | 4,67,511 | – 1 | 1 | – 4,67,511 |
| 1981 | 6,28,050 | 0 | 0 | 0 |
| 1991 | 8,64,558 | + 1 | 1 | + 8,64,558 |
| 2001 | 10,97,968 | + 2 | 4 | + 21,95,936 |
| Total | $\Sigma Y$ = 33,94,645 | $\Sigma X$ = 0 | $\Sigma X^2$ = 10 | $\Sigma XY$ = 19,19,867 |

Now, $Y = a + bX$ ....... (1) or, $\Sigma Y = na + b\Sigma X$ ....... (2) and $\Sigma XY = a\Sigma X + b\Sigma X^2$ ....... (3)

We substitute the values shown above in the equations (2) and (3), solving them, we get

$$a = 678929 \text{ and } b = 191986.7$$

We put the values in equation (1), we have $Y = 678929 + 191986.7\,X$

After getting this equation, we can find the population strength of any census year.

Suppose for census year 2011, the population,

$$Y = 678929 + 191986.7 \times 3 = 1254889.1$$

For census year 2021, the population,

$$Y = 678929 + 191986.7 \times 4 = 1446875.8$$

And for census year 2051, the population,

$$Y = 678929 + 191986.7 \times 7 = 2022835.9$$

If we compare the population of 1961, the population of 2051 will be six times more. All people especially the rural people have to response to the family programme for their own benefit in particular and for the state in general.

Again with the same procedure we can calculate to see the population density. The population density in 2011, 2021 and 2051 will be 14.80, 17.00 and 23.60.

**Growth of Non-Tribal Population:** The tribal communities in north-east India who constitute a very high percentage of the total population being economically week and socially backward, are usually dependent on natural resources for their existence. This is so because the tribal people are basically forest dwellers and from pre-historic age, they have been found to live as a close component of natural resources particularly to forest ecosystem. Forest and tribal people have a symbiotic relationship and the existence of both is mutually beneficial. The life of these primitive people is woven around forest ecology and forest resources. Forest satisfy a great range of human needs which vary from tangible raw materials (economic goods) like fuel and fodder, food and shelter, to intangible environmental benefits. The intangible vary from aesthetic enjoyment to protection against soil erosion and regulation of water supply. The primitive tribal communities collect their livelihood needs through hunting, gathering, and fishing, food production mostly at subsistence level. The forests not only provide them food, material to build house, fuelwood, fodder for the cattle, but also satisfy the deep rooted tribal sentiments. It is also necessary to note that woman and children of these communities are found to be engaged in most of the subsistence activities within the forests. Hence, the management of the forests must be for the satisfaction of the day-to-day needs of the tribals and the forest dwellers in respect of firewood, leaf fodder, small timber, edible fruit, leaves, gums, medicinal plants, resins, etc.

The indigenous people have a unique understanding of tropical forest ecology and resources because their culture has been evolved with the forests. They have learned over the centuries how to utilize the bio-resources in sustainable manner. No other person understands and loves forests as the tribal. Their lifestyle totally depends upon the forests. They are integral part of the forest ecosystem. Their biodiversity management and conservation

**Table 12.5 : Tribal Population (in %)**

| Census Year | % of Tribal People |
|---|---|
| 1961 | 88.76 |
| 1971 | 79.02 |
| 1981 | 69.82 |
| 1991 | 63.65 |
| 2001 | 64.22 |

**Source:** Different Census Issues.

system has proved to be an ideal system. If we see the census data since 1961, we get the following percentage of tribal people in the state shown in Table 12.5. If the trend keeps its same motion, we can calculate the future trend with the help of Least Squire Method taking 1981 as origin shown in Table 12.4.

***Transportation:*** Till 1947, there were only three jeepable roads between Pasighat and Kobo by 35 kilometers, Sadiya-Tezu-Denzing by 77 Kilometres and still well road 56 kilometers. So, the total length of roads was only 168 km, till 1947. Before independence the colonial government did not take any effort to initiate the development process and the British indifference towards the area was mainly due to the fact that the area did not possess any readily exploitable resources. After the independence of the country, the Government of India undertook the development of transport and communication with a view to open up this remote state of India and therefore to facilitate the rapid development of the state. In the development plans, the government has been attaching high priority to the construction of roads and as a result the total length of roads constructed in the state stood at about 15021.80 kms. including 399.80 kms under National Highway giving the road density of 17.9 kms per 100 sq.kms of area at the end of March, 2004. The development of roads and its density (Road length per 100 sq. kms.) are shown in Table 12.6.

**Table 12.6 : Category-wise Length of Roads and Its Density during 9th and 10th Plan**

(In. Km)

| Year | Total length of roads | Density of roads |
|---|---|---|
| 31.03.2000 | 13982.20 | 16.70 |
| 31.03.2001 | 13982.20 | 16.70 |
| 31.03.2002 | 13982.20 | 16.70 |
| 31.03.2003 | 14450.47 | 17.26 |
| 31.03.2004 | 15021.791 | 17.94 |

**Source:** Directorate of Economics and Statistics, Govt. of Arunachal Pradesh, Itanagar

**Note:** Density of Road = Total length of roads ÷ total area.

The impact of road transport is wide ranging which includes agriculture, industry, trade and commerce which cumulatively affect overall development of a region. But at the same time the state has to face deforestation and thereby to destroy the herbs.

---

**NCAER** Techno-Economic Survey of NEFA, 1967, p. 91.

***Industrialization:*** At present there are 14 district industries centres in the state. Three DICs provide all possible help and guidance to the prospective entrepreneurs for taking up industrial ventures and provide services for identification of suitable schemes, preparation of project reports, supply and management of raw materials and marketing of finished product, etc. The DICs also organizes trainings at district level to create awareness amongst the entrepreneurs. They also assist entrepreneurs to avail incentive packages and facilities given by both central and state government. In Arunachal Pradesh at the time of independence, there was almost absence of industry except cottage industries in the village. But at present there are 15 medium scale industries which are mostly saw mill, plywood and 11 veneer mills functioning in the state. In spite of many obstacles in the way of development of large and medium scale industries, significant numbers of small-scale industrial units have come up in the state over the year due to active support and positive policy of the government. There were 471 registered small scale industrial units functioning at the end of March 2003 mostly engaged in activities like black smithy, tin smithy, carpet making, carpentry, wool knitting handloom and weaving, cane and bamboo works, printing press, etc.

**Mining and Querying Activities:** In north-east region the unsystematic extraction of minerals is creating environmental problems thereby ruining the region's land, water, forests and air. Mining practices in large scale has made agricultural and forest land into stockyards, townships, roads etc. and also removed vegetation and topsoil. Further, constant air pollution occurs due to disposal of mining waste and mineral dust from mines and also reduces agricultural productivity. Moreover, water resources get polluted, as rain water that passes through mineral wastes, are flowing into rivers and streams. Furthermore, large-scale deforestation, soil erosion result due to mining operation, which is again responsible for various health hazards to the people.

## Impact of Deforestation

***Environmental Problems:*** Deforestation and burning of fossil fuels contribute to global warming, which has now become a local issue for every citizen for action. Therefore, restrictive exploitation of forests now in Arunachal Pradesh leads to reduction in Greenhouse Gas emissions which are the main causes of global warming. Reduction in Greenhouse Gas emissions in Arunachal Pradesh will benefit all mankind on planet earth. This state is, therefore, now contributing its bit in fighting global warming.

Deforestation does not take long, while a forest takes a very long time to develop, often hundreds of years, through a series of successive species, before it becomes a self-contained, viable eco-system. The strength of a forest system lies in its variety and the inter-dependence of its various elements. A forest maintains the humidity of the soil, its dry leaves, bird droppings and the remaining of the living organisms to add to its fertility, and the various species to support one another. The animals and insects living in the forest maintain a food chain and a balance in the production of the various species. Without forests, agriculture would die. Forest acts as a pumping station as reservoir, hoards an enormous amount of water in the leaves, stems, and roots of trees during the rainy season, and releases it slowly over the year. Without forests, the agriculture would be without water for most of the year, and there would be nothing to resist soil erosion during the months of heavy rains. Forests are necessary for maintaining the balance in the agriculture system. No less important is the need for a sound statistical base on forests, so that the policy-makers are aware of what is going on, and are able to implement a system of forest management which augment the total 'stock' of forests while at the same time producing enough of the annual 'flow' to take care of the needs of the country's economy for forest products. Selection of trees is an equally important matter, and again their impact on other species, animal husbandry, and agriculture would have to be examined, in addition to the revenue generating capacity of those trees. While a commercial approach cannot be avoided, this alone should not be the criterion, regardless of its impact on both the physical and the social environment.

The rich and varied altitudinal and climatic conditions in the territory have given rises to a wide spectrum of vegetation in which several of the important forests occur. These are tropical rain forests, the sub-tropical forests, the temperate forests, the sub-alpine forests. The tribal people depend mainly on forests for their survival, livelihood, occupation and employment. The way they exploit forests has pervasive effect on all other aspects of culture, and the socio-culture milieu emerges as an interlocking system in which case and effect are intertwined in a manner that when one element is significantly altered, it has direct and indirect repercussions on the other parts of the system. The tribal people living near the forest areas depend solely on forests and its produce. A house in a tribal village is almost made of forest produce—the roofing leaves, the posts and the walls made of bamboo and small timber, the tying canes etc. Strips of canes are used as fasteners for the rafters while building houses. The household utensils, the bamboo plates, pipes for carrying water, spoons and ladles, and the drinking cups are all shaped out of the forest produce. The people of the interior areas use beaten barks of forests trees as clothing material for specific uses. They collect many types of tuber, fruits and seeds which help these people to survive during the period of food deficit. The berries, nuts, honey, fruits and roots of all kinds abound and in the process of socializations, the tribal learns to grow which roots, berries and fruits are edible, where these are available, when and for how long etc. Hundreds of such edible items and the time of their availability are commonly known. He learns how to distinguish between poisonous and non-poisonous edible mushrooms which grow abundantly in the rainy season. Certain organic substances, leaves, flowers, roots are known to have intoxication, catalytic and decomposition and medicinal properties. Some of these are used for intoxicating fish while doing river fishing, for fermenting rice and millet beer called *Apung*, for making dyes and extracting vegetable fiber. For medicines, the tribal discerningly distinguish between various kinds of plants, weeds and herbs which have therapeutic value both curative and preventive. Some of the folk medicines of the main tribes of Arunachal Pradesh namely *Nyishi* and the *Apa Tanis* are very important. Various types of timber, bamboo, cane, leaves and fruits of medicinal value and the bark of the trees are the common items which are collected by the tribal from the forests and are sold to the people of the plains. The forests provide a good amount of animal protein to the tribal people who are now supplemented to a considerable extent by domesticated and semi-domesticated animals and poultry. A bulk of the tribal population is still depended directly or indirectly on forest and forest produce. It will remain so, unless there is drastic change in the way of life. They use herb and medicinal plants to cure their diseases. They have evolved their own system of soil and forest conservation because they are vitally concerned with preservation and continuance of forests and exemplify the age-old pattern of co-existence between man and nature.

The forest provides a good amount of revenue to the state exchequer. Other factors responsible include lack of research and market exploration, incentives to develop logging, lumbering and forest-based industries apart from paper, personnel trained in commercial management of forests and modern equipment. With the growing pressure on natural resources various forms of environmental degradation are evident in different parts of the country-especially in the north-eastern states. Wildlife resources are highly sensitive to such degradations as habitat destruction which leads to extinction of species in the majority of cases.

The status of wildlife in any area, therefore, may act as a good bio-indicator to measure environmental quality in the natural ecosystem. The important natural resources are land comprising soil, water and associated plant and animal life involving the total ecosystem. Our future depends on the preservation and improvement of the natural resources. Today, on one side we are concerned about the nature and its preservation and on the other side degradation is taking place in land, water, air etc. Soil, water and forest are land-based resources. They exist in a dynamic equilibrium with interaction among all living and non-living components of the ecosystem. Man is the only component of the ecosystem which in spite of being a part of the dynamic milieu, tends to place himself 'apart' from it, and by doing so causes great damage. In reality, the effect of humanity on the ecosystem since the dawn of the modern era has so increased that it has now become a bio-geochemical factor itself.

According to Gandhi "there is enough on earth for everybody's need, but not enough for anybody's greed". So need and greed have to be differentiated and, we must not over use or over-exploit the natural resources in the guise of development. Gandhi advises us to contain our greed and to allow our future generation to taste the fruit of real development. Spirituality helps in keeping our greed for materials and resources in check and sustainable development can take place when we use the resources for our needs and not for our greed. His advices are antidote not only to our consumerist culture but also can save the mother earth from most dangerous phenomena called "Global Warming and Climate Change".

Undoubtedly, because of deforestation the area, quality, quantity, and diversity of forest are fast decreasing. This is mainly due to the rate of deforestation, which is alarmingly faster than the natural regeneration. If a vast area is deforested rapidly, re-growth of forest over that area may take a long time depending upon the rate of regeneration in that climatic zone. Moreover, it may or may not reach to climax regeneration in foreseeable time. Due to cutting of trees not only in forest area there occur innumerable changes in the ecosystem, especially related with depletion of plant and animal species. In fact, the clearance of forest has already caused extinction of a number of species and many are either threatened or at verge of extinction. The World Commission of Forests and Sustainable Development (WCFSD) in their report (1999) has mentioned that survival of about 12.5 per cent of the world's 270,000 species of plant and 75 per cent of the world's mammals is threatened by the decline of the forest cover. The decline in the forest cover would also affect 350 million people of the world who depend entirely on forest for their subsistence (Hussain, 2002).

Loss of biodiversity and disturbance of the ecosystem continue to be a major global threat to future development, says the Fourth Report of the Global Environment Outlook (GEO) brought out by the United Nations. Disbalance in the distribution of land, fresh water and marine biodiversity is more rapid than at any time in human history. Ecosystem such as forests, wet lands and dry lands are being transformed, in some cases, irreversibly degraded. The rate of species extinction is increasing, and a great majority of them, including the commercially important fish stocks, is declining in distribution or abundance or both. Biodiversity plays multiple roles in the daily lives of people through the supply of ecosystem services. In agriculture, biodiversity contributes in regulating and supporting services through soil formation, nutrient cycling, and pollination. The Report says that poor people in rural and remote areas tend to be most directly affected by the deterioration or loss of ecosystem services. In view of this, many governments have established and adopted the 2010 biodiversity target to reduce the rate of loss of biodiversity at global, regional and national scales. Though there have been local success stories of sustainable use of biodiversity, at a global level, and in most regions of the world, biodiversity continues to be lost because current policies and economic systems do not incorporate the values of biodiversity effectively in either the political or the market systems, and many policies that are already in place, are yet to be fully implemented, says the report (*The Arunachal Times*, 2007). North-east India is a home of many endemic fauna and flora and many valuable wildlife products which originates from this region. These resources are degrading rapidly due to demand from international trade. Despite strict legislative provisions certain elements resort to illegal and unauthorized wildlife trade. The insurgency and disturbed conditions have made the law enforcement difficult and complicated the matter. Further, 98 per cent of the north-east India border is with neighbouring countries. This border is very porous and constant source of smuggling activities. The region is a storehouse of biodiversity with its species richness of flora and fauna. The NER represents a wide range of physiographic and eco-climatic conditions and is endowed with vast and luxuriant vegetation ranging from tropical to alpine with rich gene pool of both wild and cultivated plant species. The flora of the region basically exhibits an Indo-Malayan affinity. However, the flora elements of other parts of India and far off countries have also contributed to its richness and diversity. India is recognized as one of the 12 mega-diversity centres of the world because of its rich diversity of biological resources. The richness of biological diversity of the NER could be established because of its 650 species of orchids, more than 450 species of grasses, 61 species of bamboo, 65 texa of rhododendrons, 42 species of impatient, 34 species of Hedychin besides a large number of canes, timber trees, ferns, lichens and wildlife. Of 15,000 flowering plants (6% of world's total) of India 33 per cent are estimated to be endemic to north-east India. Nearly 500 plant species are threatened. Since north-east India is an area of rich endemism, a large number of endemic plant species of the region are threatened. Mammal fauna comprise of 372 species of which 63 per cent are found in Assam alone and a good number of fauna are threatened due to loss of forest covers (B.K. Sarma, 2002).

The most important natural resources are land comprising soil, water and associated plant and animal lives involving the total ecosystem. Our future depends on the preservation and improvement of the natural resources. Today, on one side we are concerned about the nature and its preservation and on the other side degradation takes place in land, water, air etc. The forest is now under threat. As a result, loss of biodiversity and disturbance of the ecosystem continue to be a major global threat to future development, says the Fourth Report of the Global Environment Outlook (GBO) brought out by the United Nations. Disbalance in the distribution of land, freshwater and marine biodiversity is more rapid than at any time in human history. Ecosystems such as forest, wet lands and dry lands are being transformed, in some cases, irreversibly degraded. The rate of species extinction was increasing, and a great majority of them, including the commercially important fish stocks, are declining in distribution or abundance or both. Biodiversity plays multiple roles in the daily lives of people through the supply of ecosystem services. In agriculture, biodiversity contributes in regulating and supporting services through soil formation, nutrient cycling and pollination. Though there have been local success stories of sustainable use of biodiversity in the state, it continues to be lost because current policies and economic systems do not incorporate the values of biodiversity effectively in either the political or the market system and many policies that are already in place, are yet to be fully implemented.

It is pertinent to mention that eastern Himalayas including Arunachal Pradesh has been identified as one of the world's 18 biodiversity hotspots. And after Rio Convention (1992), the global concern for preserving the biological diversity has increased tremendously. Forest has been playing an important role in socio-economic development of this region, specially hill tribal inhabited region, as a source of subsistence, employment, and raw-materials for industry. The indigenous people's role in ecological balance, environmental stability and sustainable development has been recognized in National Forest Policy, 1988. The forest resources of the region are under tremendous pressure due to increasing demand for human and livestock. Too much of extraction has led to forest degradation and disaster in ecological balance in recent time in this region. It is clear that north-eastern India has been fast losing its pride of place in the matter of environment and ecology. *There has been exodus of population to the hills causing damage to the forest resources.* All these have created severe problems to the whole region in the form of land sliding in the hill and siltage in the rivers. This tells upon not only on the atmospheric condition of the area but also on the livelihood of the people dependent either on forest or on agriculture or on both. Forest dwellers, belonging to different communities, tribes and religion, enjoying for long the traditional and usufractory rights over forest and other natural resources are feeling threatened by the forest policies pursued now. There has been a sense of insecurity for the great majority of the rural people who are not only threatened about their present livelihood but also very apprehensive about the future generations. The government, the NGOs and other statutory bodies concerned with improvement of environment should take appropriate and adequate initiatives. All such initiatives should aim at ensuring participation of the broad masses of tribal population. This can only be done by guaranteeing their rights on the forests and lands of the region.

**Natural Environment and Ecological Balance:** There is a great need today to create a comprehensive awareness of the need to have adequate safeguards against the destruction of the natural environment. The concern for preservation of environment is multi-dimensional and it relates itself to many disciplines and facets of the administration. The protection of environment and ecological balance are the concern of the people all over the globe. The north-eastern region of the country, which forms major part of the Indian portion of the eastern Himalayas, is not only rich in forest and related natural resources, but also very much rich in bio-diversity. It has myriads of complex problems with distinct constitutional and legal features.

Wildlife in the natural situation constitutes the most important component of the ecosystem, which participates affectively in the energy flow and bio-geo-chemical cycling. Animal–plant, plant–plant and animal–animal interactions are the basic milestone of the success of an ecosystem and its productivity. As such, the richness of the ecosystem means the capacity of hold high species diversity but deforestation has threatened the very fabric of the survival of wildlife and the ecosystem in the region. Forests are scarce and are becoming increasingly scarce due to pressure on it. It can be attributed to increase in population and demand for forest resources. The forest resources of Arunachal Pradesh are under tremendous pressure due to increasing demand for human and livestock. Too much of extraction has led to forest degradation and disaster in ecological balance in recent time in this region and this led to famous Supreme Court verdict on 12 Dec. 1996 banning exploitation of forest resources specially industrial wood in Arunachal Pradesh and other states. Timber extraction in the state was taken up on a large scale till 1995-96. Hence, a large number of woods based industries cropped up. A timber trade in the state had also increased through the operation of tree permits. There was halt on this trade after a Supreme Court judgment on 12 December, 1996 on a writ petition (civil) No. 202 filed by Shri T.N. Godavarman Thirumulkpad. In recent years, the state's rich biodiversity has increasingly come under threat. The hastening paces of developmental activities in the last three decades, and the improvement in the communication network, have meant increased access. Road building has established communication but the blasting process involved has meant the loss of valuable habitat. The rapid monetization of the barter economies has meant increased trade in timber. A number of hydropower projects have been commissioned, and these projects are at various stages of progress. The urbanization process has meant the destruction of the forest cover adjacent to the new townships that have come up. Another significant threat to the fragile ecosystem and biodiversity of the state is due to the shifting cultivation and the shortening of the *jhum* cycle and introduction of commercial plantation.

Loss of forests can be interpreted in another way which has a long run implication on our live. Destruction of forest disturbs ecological balance also. The forests regulate the earth's temperature regime, water cycle, control floods and droughts and help to balance the $CO_2$ and Oxygen in the atmosphere. Another cost of deforestation is the loss of biodiversity in the nature. The biodiversity treaty calls for the conservation of ecosystem (Rio Summit, 1992). Because of reckless destruction of forest for domestic fuel and for commercial gains about 17,000 living species are destroyed annually.

In addition, there is the illegal trade of forest projects such as timber, medicinal plants, orchids, animal hide, musk gland and birds, which are smuggled out of the state by poachers. Bio-piracy is a new challenge manifested in a number of ways. Sometimes, the operators enter the state, develop contracts, and smuggle out valuable species, mainly of flora, without the knowledge of the government. Given their highly sophisticated methods of operation, this type of bio-piracy is very difficult to detect. The creation of public consciousness, apart from the enhanced vigilance of the government, can help to control this problem. We know that each of the flora and fauna has its special genetic qualities. Different tree species has specific root system and feeding habits. The Botanical Survey of India has identified 47,688 of plant out of which 10,400 are known for their rich medicinal properties. In the north-east India, as a result of deforestation, about 650 species of plant and 70 species of animal have been listed as endangered. The region has about 50 per cent montane plants species in India of which many are endemic in nature.

Environmental problems in the state may be attributed to two major reasons: (i) due to negative effects of the process of economic growth and development and (ii) due to conditions of poverty and under-development. As per the Forest Report of 1997 based on visual and digital interpretation of satellite data pertaining to 1995-96, the total forest cover in India is 6,33,397 sq.km which is 19 per cent of the total geographical area of the country. During the period (1989-95), forest cover in north-east India was reduced by 2,037 sq.km while in the rest of the country it was increased by

933 sq.km. This reduction of forest cover in the north-east India is quite alarming.

**Medicinal Plants under Threat in the State:** Due to the shifting cultivation, growth of urbanization, growth of population, growth of transportation, growth of industrialization and overall development programmes, the hitherto virgin vegetation has become a victim of sudden large-scale changes upsetting the balance of nature. At conference in Guwahati, experts from the State Forest Research Institute, Itanagar, Botanical Survey of India and the G. B. Pant Institute of Himalayan Environment and Development, Itanagar made an assessment of 47 plant species lying under threat. Out of the 47, five are threatened at the global level and are red listed by the International Union for Conservation of Nature (IUCN). This endemic species include *Amentotaxus asamica, Coptis teeta, Gymnocladus assamicus, Piper Pedicellatum, P. Peepuloides, Aquilaria malaecensis, Dienia muscifera, Rauvolifia serpentina* and *smilax glabra* are reported to be critically endangered.

***Medical Tourism Exports by India:*** Now-a-days, India is in a position to give world class medical treatment at a low cost in comparison to the developed countries. India has advantage due to low cost of treatment, large number and high quality of Indian health care professionals, and presence of world class corporate hospitals (Apollo, Escorts), in niche areas. Presently, patients from developing and developed countries are coming to receive treatment in Indian hospitals. Health tourists from Middle-East, CIS countries, neighbouring countries, Non-resident Indians from developed countries, foreigners from some developed countries are coming every day. It is ovserved that 130,000 international patients came to India (2003) from South Asia, Africa, Gulf mainly for treatment in India. Again, many foreign patients seek treatment in traditional and alternative medicine (unani, ayurvedic, herbal treatment). The north-eastern region is the home of ayurvedic and herbal medicine. 90% herbal medicine of India is seen in this Himalayas belt. The state like Arunachal Pradesh where almost all of herbals are available has a bright scope to attract health tourists to give treatment at a low cost.

The Central Council for Research in Ayurveda and Siddha, Department of Ayush, Ministry of Health and Family Welfare, Government of India has initiated research programmes in this state from the early seventies. Accordingly it has taken up a special survey tour programme to study the traditions, culture, customs, folk medical practices and the extent of availability and the quality of the medicinal plants in the state. Consequently, the council has also initiated other important research programmes, such as clinical research programme in the state and established Regional Research Centre at Itanagar in May 1979. The status of the centre has been upgraded to Regional Research Institute with effect from 9 September 1999 with the following aims and objectives.

## Aims and Objectives of the Regional Research Centre

- Intensive clinical evaluation of selected therapies in assigned diseases.
- Specialized ayurvedic treatment in at OPD and IPD level.
- Morbidity, survey of population, health education, herbal medication and medical aids in tribal village.
- Medico-botanical exploration of Arunachal Pradesh.
- Collection and compilation of information on local healing practices from rural tribal areas.
- Development and maintenance of medicinal plants garden and supply of genuine drug materials to the research organization working under the council.

**Hydro Power Potential:** Arunachal Pradesh, having untapped estimated hydro power potential of 49,000 MW, may emerge as power house of India when this potential is fully harnessed*. Even if a part of the available hydro potential is harnessed, the state will not only be self-sufficient in meeting its own power requirement but at the same time it can earn revenue by supplying power to the other neighbouring states of the country. During 2002-03, 35 numbers of micro/mini hydel projects with an installed capacity of 32.48 MW and diesel sets with an installed capacity of 27.12 MW are the main sources of power supply in the state though the actual power requirement is 95 MW. So the state is highly deficient in power generation.

## SECTION-II

## CONSERVATION OF BIODIVERSITY UNDER SUSTAINABLE DEVELOPMENT

**Sustainable Development:** It appears that the term Sustainable Development (SD) was first used in the context of environmental degradation across generations (Raskin, 1996). However, its scope has since widened to incorporate the new realities of changing times in almost all areas of human concern. Before elaborating on the various dimensions of SD we first explore its meanings.

***Source:** Department of Power, Government of Arunachal Pradesh

The notion of SD is derived from two words—sustainable and development. Sustain means 'to maintain' or 'to uphold' something (e.g., a life, a system, etc.) by providing a minimum necessary support and/or a conducive environment. Sustainable implies 'capable of maintaining' or 'capable of upholding' and has the objective and subjective dimensions of viability and desirability respectively. Finally, Sustainability refers to the capacity or capability of systems for achieving the viable and desirable results from an activity under consideration.

Sustainable Development means 'development of the needs of the present without compromising the ability and future generations to meet their own needs'. That is, sustainability implies meeting of current human needs while preserving the environment and natural resources needed by future generations. World Bank Report speaks the sustainable development "a process of managing portfolio of assets to preserve and enhance the opportunities people face". Sustainable Development includes economic, environmental, social sustainability which can be achieved by rationally managing physical, natural and human capital. This term being used by economists and politicians all over the world and the term is constantly being refined. 'Intergenerational' equity would be impossible to achieve unless the groups stops exploitation of other groups or community living in other parts of the world.

Historical example reveals that greater economic development was achieved at the cost of inequality, unemployment, weak democracy, loss of cultural identity, over exploitation of natural resources leading to ecological and economical imbalances resulting in a dire threat for both flora and fauna. To be sustainable, we must rely on certain amount of natural resources available in nature to absorb pollution and regeneration of resources.

In Rio de Janeiro in June 1992, United Nations Conference on Environment and Development, 1992, para 2.1, it is declared, "Human beings are at the center of concern for sustainable development. They are entitled to a healthy and productive life in harmony with nature". Sustainable development assumes high substitutability among different, components of national wealth. Depletion of natural resources can be compensated with high investment on education, i.e., human development and physical capital development which make ways for replacement of old technology to new technology to have effective usage of non-renewable resources at lesser level.

Economic development comes through the judicious and efficient application of three forms of capital—human capital, physical capital and natural capita. The first two types of capital are known as produced capital whereas natural resources are defined as assets gifted by the nature. Non-renewable natural resources such as mineral resources and some other, though renewable like forests and fish resources, may be exhausted if the rate of exploitation exceeds regeneration rate in the process of economic exploitation. As a result the scope of future development stands limited because of the irreversibility and non-substitutability character of most of the natural resources. To achieve 'sustainable development *i.e.*, uninterrupted long term development, we have to keep ourselves very alert on our exploitation of our natural resources. Sustainable development does not forbid the use of natural resources but restricts their use in such a way that enough, or as much as possible, is left for the future generation; not only for future but even for day-to-day use. When poor people have little access to the capital available in the 'organized' or market economy, they meet their most basic needs as best they can through subsistence activities. The poor live within a biomass-based subsistence economy; all their fundamental needs (food, fodder, fuel-firewood, cow dung, crop-wastes, fertilizer-dung, manure leaf-litter, building materials-timber, thatch, and herbal medicines) are collected (often freely) from the immediate environment.

The traditional knowledge of the biological materials of these tribes is very vast which is often kept secret and passed to next generation through verbal tradition as well as through the individuals gifted with a state of spiritual embodiment possessing quality of rare eloquence and power of observation. The system has tremendous potential to evolve planning strategies for conservation and management of biodiversity and improving indigenous economy as well as environmental security of tribal habitat and thus sustainable development of the state.

Major causes of forest degradation are legal and illegal land-use changes; use pressure from villages inside and outside the reserve in the form of fuel wood collection and grazing of livestock; and institutions that fail to manage the forests. The grabbing of common land by the individual has been observed to a significant extent. In consequence, average distance to be covered by a household to collect CPR products has increased significantly. The size of human and livestock population, scarcity of resources (emergence of new-rich class with commercial interests), distance of the reserve area from the residential area and the quality of the management etc. are some of the important factors that determine the extent of degradation. Market close to the villages cause more severe degradation of forest resources, i.e. market plays the promotional role of forest degradation. Scarcity of commons in relation to population leads to its degradation. Though the imposition of a ban on the extraction of forest and forest products by the Supreme Court in 1996 has formally checked the illegal felling of trees, the emerging neo-merchant class are taking the advantages of local power to exploit the forest resources, and in consequence, the state ownership and management have failed to prevent the conservation and degradation of many forests.

1. A periodic exploitation of natural forest should be done on scientific basis. This will help in removing the diseased and unwanted trees to maintain a health density of forest. This, however, should not affect the bio-diversity of the region.
2. People living in and around the forest and largely depending upon the forest resources should be allowed to collect forest products for their subsistence and survival. Even the government is planning to suggest to the Supreme Court to reconsider its decision on the total ban on felling of trees in such areas. In fact, a local need-based forest policy can be framed and implemented for forest management, which will keep in mind the interests of the forest and its dwellers. A family depending entirely on forest may even be permitted to collect forest products and sell them to earn enough for their livelihood, of course, not for any big commercial purpose. There is a clear-cut distinction between the minimum needs of the family and the commercial exploitation of the forest.
3. Ecosystem-based forest management has to be adopted to maintain ecological balance. For example, cutting of forest of tropical belt is much more dangerous than that of the temperate belt. It is because, the nutrients are looked up in the biomass in the former, and in the soil in the later, i.e., organic cycle and physical cycle, respectively. Hence, cutting of the tropical forest leads to breakdown of the ecosystem itself, giving rise to number of environmental problems. Therefore, forest or trees should be grown in the tropical belt, because here nutrient cycle is 'biological'. In the deforested areas of the temperate zone, crops should be grown, as nutrient cycle is 'physical' here, means all the nutrients are in soil, not in the forest cover. This will give optimum results.
4. Each village, town, industry, and those who need forest products should own tree fields to meet their respective demands.
5. All virgin forest should be declared 'sacred groves' to preserve them for posterity.

***Plantation of Jatropha: An Alternative way for Income of Rural People and Fuel for Future:*** Jatropha curcus is a drought resistant perennial plant growing well in marginal and poor qualitative soil. It is easy to establish, grows relatively quickly and produces seeds for 50 years. The plant produces seeds with an oil content of up to 37 per cent in it. The oil can be combusted as fuel without being refined. It burns with clear smoke-free flame, tested successfully as fuel for simple diesel engine. The by-product is press cake a good organic fertilizer. Its oil contains also insecticide. It is now cultivated in many parts of the country and easily survive with minimum inputs in wastelands. It has also many medicinal values for diseases like cancer, piles, snake-bite, paralysis, etc. A good crop can be obtained with little effort. Oil can be extracted from the seeds after 2 to 5 years after plantation. This can be an important source of income of rural people and thereby diverting the *jhumia* from their shifting cultivation. But it is not economically viable and very much labour intensive cultivation. But from the ecological point of view only barren land can be used for the purpose.

***Incentive and Encouragement to the Poor People:*** Financial credit, technical assistance and organizational support can help to relieve constraints related to rural poor household's awareness, technology, capacity to invest and local institutional capacity. Co-investment with local communities may be used to mobilize longer term investments through group or micro-credit with labour mobilization or provision of key inputs. Well-organized local participation in project design and management is essential.

Tribal should be encouraged to take *up horticulture, floriculture, agro-forestry, growing of medicinal and aromatic plants* on hill slope which will not damage the fragile hill ecology. These can play a crucial role in relieving constraints related to a lack of technologies suitable for poor household. Such technologies and resource management systems must raise overall productivity, both increasing household income (to reduce poverty) and protecting or improving the natural resource. Poor rural households have few economic incentives to manage their natural resource more carefully.

***Natural Resource Based Entrepreneurship in North-East:*** In north-east there is tremendous scope for agro-based industries, agro forestry, horticulture, mushroom farming, herbal, medicinal and aromatic plants, bio-technology, fruit and vegetable processing, handlooms and handicrafts, bee keeping, meat and poultry products, cereal-based products, consumer industry, milk and milk-based products, food processing, paper products, jute and mestas products, cattle rearing, fishery, edible oil, processing of oils and fragrances, gas-based intermediary products, floriculture-spices production and processing wood-based products, etc.

***Exploration of Natural Resources in Planned way:*** People should be made aware of the consequences of the degradation of natural resources due to exploration of natural resources and the need to minimize them. Efforts must be made for ensuring optimum utilization and conservation of natural resources which will not only increase national output but also will improve living condition of the people. The schemes of afforestation and tree planting should be extensively done specially by the NGOs and government agencies and proper steps should be taken for continuous maintenance of those areas at least in the initial stages. It may be mentioned that though this type of schemes were undertaken earlier but could not give desired result due to lack of proper maintenance. People should also realize the potent dangers of deforestation and take active interest for successful implementation of the afforestation schemes. In this regard Environment Awareness Schemes seem to be fruitful if the message can reach the remotest corner of the region. Efforts should be made to ensure optimum utilization and conservation of natural resources, which will increase both the national output and improve the living standard of the people of the region.

Forestry development in the region can take place through harnessing the community institutions for the purpose of food-fodder, fuel and timber extraction requirement of the people. Further it is also essential to ensure greater coordination between the government machinery, people and voluntary organizations in regard to enhancement of productivity of forest and forest land under protective care and supervision. Private sector investment should also be encouraged upto some extent. Aforestation of identified areas (wastelands, catchment areas of hydroelectric projects and watershed management projects) and regeneration of forest in abandoned *jhum* land will be helpful in improving the environment sustainability. The centrally sponsored programmes related to agro-forestry, social-forestry, wasteland development and other employment generation programmes should be given more emphasis on this region.

***Land-use Pattern:*** Basically, the land-use pattern of a particular region is by and large determined by the nature and general lay out of the physical as well as cultural elements. Primarily, the physical factor like climate, topography set the broad limits upon the capabilities of the land; subsequently, the human factors like length of occupation of the area, density of population, social and economic factors, especially system of land tenure and the technological levels of the people, determine to an appreciable degree the extent to which the physical capacities of land are utilized. Efforts should be made for more intensive people's participation in forest management. It is the people's involvement that will be able to create mass awareness more effectively for preserving the forestry of the region.

Innovations are needed to facilitate poor people's access to natural resources through its more sustainable use whether it is owned or controlled by or shared with others. Land reforms process if taken up in the near future, must ensure secure access by the poor households for both productive and consumptive uses, yet make provision for environmental uses of village commons. Formal arrangements are needed for access to critical resources by the increasing numbers of temporary migrants (e.g., from natural disasters), to limit over-exploitation and conflict. Groups of poor people can be involved in land-use planning efforts to ensure that their existing use patters and future needs can be met without increasing poverty or resource degradation. Finally, poor households need insurance systems—cash payments, in-kind provisions or public works employment—to provide subsistence needs after crop failures so natural resources are not over-exploited as emergency reserves. Governments, non-governmental organizations (NGOs) and the private sector should to co-invest in the rehabilitation or improvement of productive on-farm natural resources that are assets of the poor households.

***Government Policy:*** In order to offset the loss of revenue from forests, the Government of India has given direct fiscal assistance to the state on the recommendations of the Twelfth Finance Commission and is promoting development of non-timber forest products particularly bamboo through a fully funded centrally sponsored scheme. Development of bamboo, cane and medicinal plants are thought to have great potentials for employment generation and economic development. The state should particularly evolve a forest sector development policy, bamboo policy and land-use policy before any further delay. These measures would go a long way in improving the environmental governance in the state.

***Government's Steps:*** 1. The state has to move away from fossil-fuel based, sustainable development processes and adopt alternative sustainable process that provide basic livelihood and social security to all people; this could be done by adopting a clear set of indicators of sustainability (for example, non-conventional energy sources).

2. All leasing of the state's remaining forest areas to mines, industries and other large-scale commercial or development project must halt immediately.

3. *Role of NGOs:* Government agencies and NGOs need to urgently facilitate communities to derive sustainable forest-based livelihoods and provide other sources of employment and livelihood including through the National Rural Employment Guarantee Act. Simultaneously the government has to identify and arrange alternative health, education and other such amenities that do not end up destroying the forest; this can best be done by building on existing traditional knowledge and process of learning rather than completely replacing them.

One of the important components of effective forestry planning is involving the people in the protection and regeneration of forest because forest can never be protected unless the people are made to feel about the necessity of the forest.

In this respect, the NGOs can also play an important role in forest conservation and preservation among the people of Arunachal Pradesh. The tribes of Arunachal Pradesh had their own system of forest conservation and management but due to modernization and introduction of monetary economy, much of it has been lost. Hence, it is the NGOs who can make the local people more aware about the age-old tradition of the preservation of forest resources and help them to conserve the forest resources of the state. It should be noted that unless social consciousness about forest promotion and conservation do not grow or revive among the people, the government's efforts will be of no use. It is the NGOs, who can motivate people at the grassroots level.

4. The state and central governments would do well to take care of the increasing signs of unrest and hostility in the regions where unsustainable development is being imposed.

***5. Forest Management:*** With the advent of scientific forestry in 1946, the effort of the State Forest Department (now Environment and Forest Department) has been to conserve the forests and wildlife, to maintain the ecological balance, and to promote sustained socio-economic development of the local people. A humble beginning was made with an area of 534 sq kms of reserved forests handed over by the government of Assam. Over the years rapid strides have been taken in bringing large areas under scientific management besides associating the people in protection, development and management of the forests. The predominantly tribal population of the state lives in close association with and depends largely on the forest resources. Therefore forest management efforts seek to elicit the involvement and cooperation of the people while safeguarding their customary rights over the land.

Hitherto, forestry has been confined to reserved forests. But now with the growing emphasis on peoples' participation, forestry is gradually catching up as a land-use practice even in the traditionally owned community lands under the schemes of social forestry, wasteland development, national afforestation programme and national bamboo mission. These activities are being taken up in joint forest management mode. For this purpose, forest development agencies and village forest management committees have been constituted in various forest divisions (SFRI Information Bulletin, No. 27, 2008).

***Arunachal Pradesh State Pollution Control Board:*** Arunachal Pradesh State Pollution Control Board (APSPCB) has been constituted under the provisions of the Central Rules—Water (Prevention and Control of Pollution) Act, 1974 by the government of Arunachal Pradesh on 6th July 1993 in order to regulate the new rules in the state. Due to increasing **concerns** for environmental issues and realization about the need for protecting the environment from various polluting ingredients, several acts have been enacted and brought under the purview of Environment Protection Act, 1986. The Board is headed by a full time chairman and a senior IFS officer as Member Secretary. The Board is required to be further strengthened. The SPCBs/ PCCs, all over the country have been entrusted with the responsibility of monitoring and ensuring the implementation of these acts by various agencies (*SFRI Information Bulletin,* No. 27, 2008).

***Arunachal Pradesh Biodiversity Board:*** The government of Arunachal Pradesh has constituted Arunachal Pradesh Biodiversity Board in March 2005 with Chief Secretary as Chairman and Director, State Forest Research Institute as Member Secretary and Chief Executive Officer. The Board has other senior officials and scientists as members.

Functions of the Arunachal Pradesh Biodiversity Board are as follows:

1. Advise the state government subject to any guidelines issued by the central government on matters relating to the conservation of biodiversity, sustainable use of its components and equitable sharing of the benefits arising out of the utilization of biological resources.
2. Regulate requests for granting of approvals or otherwise for commercial utilization or bio-survey and bio-utilization of any biological resource by Indians.
3. Perform such other functions as may be necessary to implement the provisions of Biological Diversity Act, 2002, or as may be prescribed by the state government.

The National Biodiversity Authority provides some financial assistance for setting up infrastructure facilities and towards running expenses of the board. Arunachal Pradesh State Biodiversity Strategy and Action Plan prepared by the State Forest Research Institute have been approved by the Central and State Government (*SFRI Information Bulletin,* No. 27, 2008).

***Compensatory Afforestation/NPV Scheme:*** In Arunachal Pradesh many developmental projects are implemented after formal diversion/ de-reservation of forest land under Forest (Conservation) Act, 1980 by the Government of India. The user agencies remit funds for undertaking compensatory afforestation as per the provisions of Forest (Conservation) Act, 1980. The Hon'ble Supreme Court of India vide their order dated 30th October, 2002 and 1st August, 2003 in IA No. 566 in WP (Civil) No. 202 of 1995 ordered realization of Net Present Value (NPV) against the diverted forest land. The user agencies now remit NPV also along with funds for Compensatory Afforestation. The central government has constituted a body called the Compensatory Afforestation Fund Management and Planning Authority (CAMPA). The funds received from the user agencies are sent to

CAMPA which in turn is released to the state for implementing the Action Plan for NPV fund and Compensatory Afforestation Scheme. Conservator of Forests (Conservation) in the office of PCCF and Principal Secretary (Environment and Forests) is the nodal agency for dealing with the F.C.A cases including implementing the NPV and Compensatory Afforestation Schemes by utilizing the funds received from CAMPA (*SFRI Information Bulletin,* No. 27, 2008).

All the government rules, regulations and schemes should be strictly carried out. The new Scheduled Tribes and Other Forest Dwellers (Recognition of Forest Rights) Act, 2006 is reframed in such a way that community should be given more chance to shoulder more responsibility to manage all the forest regulation Acts.

The debates and developments with regard to the draft of National Environment Policy (NEP), 2004 and the Scheduled Tribes (Recognition of Forest Rights) Bill (STB), 2005 were illustrative in different ways of the manner in which social concerns were dealt with in environmental policy and legislation in India. Yet, while the pros and cons of specific policies and legislations had been central to the academic debates on the environment, very little attempt had been made to trace the changes in environmental policy-making and the way of social concerns still remains problematized.

The government schemes that should have helped communities with securing livelihoods have sometimes done the reverse. For instance, Joint Forest Management (JFM) was meant to create spaces for vulnerable sections of the community to benefit from regenerated forest resources. Certainly in several sites this has helped. However, very often the participation of local people has remained on paper; in any case, the governance framework of JFM is not conducive to power-sharing between the forest department and the communities. In addition to this, JFM has in many cases been superimposed on Community Forest Management (CFM), undermining existing institutions that communities have created.

***Community Rights:*** Our specific focus with regard to social concerns is community rights to resources—a concern that is central to many of the debates on natural resource management. Three arguments are put forth: (i) that while the environment has at one level assumed a non-negotiable presence in policy, social concerns are only highlighted to the extent that they are deemed not to be environmentally destructive, (ii) that the discursive terrain through which social concerns are deemed harmful is overly simplistic and in need of re-examination and (iii) that the changing nature of environmental discourse can only be understood within the wider shifts in development policy. Although there are many who would claim that the environment itself receives an inadequate attention in development policy, a contention that is at least partly true, we are concerned herewith how emerging policies and legislations tackle social concerns given the socially constructed nature of the environment.

While the discursive thrust of much of environmental policy-making in the late 1970s and early 1980s was on incorporating environmental principles in sectoral planning, something that was matched with legislative intervention, the latter part of the 1980s saw the focus shift towards sustainable development. The importance of this shift was that the link between social and environmental concerns was more forcefully articulated.

The 1988 National Forest Policy (NFP) was the first "environmental" policy document in India that explicitly recognized the linkages between environmental and social concerns in terms of community rights to natural resources. Unlike the previous forest acts that privileged revenue and commercial interests, the NFP was strikingly different. Section 4.6 of the policy highlighted the symbiotic relationship between tribals and forests and the need to involve tribal communities in the management of forests. It also emphasized that domestic requirements of firewood, fodder and minor forest produce should be the first priority of forest management, not commercial or industrial needs.

The 1990 government order on JFM, while giving communities adjacent to reserved forests usufruct rights, was also aimed at improving the protection of forests. As Kolavalli (1995) has argued, citing a number of state-level government orders, JFM was the forest department's way to involve communities in the management of forests as it was incapable of doing it on its own.

But JFM has remained a policy and has not been incorporated into the Forest Act. Thus, while the NFP recognized the symbiocity of forest dependent (tribal) communities with forest, right afforded to these communities have been limited and often no more (sometimes less) than existing settlement rights.

In 2000, the ministry of environment and forest (MoEF) actually gave an NGO Kalpavriksh, the coordinating role in preparing a national biodiversity strategy and action plan (NBSAP) in consort with 15 members Technical and Policy Core Group. In terms of strategies, the report specified that "empowered local community institutions" should be the implementers of the plan. It would have appeared, therefore, that a good opportunity for decentralized natural resource management where communities were given rights to resources was on the anvil (Kothari, 2004). However, before the NBSAP was completed in 2003, the National Biodiversity Act, 2002 was passed, although one of the explicit objectives of the Act was the recognition of local rights to biodiversity. The National Biodiversity Act, 2002 does recognize the need for local biodiversity committees; the actual powers given to these committees again are mostly managerial in nature. Under Section 41, these committees are constituted for "promoting conservation, sustainable use and documentation of biological diversity including preservation of habitats, conservation of land races, folk varieties and cultivars, domesticated stocks and breeds of animals and micro-organisms and chronicling of knowledge relating to biological diversity" [NBA, 2004:20].

These three cases have a number of things in common. First, different policies, programmes and laws within particular sectors are often not in consonance with each other in terms of their normative position vis-a-vis community rights. For example, while the National Environment Policy (NEP) has made some headway by recognizing tribal rights to forest produce, JFM as a programme has actually given limited usufruct rights to only those who are part of FPCs. Moreover, the Forest Act has remained un-amended with no room for community-based forest management except in the context of village forests (Menon, 2006).

***Conservation of biodiversity:*** The Convention, which was signed by majority of the Nations during the UNCED Earth Summit held in Rio de Janerio in June 1992, is now an International Law. The World Conservation Strategy takes into consideration the human impacts and the perils that may threaten the future of the world's life supporting systems. It clearly defines three global objectives of living resources conservation:

1. To maintain essential ecological process and life support systems
2. To preserve genetic diversity
3. To ensure the sustainable utilization of species and ecosystems.

Conservation of biodiversity is the management of human use of the biosphere so that it may yield the greatest sustainable benefit to present generation, while maintaining its potential to meet the needs and aspirations of future generations. In this respect, the NGOs can also play an important role in forest conservation and preservation among the people of Arunachal Pradesh. The tribes of Arunachal Pradesh had their own system of forest conservation and management but due to modernization and introduction of monetary economy, much of it has been lost. Hence, it is the NGOs who can make the local people more aware about the age-old tradition of the preservation of forest resources and help them to conserve the forest resources of the state. It should be noted that unless social consciousness about forest promotion and conservation do not grow or revive among the people, the government's efforts will be of no use. It is the NGOs, who can motivate people at the grassroots level.

***Systematic Study:*** It is very important to do a systematic study of these forests products to evaluate their nutritional and medicinal values. On the basis of such study the forest planner may consider the viability of growing such plants commercially for use by a wider array of people.

## Other Preservation and Sustainable Use, Restoration and Enhancement

- In situ and ex situ conservation of forest genetic resources through establishment of biosphere reserves, national parks and sanctuaries.
- Protection of exceptional and rare trees in preservation plots.
- Creation of public awareness of rational utilization of valuable forest resources.
- Promotion of public involvement in the management of protected areas.
- To increase areas under preservation plots to include all forest types and scientifically monitoring of the plots.
- Promotion of eco-restoration of degraded forest areas.
- Regeneration of rare and threatened species and introduction of such plants in suitable habitats.
- Establishment of ethno-botanical forest parks.
- Vigorous community participation to medicinal and rare plant conservation.
- Creation of State Information and Data Base (SIDB) centres of forest species, medicinal and aromatic species. Wild relatives of cultivated species, wildlife species along with establishment of bioresource centres.
- Identification of traditional knowledge-base and species exploration to conserve diversity in agro-ecosystems and for promoting sustainability in farming systems.
- High raised areas should be developed in National Parks and Sanctuaries for protection of wildlife during flood and other natural calamities, so to prevent from migrating wild animals during flood and drought.
- Reduction and replacement of areas under shifting cultivation system by alternative farming systems.
- Environmental educational awareness building and motivation should form strategy in conservation issues.
- Implementation of clear cut forest policy implementation.

Human interference has greatly threatened the natural ecosystem of the region. The forests of the region have dwindled to a great extent due to indiscriminate human intervention, endangering large number of plant and animal species which are facing extinction.

We have to grow trees for timber, fuelwood, fodder medicine and other uses on land not meant for agriculture. Trees, especially the timber trees, have to be cultivated on non-agricultural land or 'tree fields'. The grown up trees can be cut to meet the demands. The tree cultivation has to be started in subsequent years in different tree fields, so that annual requirement can be fulfilled from the matured trees in different years. This will enable the tree cultivator to reap the harvest every year or whenever the trees are cut for use. This time-based cultivation of trees would ensure sustainable availability of timber and other forest based products. It is worth mentioning that such practice has already started in various parts of the North-East India.

***Local Industries:*** The absence of local industries to process the forest resources inside the state is another problem. Since no such industries existed or established, the resources have to be exported to outside only. If there is local consumption through industries, finished products will only be exported to outside and the resources will be able to be utilized in a planned way that will not deplete the natural stock. The government should try as much as possible to establish local industries based on local resources.

***Other Forest Management:*** This task of managing forest resource cannot be done by foresters alone. Local communities have to realize this and have to come forward to join hands with foresters for protecting and conserving this primary source. Arunachal Pradesh has been declared as one of the hotspots of mega biodiversity in the world.

Forest management practices are implemented in the reserved forests and protected forests only and under the control of the state government, that is, through the approved working plans. So, far the remaining forest of the state under the control of the autonomous district councils and private ownership are without working plans which are very essential for the sustainable harvest and management.

***Land Tenure System:*** The state has a peculiar land tenure system where large extent of the land belonged to the community, villages, clans and private individuals. Enforcement of rules and regulation becomes a difficult task. No doubt the system is very good but proper scientific and systematic management is very difficult especially on the part of exploitation and utilization of forest resources.

***Lack of Awareness:*** In general, the awareness on the environmental aspect is far from expectation. The rural population is supposed to be the main group which lived and depend on forest resources, but they are unaware of the importance of conservation and utilization. Due to their ignorance they are being exploited to the extent that may be detrimental to their existence.

***Publicity:*** Increase appreciation and awareness of environmental values and importance of conservation have to be promoted in order to get a satisfactory result. Through mass communication, awareness programmes, trainings and interactions, seminar, and symposium the people are to be made aware of the things around them. Related institutions both governmental and non-governmental will have to be involved to make the population understand the importance of environment.

***Forest Protection Force:*** A handsome amount of fund is required to fully equip the forest protection force with sophisticated arms and ammunition against the fully armed timber smugglers and also to carry out regular eviction operations to drive out the encroachers from lands.

## Suggestions

No doubt management of forest is one of the most important and complicated subject and is guided by the variety of factors. The important factors may be forest resources condition, forest policy, local requirements, industrial commitments, economic and ecological considerations etc. Once the decision about the objectives of management of the forest is taken, the detailed procedure of felling trees, regeneration management systems, control of yield and other operations can be easily worked out.

In the physiographical and socio-economic condition of the region, where tribal communities have to depend heavily on traditional practices of forest exploitation, the right approach to forestry is to plan forest development in such a manner that there would be a net addition to a perpetuating stock even after meeting the essential food, fodder, fuel and timber requirement of the people, as well as, the growing requirement of commercial exploitation. It is also necessary to focus other important aspect namely, the conservation of forest resources and control of harmful exploitation. It is worthwhile to introduce the basic elements of community forest management strategy with the community as the unit management. This will help forestry to play a si nificant role in rural development, maintenance of stream flow and preventation of floods in the plains. Strategies will have to be developed for tackling various problems in connection with forest management in the region.

In India, 1972 Wildlife (Protection) Act was introduced with specific provision to control trade and commerce of wildlife and its products. The Act has been amended thrice, i.e., in 1982, 1986 and 1991. Gradually this trade was discouraged. Initially the Act has divided Animals in five schedules. By Wildlife Amendment Act, 1991 a new schedule VI was added with imported legislative protection to six species of plants becoming rare and facing extinction. The Act as amended till date prohibits trade in all species of animals included in Schedule I and Schedule II (Part II) and increased penalty for violators. No fresh hunting can be done for commercial purpose (Diksit, 2002). But it is a matter of sorry to say that meat of wild animals are sold in open markets of every district headquarters even in capital market, Itanagar till this year, 2009.

If villagers are made partners in the use of potential and over the benefits of, they are more likely to take interest in its protection. A food for work programme may be an example for a successful management. Sharing the responsibilities with local communities and NGOs to interact with all user agencies through forest collaboration, can go a long way for sustainable management of forest and development of society. It is realized that poverty, environmental degradation and population growth are inextricably related and that none of these fundamental problems can be successfully addressed in isolation. However a commonly acceptable sustainable development still remains a challenge for all engaged in development process. One of the important components of effective forestry planning is involving the people in the protection and regeneration of forest because forest can never be protected unless the people are made to feel about the necessity of the forest.

In the pretext of change in forest policy in 1988, the idea of Joint Forestry Management came and it was adopted by various states of the country. However, the JFM model will require suitable modifications to be workable in the hill state like Arunachal Pradesh where 62.17 per cent of the total forest areas are mainly under the traditional ownership of local village committees. At the same time, there is enough scope to shift focus from government forests by bringing more virgin USF to JFM. network. The concept of *Apna Van* has received enthusiastic and wide acceptance among some of the local tribes in Arunachal Pradesh.

## Conclusion

In the exploitative development model, the forests were looked upon by man as a resource pool of only timber and other industrial raw materials. This idea has since been changed. Forest now managed also for wildlife, medicinal and other beneficial plants, eco-tourism, and soil and water conservation as well as for meeting the local and industrial needs. However, research efforts are necessary to explore new avenues for development and at the same time for restoration and maintenance of ecosystem. Moreover, large patches of the forest in the world still exist as virgin forests which provide a niche to a large number of species of great biodiversity. These offer an excellent situation for study of ecosystem without human influence. Assessing the economic impact of ecological degradation requires an understanding of the value of ecosystem. Particular attention is required to be given to environmental value of the forest because the ecosystems still continue to contribute to the well being of the people. Given such multi-facet dimension of complexity, conservation and management of forest resources, including eco-development of the region continue to remain a special challenge.

The interests of people depending on the forests products for their livelihood would have to be protected by providing training and employment opportunities in alternative occupations. The population increased and modernization are realities of the day when we plan for the future, new ideological statements are not enough, but one should have proper action plan. It is necessary that a systematic forestation and plantation programmes to be undertaken to increase the forest cover. It is worthwhile to consider allowing barren land to be brought under forest cover by private sector.

For conserving and managing natural vegetation the *jhum* cultivation and illegal felling of trees, which are the root cause of deforestation, must be stopped immediately but not without rehabilitation of the *jhumias*. If the government is successful to protect the natural vegetation, the state will be the richest in having the Herbs which can be sold in national and international markets. Hence, it is necessary first to develop the market for Herbs within the state where the local cultivators will be benefited economically. It will give an incentive to the local people to protect the valuable Herbs from extinction.

For the betterment of lives, urbanization, transportation, industrialization are necessary but we can try to minimize the deforestation due to shifting cultivation and illegal falling of trees which are the main cause of disappearance of flora and fauna in Arunachal Pradesh. The central government as well as the state government should give top priority to protect the herbs of economic value in the state which are endowed more than 50 per cent of herbs of the country. Days are not far when the governments can generate employment as well as earn foreign currency from the export of the state's herbs if they try to take kin interest to protect the existing herbs from disappearance due to impact of the factors mentioned above.

The foresters, wildlifers, conservationists, ecologists, geographers, pedologists and agronomists collectively need to have a good deal of co-ordination with sociologists, and anthropologists for understanding the bad effect of degradation of natural resources and work in the same view for its conservation. A synthesis of traditional knowledge and modern scientific outlook is necessary to evolve a method for improving tribal tradition economy confirming to security.

It is clear that there is a need for conservation of forest in the region. As there are many people maintaining their livelihood from forest, we should chalk out proper aforestation programme which will ultimately satisfy the growing demand for products. But at the time of aforestation we should use multiple species for plantation. Environmentalists have been warning about the damage of planting a single species over a large area. This is because any insect or disease outbreak can wipeout the entire tree plantation, leading to ecological and financial crisis. Monoculture may deplete the nutrients at a particular profile of the soil and cause nutritional deficiency in the long run. The principle behind bio-diversity is to encourage the conservation of a wide range of flora and fauna in a given area to ensure an ideal nutrient cycle, as well as, food chain which are important aspects of ecological balance. Preservation of plants and animals are necessary, because our present knowledge about them is confined to a small number of species and the benefits of the remaining millions of plants and animal species are not known to us today. Nevertheless they play an important role in maintaining the ecological balance (Hegde, 1994).

Total comprehension of the problems is essential and this can only emerge if there are attitudinal changes in both the government and the people. Education on environment from lower classes and training at different levels will go a long way to solve some of these problems.

Development of overall environment will be a nursery bed of co-operation and harmony as opposed to mindless competition and conflicts. We must dare act and go beyond and behind nature to seek the main purpose of existence. Saving the tree is only a first step for saving ourselves. Only then sons of the earth will repossess the earth and an enjoyable period of time will be ushered in.

It is found that accessible natural forests particularly in the foothills of Arunachal Pradesh are under great pressure to a large scale due to extraction of timber and illegal felling of trees. Although the demand for wood for local consumption is relatively low due to low population of the state but in view of the increasing demand for industrial timber within the state and other parts of the country, the forest in the state are under great pressure. As per the official estimate, the state contributes to nearly 50 per cent of the timber supply made from the north-eastern region of India. At the same time, it is observed that there is large scale illegal felling of trees, which is many times more than the official permits issued for felling of trees. The tree permit system in unclassified state forest (D.S.F.) which was introduced to enable the local people to earn their livelihood in logging and extraction of timber with a view to generate income has led to the emergence of a 'neo-rich' class in the traditional tribal society to make easy and quick money in collaboration with private forest contractors. There is a growing social and political pressure to over exploit the forest and the protection of forest are becoming increasingly difficult.

China and Southeast Asian countries have already demonstrated their capability in bio-resource management. China in particular has made great strives in transforming its rural economy through bamboo. Chinese people have replaced wood by bamboo in almost all their industrial, construction and domestic applications. This has considerably reduced pressure on their natural forests. Forest cover in China has increased while India's has remained stagnant. There is, therefore, need for this state to learn about bamboo sector from China particularly in the areas of policy, legal and institutional arrangements which were behind their success story on bamboo (*SFRI Information Bulletin*, No. 27, 2008).

## REFERENCES


1. Azad, N.A. (2004), "Poverty and Sustainable Development", in S. Bhatt (ed.) *Poverty and Food Security in India*, Aakar Books, Delhi, pp. 106-110.
2. Bhattacharjee, R.P. (2000), *Economic Development of Arunachal Pradesh*, Himalayan Publishers, Delhi, Itanagar, pp. 17-18 and pp. 45-49.
3. Bhattacharjee, R.P. (2006), "Forest Economics in Arunachal Pradesh and its Impact on State Economy", *Arunachal Review*, Vol. VIII, No. 18, June-August, Naharlagun, Govt. of Arunachal Pradesh.
4. B.K. Sarma & *et.al.,* (2002), "Dwinding Forest Biodiversity of North East India" in Roy B.Datta and Alam K. *Forest Resources in North East India*, Omsons Publication, New Delhi.
5. Diksit, V.K. (2002), "International Wildlife Trade and Its Impact on Wildlife Resources" in Roy B. Datta and Alam K., *ibid.*
6. Ghosh, A.K. (1990), "Impact of shifting cultivation in Living Natural Resources", in Majumdar, D.N. (ed): *Shifting cultivation in North-East India*, Omsons, Publications, Guwahati and New Delhi, pp. 178-197.
7. Govt. of Arunachal Pradesh (2006), *Economic Review*, Directorate of Economic and Statistics, Itanagar.
8. Govt. of Arunachal Pradesh (2006), *Arunachal Pradesh: Human Development Report 2005*, Rajiv Gandhi University, p. 171-72.
9. Hegde, N.G. (1994), "Biodiversity and Ground Realities", *Yojana*, February.
10. Hegde, S.N. (1988): "Coptis Teeta Wall (Mishmi Teeta): A Rare Medicinal Plant from Arunachal Pradesh", *Arun for News* 6(I), p. 27-29.
11. Hussain Zahid (2002), "Tree Cultivation: A Need of the Hour in Forest Management" in Roy B. Datta and Alam K., *op. cit.*

12. Josh, M.C. (1997), "Role of Herbs and Drugs in Economic Development" in Pandey B.B. (ed.) *Patterns of Change and Potential for Development in Arunachal Pradesh*, Himalayan Publishers, Itanagar, New Delhi, p. 174-184.
13. Kanjilal, U.N., Kanjilal, P.C. and Das, A. (1934), *Flora of Assam*, Vol.I, Govt. of Assam, Shillong.
14. Mandal, R.K. (2006), "Sustainability of Medicinal Plants and its Economic Viability in Arunachal Pradesh", *Resarun* (Journal of the Directorate of Research), Govt. of Arunachal Pradesh, Itanagar, Vol. 31, p. 1-10.
15. Mandal, R.K. (2005), *Arunachal Economy: Socio Economic Transformation*, Champion Publishing, Itanagar, p. 116-117.
16. Mandal, R.K. (2007), "Flora and Fauna in Arunachal Pradesh: Economic Viability and Sustainability" *Arunachal Review*,Vol.VIII, No.23, Sept.-Nov., Naharlagun, Govt. of Arunachal Pradesh.
17. Mandal, R.K. (2005), "Arunachal Pradesh Emerging as Power House" *Journal of Global Economy*, Vol. 1., No. 4, Research Centre for Social Sciences, Mumbai.
18. Menon, Ajit (2006), "Environmental Policy Legislation and Construction of Social Nature", *EPW*, January 21-27, Vol. XLI, No. 3, p. 188.
19. Narayana. K.S. (2006), "Biodiversity Conservation should be the Mantra of the Century". *Kurukshetra"*, Vol. 55, No. 2, pp. 3-4.
20. Pandey, H.C. (1988), "Some Healing Herbs of the Monk's Amongst the Minor Forest Produce", *Arun for News* 6(I), pp. 1-10.
21. Rao, V.M. (2003, *Tribal Women of Arunachal Pradesh*, Mittal Publications, New Delhi, p. 21.
22. Sharma,T.C.(1976), "The Prehistoric Background of Shifting Cultivation" in Pakem, B. *et.al., Shifting Cutivation in North-East India*, NECSSR, Shillong.
23. Wani, Milind and Kothari Ashish (208), "Globalisation Vs. India's Forest", *EPW*, September13-19,Vol. XLIII, No. 37.
24. *The Arunachal Times*, Vol. 19, No. 154, November 11, 2007.
25. "Forest and Forestry in Arunachal Pradesh", *SFRI Information Bulletin*, No. 27, Director, State Forest Research Institute & Mission Director, State Bamboo Mission, Itanagar.
26. Website: www.sfri.org.
27. Arunachal Front, March 21, 2009, Vol. 17, No. 201.
28. Sinha,G.N. (2008), "Forest and Forestry in Arunachal Pradesh", *SFRI Information* Bulletin No. 27, Issued by Director, State Forest Research Institute & Mission Director, State Bamboo Mission, Itanagar, Arunachal Pradesh.

# Index

A

Abbasi, Faiza, 27

Agrawal, Kamlesh, 129

Agriculture, 154

*Ailurus fulgens*, 44

Alatas, Sharifah Munirah, 11

Aquatic organisms as bio-indicators, 123-128

- animal indicators, 124
- coral reef indicators, 125-126
- marine/tidal bioindicators, 125
- microbial indicators, 124
- non-coral bioindicators, 127
- plant indicators, 123-124
- scleractinian coral bioindicators, 126
- tiniest bioindicators, 124
  - water fleas, 124-125

*Aquillaria malaccensis*, 42

Arunachal Pradesh, 39, 61, 151

Assam, 39, 61

Australia, 31

*Azadirachta indica*, 56

B

Badawi, Abdullah, 22

Bamboos, 65

Banteng, 46

Benthos, 125

Biodiversity Act, 2002, 112

Biodiversity and traditional knowledge, 104

- treats of traditional knowledge, 105
- value of traditional knowledge, 105

Biodiversity Management Committees, 116

Biodiversity, 1-10, 148-191

- aims and objectives of the regional research centre, 172
- benefit sharing, 5-6
- biodiversity and the international regime, 2-3
- causes of deforestation and its impact, 151-157
- community rights, 181-183
- impact of current development on forest, 157-163
- impact of deforestation, 163-171
- Indian constitution and equitable benefit sharing, 6-8
- introduction, 1-2, 148-149
- meaning of biodiversity, 2
- medicinal plants under threat in the state, 171
- other preservation and sustainable use, restoration and enhancement, 184-186

permanent sovereignty over the natural resources, 5
shifting cultivation, 153-156
suggestions, 186-187
sustainable use, 3-5
traditional knowledge, 6
what is biodiversity, 149-151
Biological Diversity Act, 2, 5 , 106, 118
Biological Diversity Convention, 2
Biological diversity, environmental ethics and traditional ecological knowledge, 39-60
biodiversity loss is big concern, 46
concept and value of biodiversity, 40-41
conservation method, 52
*ex-situ* conservation, 53
*in-situ* conservation, 52-53
deforestation and lopping, 49
ecosystem diversity, 45
ecotourism, 51-52
factors responsible for deterioration of biodiversity, 48
habitat degradation, 48
habitat loss, 49
flood, 50
fragmentation, 50
how to work, 56-59
human and wildlife conflict, 46-47
moral ideals behind conserving diversity, 53-54
natural cause of extinction crisis, 51
degree of specialization, 51
dispersal ability, 51
intrinsic rate of population increase, 51
longevity, 51
population variability, 51
rarity, 51
trophic status, 51
over-exploitation and poaching, 50-51
people-government conflict, 47-48
phytodiversity of the region, 41-43
religious ethics and biodiversity conservation, 54
traditional knowledge and biodiversity, 54-56
Biosphere Reserves, 109
*Bos javanicus*, 46
Botanical Survey of India, 108
Brown-Antlered Deer, 45
*Bubalus bubalis*, 46
Buddhism, 54

C

Carbon Tax, 142
*Catharanthus roseus*, 104
CBD convention and sharing of resources, 105
Centre for Cellular and Molecular Biology, 113
China, 16
Chlorofluorocarbons (CFCs), 141
Chlorophyll, 28
Choudhary, Bal Krishan, 39
Choudhury, Hiranjit, 61
Climate change, 148
Coix, 75
Cold War period, 17
Colocasia, 75
Community Biodiversity Committees, 5, 106, 116
Community Forest Management (CFM), 181
Compressed natural gas, 140
Conflict and ecological security, 11-26
Conflict and ecological security: clarification of terminology, 12
conflict, 15-16
considerations in security studies, 16-18

ecology, 12-14
ecosophical approach to a scarcity-conflict-security nexus in the Malaysian context, 22-24
environment, 12
environmental scarcity and ecological security in Malaysia, 18-22
introduction, 12
natural resources, 14
scarcity/environmental scarcity, 14
security/ecological security, 15
Conservation, 46
Conservation education, 59
Conservation of biodiversity under sustainable development, 172
Conservation of Biological Diversity Act, 6
Constitution of India, 6, 7
Convention on Biodiversity, 103, 105
Convention on Biological Diversity, 1, 55
Cropping of forest areas, 154

D

*D. turbinatus*, 42
DAC, 114
Dam-construction, 20
DARE, 114
Darwin, Charles, 28
Deforestation, 21
Deforestation, 66
Developmental activities, 66
*Didermocerus sumatrensis*, 48
*Dipterocarpus tuberculatus*, 42
Directive Principles, 6
District Council, 58
Drainage and Irrigation Department (DID), 20
Dubey, Vivek, 102

E

Ecosophy, 13
Eco-taxes, 139
Environment Impact Assessment, 47
Environmental Equality Act (EQA), 21
Environmental policy, 139
*Epipogeum roseum*, 42
ESCAP, 18
Ethics of biodiversity conservation, 27-38
development and biodiversity conservation, 28
inhospitable urban, industrial and agricultural expansions, 28-29
limitations of the protected area approach, 29-31
ethics for integrated habitats, 31
biodiversity in urban green spaces and the built environment, 33-35
protecting and managing inland wetlands, 32-33
using sustainable agriculture practices, 35-36
introduction, 27-28
European Restriction of Hazardous Substances (RoHS), 133
European Union, 16
E-waste, 129-138
definition, 130
e-waste
generation, 131-132
management in India, 133
management, 132
implications, 130-131
introduction, 129
methodology, 129
objectives, 129
recommendations for action or guidelines for future work on
benefits, 136, 137
e-waste, 135
government responsibilities, 135-136

recycling, 136
redesign, 136
repair, refurnish or upgrade, 136-137
reuse and donations, 136
sale or trade, 137
some companies responses to e-waste, 135
Austria, 134
California, 134
China, 134
European Union, 133-134
Japan, 134
Netherlands, 134
OECD, 134
San Francisco, 134
sustained campaigns, 134
United States, 133
suggestion to customer, 137-138

F

Five Elements of Ecology, 149
Flood, 50
Floristic diversity, 61-71
Floristic diversity, 64
conservation status, 68-69
conservation strategies, 69
endemism, 65-66
forest cover, 62-63
introduction, 61-62
threats to biodiversity, 66-68
vegetation types, 63-64
Flowering plants, 41
Fossil fuels, 141
French-Algrian war, 17

G

*Galeola falconeri*, 42
Gandhiji, 148, 149
Genetic diversity, 40
Global Environmental Facility, 107
Global warming, 148
*Gnetum gnemon*, 42
Great Andamanese, 83
*Grus antigone*, 36
Gulf of Mannar, 110

H

*Helicoverpa armigera*, 30
Hindu, 54
Home sapiens, 29
Homo sapiens, 41

I

Idu Mishmi, 47
India flora and fauna, 39
India, 30, 153
Indian initiative for protection of ownership issues in respect of indigenous people, 117
Indigenous people, traditional knowledge, 102-122
capacity building, 109
coastal areas, 111
criteria for benefit sharing, 120-121
enhancing financial capacity to implement the convention, 117
ensuring fair and equitable sharing of benefits, 116-117
exploration of traditional knowledge of Kani tribe, 107
facing threats from invasive alien species, 114
forests, 110
implementation of CBD in India, 107
implementation of CBD in India: nodal implementing agency in India, 107
*in situ* conservation, 109-110
introduction, 103-104
livelihoods, local food security and health care, 115

national reports, 108
overview of the status and trends of conserving biological diversity in India, 108
policy support, 111-113
promoting conservation of
genetic diversity, 113-114
species diversity, 113
protecting traditional knowledge, innovations, and practices, 115-116
reducing pollution and its impacts on biodiversity, 115
rivers and wetlands, 111
strategies, 108
survey and documentation, 108-109
Indo-Burma, 61
Indo-Chinese, 61
Intellectual property rights (IPRs), 56, 106, 120
International Community, 2
Introduction to ecotaxation and environmental levy, 139-147
criteria for electing a policy option, 141-143
economic instruments providing the greatest environmental benefits, 145-146
effectiveness of ecotaxation, 143-145
environmental effect, 143
incentive effect, 143
introduction, 139-140
types of ecotaxes, 140-141
Israel-Palestine, 17

J

Jaman, Samsur, 139
Jamir, S.A., 72
Japan, 16
Jarawas, 83
Jewels of Arunachal Pradesh, 43
*Jhum* or shifting cultivation, 30, 57, 62, 66, 73, 153, 154, 157
*Jhumia*, 154, 155, 176

K

Kaziranga National Park, 44
Khandu, Dorjee, 156
Klang Valley, 19, 22
Kyoto Protocol, 13

L

Larvae, 30
Lecpha Ethnobotanical Plants, 93
Lecpha society, 91
Lecpha-nature relation, 85
events of life, 86
Lecpha
concept of balancing ecology, 88
culture, 91
folktales, folksongs, 89
literature, 89
material culture, 88-89
medicinal knowledge, 86-87
mythology of origin, 85
personal names, 90
religions practice, 85-86
traditional ecological knowledge, 87-88
village name, 90
occasions, 92
places, 90
rituals, 88
rivers, 89
Lichens, 123
*Lilium mackliniae*, 42
Local ecological knowledge (LEK), 55
Loss of Biodiversity, 1
Love Our Rivers (*Cintai Sungai Kita*), 20

M

*Macaca arctoides*, 44
Maize, 75

Malaysia, 11, 18
Malaysian Environmental Quality Report, 2000, 21
Malaysian society, 12
Malthus, Thomas, 17
Mandal, Ram Krishna, 148
Manipur, 39, 61
Medicinal plants, 67
Meghalaya, 39, 61
*Melanorrhea usitata*, 42
Millennium Ecosystem Assessment, 27
Mining, 66
Mizoram, 39, 61
*Monoropa uniflora*, 42
Mother Nature, 91
Mount Saramati, 72-81
    biodiversity status, 75-76
    ecotourism, 77-78
    future strategies, 78-79
    introduction, 72-73
    results and discussion, 74
    study area, 73-74
    village profile, 74-75
*Muntiacus putaoensis*, 43

N

Nagaland, 39, 61
Nanda Devi, 110
National Biodiversity Authority (NBA), 115, 116, 118
National Bureau of Plant Genetic Resources (NBPGR), 113
National Forest Policy, 1981, 109
National Gene Bank, 114
National Lake Conservation Plan (NLCP), 111
National Parks, 72, 109
National River Conservation Directorate, 115
National River Conservation Plan, 111
NATO, 16
Natural hazards, 83
*Neofelis nebulosa*, 44
*Nepenthes khasiana*, 42
Nepenthes sanctuary in Meghalaya, 69
Network of Medicinal Plant Conservation Areas, 115
New Forest Policy, 153
NGOs, 22, 152, 176
Nilgiri, 110
Non-point source of pollution (NPSP), 140
Northeast India, 40
Northeast, 39
Nuclear powers, 16

O

Odyuo, Nripemo, 61, 72
OECD, 144
Onges, 83
Origin of Species, 28

P

Paleo-artic flora of Tibetan highland, 64
Panchayat, 115
*Panthera pardus*, 44
Pitcher plant, 42
Plant species, 68
Plant, 65
*Podocarpus nerifolia*, 42
Pollution in Malaysia, 22
Power politics, 17
Prasanna, Sai, 129
Protection of plant varieties and farmers rights Act, 2001, 117
Public transportation, 22
*Python Molurus bivittatus*, 45
Python reticulates, 45

R

Rajasekar, G., 1
*Rawalfial sepentina*, 56

*Rhinoceros sondaicus*, 48
*Rhinoceros unicornis*, 44
Rhododendron sanctuary, 69
Rice, 75
Rio Declaration, 13
Roy, Dulal Chandra, 82
Russia-Chechnya, 17

**S**

Saha, Amartya, 102
Salim Ali Centre for Ormithology and Natural History, 30
Sapin, 35
Sarus crane, 36
Saujanya, J., 129
Saxena, Amita, 123
Scheduled Tribes, 84
Selaginella, 42
Sentinelese, 83
Shifting cultivation (jhum), 49, 73, 154
Shompens, 83
Sikkim, 61
Singh, J.J., 156
Siroy Lily, 42
Stockholm Convention in 1972, 13
Submerged aquatic vegetation, 125
Sunderbans, 110
Supreme Court, 4, 152
Sustainable use, 4

**T**

Taxes on polluting inputs, 140
Technical Report, 112
Toxic metals, 130
*Trachypithecus geei*, 43
*Trachypithecus phayeri*, 43
*Trachypithecus pileatus*, 44
Traditional ecological knowledge (TEK), 54
Traditional Knowledge Digital Library (TKDL), 115
Traditional knowledge, 104, 118
Tribal relation with nature, 82-101
Tribal relation with nature: introduction, 82-84
Tribes, 82
Tripura, 39, 61
Tropical evergreen, 63

**U**

UK landfill tax, 143
UN Convention on Biological Diversity, 4
UNCED, 15
UNCHE, 149
UNDP, 17
UNEP, 107
UNFPA, 18
United Nations Convention on Environment and Development, 3
Upadhaya, Krishna, 61, 72
Urbanization, 18

**V**

Verma, Vinod Kumar, 123
Vijay, Bindu, 102
Vijayan, V.S., 30
Village Communities, 58

**W**

Waste piling, 132
Water (Prevention and control of Pollution) Act, 1974, 149
Water Buffalo, 46
Water flea, 124
Waterfowl Habitat, 32

Wetland purification, 32

Wildlife Protection Act, 1972, 149

Wildlife Sanctuaries, 68, 72, 109

World Bank, 112

World Commission on Environmental and Development, 148

World Conservation Strategy, 3

Writ of Mandamus, 8

**Y**

Yimchunger tribe, 77

**Z**

Zingibers, 67

Zoo, 53

Zooanthiniaria, 126

Zoo-cum-Botanical garden, 53

Zoodiversity of the region, 43

Zoodiversity, 58

Zoological Survey, 109, 113

Zooplankton, 125

Zooxanthellae, 126